EYEWITNESS TO CHAOS

EYEWITNESS TO CHAOS

Personal Accounts of the Intervention in Haiti, 1994

WALTER E. KRETCHIK

Potomac Books
AN IMPRINT OF THE UNIVERSITY OF NEBRASKA PRESS

∞

All photographs courtesy U.S. Department of Defense (DOD).
The appearance of DOD photographs does not imply or
constitute DOD endorsement.

Library of Congress Cataloging-in-Publication Data
Names: Kretchik, Walter E. (Walter Edward), 1954–
Title: Eyewitness to chaos: personal accounts of the
intervention in Haiti, 1994 / Walter E. Kretchik.
Other titles: Personal accounts of the intervention in Haiti, 1994
Description: Lincoln, Nebraska: Potomac Books, an imprint
of the University of Nebraska Press, [2016] | Includes
bibliographical references and index. Identifiers:
LCCN 2016026092 (print)
LCCN 2016040492 (ebook)
ISBN 9781612347240 (cloth: alk. paper)
ISBN 9781612348667 (epub)
ISBN 9781612348674 (mobi)
ISBN 9781612348681 (pdf)
Subjects: LCSH: Haiti—History—American intervention,
1994–1995—Personal narratives. | United States. Army—Officers—
Interviews. Soldiers—United States—Interviews. | United States.
Army—History—20th century. | United Nations Mission in
Haiti. | United Nations—Armed Forces—Haiti. | United States—
Relations—Haiti. | Haiti—Relations—United States.
Classification: LCC F1928.2 .K738 2016 (print) |
LCC F1928.2 (ebook) | DDC 972.9407/3–dc23
LC record available at https://lccn.loc.gov/2016026092

Set in Lyon Text by John Klopping.

To those who served

CONTENTS

ILLUSTRATIONS

Maps

ACKNOWLEDGMENTS

The author wishes to thank everyone who made this work possible. Special recognitions are in order for the military and civilian men and women who kindly volunteered their oral histories in the 1990s after having lived through what are now historical events. I am indebted to colleagues Dr. Robert F. Baumann, Dr. John T. Fishel, and the many military officers who conducted oral history sessions in the United States and Haiti. Col. Jerry D. Morelock (Ret.), past director, Combat Studies Institute, Fort Leavenworth, Kansas, provided time and resources in the 1990s to make this book possible decades later. Manuscript reviewer Professor Philippe Girard offered thoughtful observations and suggestions that improved the work. I am indebted to copyeditor Joy Margheim for strengthening the manuscript. The University of Texas–Austin's Perry-Castañeda Library provided maps. The U.S. Department of Defense furnished photographs. The professional librarians and staff at the Combined Arms Research Library, Fort Leavenworth, Kansas, archived and catalogued the documents and oral history tapes for public education and historical purposes. Erin Girard of Speedy-Script Transcription Services transcribed hours of video and cassette tapes rife with military acronyms and jargon. Particular thanks go to the Global Special Operations Forces Foundation and retired Special Forces associates for research assistance. I am most grateful to the University Press of Nebraska's editorial staff. My wife, Pamela J. Kontowicz, afforded support, transcribed tapes, indexed the manuscript, and critically commented on all drafts. Of course, none of these people are responsible for what is written here and all errors are mine alone.

INTRODUCTION

From September 19, 1994, to March 31, 1995, the U.S. government intervened militarily in Haiti. Conducted under UN Security Council Resolution 940 and Chapter VII of the UN Charter, Operation Uphold Democracy was the most convoluted military invasion in American history. Due to former president Jimmy Carter's successful last-minute negotiations with an illegal junta, President William J. Clinton turned around about one hundred aircraft and airborne troops twenty minutes before hostilities were set to commence. Commanders and their units then prepared to enter the country peacefully, scrambling to switch from a war mentality to a peacekeeping mind-set overnight. Operational disorder ensued for weeks even as thousands of multinational forces and numerous agencies entered the country to advise and support Haiti's fledgling democratic government. With mission handover to the United Nations Mission in Haiti (UNMIH) on March 31, 1995, many U.S. troops departed while others donned blue berets to serve under UN command. For fifteen months, UNMIH troops, 40 percent of them from the United States, assisted Haitians and their government in furthering democracy before mission transfer to yet another UN force, the United Nations Support Mission in Haiti (UNSMIH).

The 1994 U.S.-led military intervention also allowed the U.S. Army major and Haitian American Anthony "Tony" Ladouceur to return to his native country. In 1967 Ladouceur left Haiti to spend his teenage years with relatives in New York City while his businessman father remained in Port-au-Prince. American citizenship and an army enlistment led to a commission through officer candidate school. As a cultural advisor and translator for the military intervention's commander, Lt. Gen. Henry H. "Hugh" Shelton, the Haiti-born major was able to visit his father's mountainside home overlooking Port-au-Prince. "I will show you a picture of it," he said. "He has a fifty-foot wall around it. He enters through three doors: a wooden door, a reinforced metal door, and then another metal door, both in the front and the back. All the windows have metal bars on them. He has a loaded shotgun and a strategic location in his house where he goes if something starts to happen. One of his neighbors was robbed and they killed his son in the house. He was hiding when they shot his son but then he came at them with a machete. They had Uzi submachine guns and they just wasted him."[1]

Three weeks later Capt. Doni Colon, U.S. Army, arrived. His participation in the military intervention began with debarkation at Port-au-Prince International Airport in October 1994. It was also his first exposure to the Western Hemisphere's poorest country. While being transported to his headquarters, Colon witnessed an airport terminal controlled by heavily armed U.S. combat troops, throngs of Haitian pedestrians and street vendors conducting their affairs along dirt streets, and American infantrymen on foot patrol circumventing heaps of human waste and rotting garbage. While nearly vomiting from the stench, Colon observed Haitians "washing themselves by throwing a bucket into the sewer and bringing water out and also cleaning their clothes and stuff in that." A subsequent safety briefing on AIDS increased Colon's growing consternation about Haiti. "I was told that Haitians do not believe that AIDS is really a disease. They believe it is done by someone to you. You can't get it if protected by a particular voodoo [vodun] religious spell. They might make a little charm or do a saying at home to protect them and it is the same with many diseases here. They just do not understand the science, the reality of it. To them, it is magic and superstition." After less than twenty-four hours in country, Colon grimly stated, "This place is in trouble."[2]

This book is about Ladouceur, Colon, and others like them who served during Operation Uphold Democracy and UNMIH from

1994 to 1996. It is an oral history of the two military interventions, as told by the men and women who personally experienced them. Because it is concerned with military incursions from a personal viewpoint, this study asks a straightforward but important question: What happens to the military men and women who plan and execute military interventions and the civilians who observe them firsthand?

In a contemporary sense, military intervention as a form of preventive diplomacy began on June 17, 1992, six months after the Cold War ended, when UN secretary-general Boutros Boutros-Ghali submitted his Security Council report entitled *An Agenda for Peace: Preventive Diplomacy, Peacemaking, and Peacekeeping.*" In it he articulated his vision for the UN in resolving post–Cold War conflicts peacefully. To the secretary-general, the ideological struggle between the West and the East had terminated but various population groups now threatened international peace through "new claims of nationalism and sovereignty." To "remove sources of danger before violence resulted," he reiterated that the UN Charter's Chapter VI allowed for peaceful intervention in international disputes. In the absence of a nonviolent solution, however, Chapter VII and Article 42 permitted a UN armed force to maintain international peace and security. Through preventive diplomacy, peacemaking, peacekeeping, or postconflict peacebuilding, the UN members' judicious application of the charter's authority and appropriate use of military force would "address the deepest causes of conflict: economic despair, social injustice, and political oppression."[3]

In the early 1990s Haiti certainly met the criteria for a UN military intervention under Chapter VI or Chapter VII. But the use of armed troops to intervene in places such as the island of Hispaniola has generated considerable debate. Historically, intervention to end human suffering is traceable to St. Augustine and Thomas Aquinas and Christian theories of "just war." More recently, Andrea Kathryn Talentino's *Military Intervention after the Cold War: The Evolution of Theory and Practice* (2005) represents those who doubt its usefulness. In the case of Haiti, Talentino concludes that armed

1. The face of military intervention: a wary U.S. soldier canvasses the Port-au-Prince streets. Source: Department of Defense.

intervention accomplished little because the effort was far too limited in scope and reflected a "one and done" attitude of get in and get out. In truth, Maj. Robert B. Geddis, U.S. Army, verified her point by remarking, "I kind of took to Haiti that it is a problem that they got to work out. We are here to help; let's do our job and then leave." Richard N. Haass, in *Intervention: The Use of American Military Force in the Post–Cold War World* (1999) also questions the value of military interventions to alleviate human suffering. His book offers recommendations for decision makers to consider when determining whether to intervene. Glenn J. Antizzo's *U.S. Military Intervention in the Post–Cold War Era: How to Win America's Wars in the Twenty-First Century* (2013) advocates for military interventions as long as objectives are clearly defined, public support is secured, and decision makers have the will to use force when necessary.[4]

These important studies take an argumentative stance to weigh the merits and drawbacks of intervening or offer an advisory perspective intended to sway policy makers. Noticeably absent from the existing literature is an attentive examination of military interventions from the standpoint of those who actually plan and execute them "on the ground."

To address that deficiency, this book uses oral histories to disclose the personal experiences of general officers, commanders, staff officers, noncommissioned officers, and others involved in Operation Uphold Democracy and UNMIH. Their insights speak to strategic, operational, and tactical planning considerations, intelligence gathering, multinational force interaction, mission execution conundrums, communications and language concerns, ethnic and cultural factors, and other topics. Collectively, they shed valuable light on what it actually means to intervene militarily in the affairs of others.

The oral histories used here resulted from a chief of staff of the army directive to produce a history of the service's role in Operation Uphold Democracy. From 1994 until 1999 I led a research team as a regular army lieutenant colonel and faculty member assigned to the U.S. Army Command and General Staff College (CGSC), Fort Leavenworth, Kansas. Professors Robert F. Baumann and John T. Fishel, along with U.S. Army reservists and CGSC students, also conducted interviews. We followed guidelines within the U.S. Army's Center of Military History publication *Oral History: Techniques and Procedures*. Department of the Army regulations for documenting ongoing military operations and distributing public information about them guided our efforts. Military participants released their oral histories as government employees and public servants. Nongovernment civilians also agreed to public release, as concerned citizens. The unclassified interview records are within the public domain and accessible through the Combined Arms Research Library archives at Fort Leavenworth, Kansas.[5]

The reasons why the UN and the U.S. government would intervene militarily in Haiti are complex and understanding them requires revisiting Haiti's position within international circles and in relation to the United States. The island of Hispaniola is strategically important, for it is but 1,530 miles from UN headquarters in New York to Haiti's capital, Port-au-Prince, equivalent to the distance from Los Angeles, California, to Topeka, Kansas. Haiti is also 690 miles off the U.S. coast, equal to the driving distance from Chicago, Illinois, to Washington DC. Soon after Jean-Bertrand Aristide's ouster in 1991, the UN secretary-general encouraged the formation of the UN Group of Friends of Haiti, a political, economic, and diplomatic assistance body including Argentina, Brazil, Canada, Chile, France, Guatemala, Peru, the United States, and Uruguay. U.S. membership has much to do with national security because of unlawful immigration and Haiti's role as an illegal drug conduit through which tons of cocaine enters America annually. Stopping illegal immigrants and countering Haitian drug smuggling composes a significant portion of U.S. counterdrug operations and expenditures.[6]

Once considered the "pearl of the Antilles," Haiti is the poorest Western Hemisphere country, with a 10 percent adult literacy rate. Only 50 percent of Haitian children attend school. The country ranks among the ten least-educated nations globally, with the other nine located in Africa. The relatively few educated Haitians are typically wealthy and attended foreign universities. They often become expats, leaving their country for the United States and other locales, such as Canada.

Haiti's loss of educated citizens creates a national "brain drain" as well as a substantial diaspora in many countries. The 2010 U.S. Census reported 975,000 Haitian Americans, concentrated in Florida, New York, New Jersey, Massachusetts, Kentucky, Louisiana, Delaware, and Wisconsin. There are prominent Haitian American judges, lawyers, politicians, military officers, entertainers, businessmen and businesswomen, artists, musicians, and models in the United States, as well as the 1991 Miss America and numerous professional athletes. Haitian Americans send millions of dollars to their relatives in Haiti each year.

Although the relationship between Haiti and North America is well established, surprisingly little has been published about Operation Uphold Democracy and UNMIH. John R. Ballard's *Upholding Democracy: The United States Military Campaign in Haiti, 1994–*

1997 (1998) conveys his personal views as a member of U.S. Atlantic Command's Joint Analysis and Assessment Team in Haiti and Norfolk, Virginia. His work is chronological and sophisticated and includes some participant interview material. A book I coauthored with Baumann and Fishel, *Invasion, Intervention, "Intervasion": A Concise History of the U.S. Army in Operation Uphold Democracy* (1998), was published by the U.S. Army's Command and General Staff College Press and focused on army operations in Haiti. Additional works include Bob Shacochis's *The Immaculate Invasion* (1999), an excellent personal story of an imbedded journalist with U.S. Special Forces units in Haiti. Stan Goff's *Hideous Dream: A Soldier's Memoir of the U.S. Invasion of Haiti* (2000) is another personal account. Lawrence E. Casper's *Falcon Brigade: Combat and Command in Somalia and Haiti* (2001) offers insights into military intervention operational and tactical decision making. Ralph Pezzullo's *Plunging into Haiti: Clinton, Aristide, and the Defeat of Diplomacy* (2006) and Philippe Girard's *Clinton in Haiti: The 1994 U.S. Invasion of Haiti* (2004) offer superb general histories of Haiti and cover specific events leading up to the military intervention and afterward. How the local populace engages UN peacekeepers is covered in Béatrice Pouligny's *Peace Operations Seen from Below: UN Missions and Local People* (2006). Several complementary works highlight the two interventions through the lenses of U.S. and Haitian economic, government, humanitarian, political, military, or social issues. They include Amnesty International's *On the Horns of a Dilemma: Military Repression or Foreign Invasion?* (1994); Charles Arthur's, *After the Dance: Haiti: One Year after the Invasion* (1995); and Karen von Hippel's, *Democracy by Force: U.S. Military Intervention in the Post–Cold War World* (2000). *The UN Security Council: From the Cold War to the 21st Century*, edited by David M. Malone (2004), includes a comprehensive chapter on the Security Council's role in the Haitian intervention. *Capacity Building for Peacekeeping: The Case of Haiti*, edited by John T. Fishel and Andrés Sáenz (2007); Ronald H. Cole, *Mission to Haiti: Direction and Support of Peacekeeping and Humanitarian Operations, 1994–2000* (2008); and

Aaron L. Wilkins, *The Civil Military Operations Center in Operation Uphold Democracy* (2012) are valuable for deducing practical "lessons learned." All of these studies assist in understanding the military intervention in Haiti.

This book adds to the body of work on military interventions in several ways. It illustrates how oral history assists in explaining past events. Those interested in foreign relations and military history should find it useful for what it says about executive policy becoming operational reality. The work further illuminates what happens to men and women in uniform when ordered into harm's way. Maj. Gen. Joseph W. Kinzer, U.S. Army, the commanding general of UNMIH, explained in his interview why the Haiti military intervention is a worthwhile study: "You should look at this and think about having to do something like it." Before taking Kinzer's advice, however, it is necessary to give some thought to military intervention in light of how Haiti's people have historically viewed the use of military power.[7]

ABBREVIATIONS

Note that abbreviations follow the publisher's house style in the use of small capitals and thus may differ slightly from forms used in military and Haitian Studies contexts.

ACR	armored cavalry regiment
BCT	brigade combat team
BCTP	Battle Command Training Program
CARICOM	Caribbean Community or Caribbean Command
CEP	Conseil Electoral Provisoire (Provisional Electoral Council)
CGSC	Command and General Staff College, U.S. Army
CINC	commander in chief
DOD	Department of Defense
DOJ	Department of Justice
DPKO	Department of Peacekeeping Operations (UN)
EXCOM	Executive Committee, National Security Council
FAD'H	Forces Armées d'Haïti (Haitian army)
FRAPH	Front pour l'Avancement et le Progrès Haitien (Front for the Advancement and Progress of Haiti)
HNP	Haitian National Police
HOHP	Haiti Oral History Project
ICITAP	International Criminal Investigation and Training Program
IPM	International Police Monitors
IPSF	Interim Public Security Force
IWG	interagency working group
JCS	Joint Chiefs of Staff

JTF	joint task force
JTF HAG	Joint Task Force Haiti Assistance Group
LIC	Light Industrial Complex
MICAH	International Civilian Support Mission in Haiti
MICIVIH	International Civilian Mission in Haiti
MINUSTAH	Stabilization Mission in Haiti (UN)
MIPONUH	Civil Police Mission in Haiti (UN)
MIST	military information support team
MNF	multinational force
MP	military police
NCA	National Command Authorities
NSC	National Security Council
OAS	Organization of American States
OOTW	operations other than war
OPLAN	operations plan
PDD	Presidential Decision Directive
POL/MIL	political/military implementation plan
PRD	Presidential Review Directive
PSYOP	psychological operations
SAW	squad automatic weapon
SF	Special Forces, U.S. Army
SOPS	standard operating procedures
TRADOC	Training and Doctrine Command, U.S. Army
UNMIF	Multinational Interim Force (UN)
UNMIH	Mission in Haiti (UN)
UNSCR	Security Council Resolution (UN)
UNSMIH	Support Mission in Haiti (UN)
UNTMIH	Transition Mission in Haiti (UN)
USACOM	U.S. Atlantic Command
USAID	U.S. Agency for International Development
USMC	U.S. Marine Corps
USSOUTHCOM	U.S. Southern Command
VSN	Milice de Volontaires de la Sécurité Nationale (Militia of National Security Volunteers, or Tontons Macoutes)

EYEWITNESS TO CHAOS

1. Haiti. Courtesy of the University of Texas Libraries, the University of Texas at Austin.

1

Haitian Culture and Military Power

"Believe me, the day the Army really intervenes, then there'll be complete silence."
—Lt. Gen. Henri Namphy, Haitian army chief of staff

Before intervening in foreign lands, preventive diplomacy advocates should consider how the recipient populace views military power. In the case of Haiti, interceding militarily through Operation Uphold Democracy and the United Nations Mission in Haiti meant fathoming Haitian culture and centuries-old societal attitudes concerning the role of various military or paramilitary units. Haiti was born through war but the island's inhabitants had experienced violence long before taking up weapons against their colonial masters. From the revolution onward, regular and irregular armed forces, both domestic and foreign, benefited and harmed Haiti's people. The result was a citizenry possessing disparate views of what military power was all about, particularly when a military junta deposed democratically elected President Jean-Bertrand Aristide in September 1991.

Conflict and War in Spanish Hispaniola, 1492–1697

Prior to contact with Western European empires in the late-1400s, Caribbean Basin inhabitants engaged in frequent intertribal warfare. The Carib people in particular conducted ferocious raids to capture male prisoners for enslavement, ritual sacrifice, and cannibalistic consumption. Their incursions affected the Taino people who occupied the island of Ayiti (land of high mountains), as Haiti was then known. While scholars have considered the Taino to be peaceful, they nonetheless defended themselves with wood and stone clubs, axes, daggers, and other dual-purpose implements used for warfare as well as agriculture and hunting.[1]

In December 1492 Christopher Columbus spotted Ayiti and called it "La Isla Española" (Little Spain Island), which later became Hispaniola. After the *Santa Maria* became stuck upon a reef and was wrecked, the salvaged wood became a tower and fort near present-day Cap-Haïtien.[2]

Columbus left a small garrison on Hispaniola in January 1493 and eventually returned to Spain. In November he returned to find the fort destroyed and his men dead from disease, starvation, or violence at the hands of the Taino's Jaragua tribe. Columbus chose to avoid further confrontation with the inhabitants by moving inland. His fifteen-hundred-man force constructed yet another fort that eventually led to a small colony with its capital, Santo Domingo, in what is now the Dominican Republic.[3]

By 1512 Spain's colony had grown to about four thousand Spanish inhabitants who forced the native people to labor in colonial mines or farms under the *encomienda* system. Brutal conditions diminished the workforce and initiated the introduction of black slaves. Hispaniola nonetheless generated far less wealth than what Aztec and Inca laborers produced in Mexico and South America. Less output meant less wealth for Spain but also that the lightly defended island was unimportant to foreign empires.[4]

Over time, ships carrying vast wealth to Spain passed by Hispaniola, and its location became strategically valuable. Without a substantial military force to defend the island's 18,704 square miles (slightly smaller than West Virginia), sixteenth-century French pirates from nearby Tortuga plundered and burned the Spanish settlement of Yacanagua in 1543. Pirate raids reflected rising international interest in the island's affairs, a circumstance that dragged the inhabitants into foreign wars. In 1585 England's Queen Elizabeth I supported Dutch separatists fighting against Spain in what became the Eighty Years' War (1568–1648). Hispaniola entered the conflict when a Crown-directed foray by the

Englishman Sir Francis Drake pillaged Santo Domingo on January 1, 1586. The Spanish paid twenty-five thousand ducats (equivalent to about $20 million in 2015) in ransom for the city's return, a move that made Spain appear weak in protecting its overseas colonies. That notion was reinforced on May 27, 1592, when Christopher Newport and his 110-man English naval force torched the ill-fated settlement of Yacanagua for a second time. In 1605 the town was attacked again, in this case through a very brief "civil war." Spanish troops acting under Crown orders destroyed it and hauled off its inhabitants to halt an unauthorized salt trade between Dutch merchants and Spain's Dominican colonists.[5]

The Spanish military action against itself proved to be the colony's ultimate undoing. The soldiers forcibly relocated colonists from several northern and western villages to Santo Domingo, where they could be controlled. Although some colonists fled into the jungle or escaped aboard passing Dutch ships, more than 50 percent of them died in the so-called Devastaciones de Osorio. Thousands of cattle were abandoned and many slaves escaped. Well into 1606, Spanish troops methodically obliterated five of the existing thirteen colonial settlements, including two in what is now Haiti: Bayaja, founded in 1578, and La Yaguana, a former Taino village.

French Military Power in Saint-Domingue, 1697–1789

Spain's use of military power to punish economically opportunistic colonists proved a significant blunder. By 1625 Hispaniola was in chaos and the western portion was virtually abandoned. Pirates from Tortuga, also called *flibustiers* or *boucaniers*, intercepted passing ships from their island settlement about one mile northwest of Hispaniola, part of present-day Haiti. Gradually some of them moved to western Hispaniola, calling it Saint-Domingue.[6]

Many pirates were of French origin, from nearby islands such as Martinique, so France claimed authority over them to justify seizing the area. In 1664 France's West Indian Company took control and Bertrand D'Ogeron, a former *boucanier*, became governor. The French navy used the pirates to attack Spanish garrisons and treasure ships transiting from the New World to the Old World, all the while encouraging immigrants to acquire land, buy slaves, and grow crops.[7]

Between 1679 and 1704 four slave conspiracies occurred in which the object was the extermination of white masters. Although quickly squelched, the incidents nevertheless established that some of the island's population accepted violence as a means of social change; this view would eventually become entrenched within Haitian culture. These incidents aside, in 1697 two centuries of Spanish domination of Hispaniola ended with the Treaty of Ryswick, validating French claims to the western portion of the island. The area was organized into the *partie du Nord* (northern part), *partie de l'Ouest* (western part), and *partie du Sud* (southern part). A capital was established at Cap-Français in 1711, present-day Cap-Haïtien.[8]

The French colony soon became the "pearl of the Antilles," the richest colonial possession of any empire in the New World. Saint-Domingue alone produced 50 percent of all French commodity exports, which soon attracted the eye of rival powers such as Britain. By midcentury France's government had secured its most precious overseas possession with substantial military force. During the War of Austrian Succession (1740–48), French naval vessels from Saint-Domingue patrolled the Caribbean and protected French shipping from British and other foreign attacks.[9]

In 1749 the town of Port-au-Prince was founded, and it became the new capital in 1770. Military forces increased during this period; by 1775 the army comprised several metropolitan regiments of infantry, voluntary grenadiers, voluntary *chasseurs* (light infantry) of free blacks and mulattoes, and a loose militia of free blacks and mulattoes. An impressive naval fleet of at least twenty-five ships-of-the-line (fifty guns or more each), fifteen smaller ships, and numerous trade and supply vessels called Cap-Français home.[10]

Some of the island's military forces participated in the American Revolution (1775–83). In March 1778 France's government signed the Treaty of Alliance with the Americans and agreed to provide military support and armament. On July 31, 1779, a 3,750-

man French force was transported by sea from Saint-Domingue to Savannah, Georgia. Free men of color in French military service fought under the command of French general Charles Hector, the Comte d'Estaing. Future Haitian rebels such as Henri Christophe learned firsthand about American revolutionary ideas, military organization, and contemporary tactics.[11]

Black slave participation in America's revolt also inspired calls for further use of such troops. France had been defeated in Canada, India, and Louisiana at a high cost in soldiers, and thus black colonial troops seemed a reasonable way to fill the ranks. But racial prejudices hindered such initiatives; some deemed mulattoes and blacks incapable of mastering more than mundane military tasks. Moreover, black slaves made up 90 percent of the population of France's Caribbean holdings. Given a history of several unsuccessful slave revolts in Saint-Domingue alone, arming slaves was considered to be foolish. Still, many trusted slaves learned to use firearms to hunt game for their masters' tables, a skill that would prove useful in the future for other purposes.[12]

Mulattoes, free men of color, could and did serve in the *maréchaussée*, a rural police force led by a seneschal that had roots dating to the French Middle Ages. In Saint-Domingue, the *maréchaussée* was established in 1721 to control the population. White officers led black conscripts, and by 1733 the enlisted component was entirely of African ancestry. Although mostly leveed into service, many members joined for pay. Serving also meant societal uplift and increased status. Members attained social and economic privileges and owned property, land, and slaves. The black policemen wore ornate uniforms and carried weapons, prestige symbols that not only fed the ego but also reflected personal wealth. The troops embraced their roles with enthusiasm, a mission that included hunting down bandits and *marrons* (runaway slaves), protecting towns and villages from lawbreakers, and upholding state power.[13]

The *maréchaussée* enlisted men commanded a certain respect within the free black and slave communities. However, the mulatto police and slaves also despised each other, for the constabularies advanced their own social status by keeping slaves in line. Moreover, their loyalty was to those who paid them. This sixteenth-century mind-set resulted in an established Haitian cultural value that military fidelity comes from money, not a sense of civic-mindedness. This viewpoint was significant during and after Operation Uphold Democracy, when foreign nationals attempted to reform the Haitian police according to Western law enforcement norms.[14]

By 1789 centuries of warfare among the Taino and Caribs, the presence of Spanish garrisons and militias, pirate occupancy and raids, international and domestic wars, slave uprisings, and the participation of Frenchmen and mulattoes in military and police forces meant that Saint-Domingue was well on its way toward becoming militarized. A robust armed force allowed the French colony's seven thousand plantations to produce 40 percent of France's foreign trade, nearly double the production of all British colonies combined. The harbor of Le Cap was one of the busiest in the world.

Saint-Domingue's Slave Uprising

France's celebrated colony was productive, but societal tensions threatened to destroy over ninety years of French-dominated life. In 1790 the colony's social hierarchy was partially maintained by armed forces, including French colonials, black militias, and the *maréchaussée*. However, the news that the Bastille had been stormed in Paris along with the issuance of the *Déclaration des droits de l'homme et du citoyen* (Declaration of the rights of man and citizens) propelled the island into revolutionary fever. The militia organization was abolished. Whites and mulattoes formed a national guard and adopted the tricolor cockade. Mobs lynched individuals who failed to support calls for freedom. As mulattoes pressed for equal political power, white colonial troops were caught between keeping civil order and taking sides.[15]

Many slaves expected to be freed due to the French revolutionaries' profound views of human rights. However, they waited as

Haiti's colonists and the French government debated liberating them. Civil unrest permeated the island. Fearful of a slave uprising, the French government sent a naval squadron with two army regiments to Saint-Domingue, arriving in March 1791. Soon thereafter, the Port-au-Prince colonial regiment mutinied, beheading their colonel and parading his pate on a pole.

On May 15, 1791, the French National Assembly voted to award French citizenship to free men of color provided that certain conditions, such as loyalty, were met. Free blacks were hopeful of becoming French citizens but soon discovered that the law would either be delayed or not enforced. In June and July 1791 armed whites and free blacks fought each other in the streets of Port-au-Prince. By August some mulattoes and slave leaders had succeeded in stirring up the masses through the use of vodun, the local religion that combined Roman Catholicism with African spiritualism. Slaves roamed the northern countryside slaughtering white men, women, and children and burning plantations in their quest for liberty. By August, upwards of fifty thousand northern slaves were in rebellion. Some had firearms or swords; others fought with sticks or bare hands. Still, the motley insurgent force withstood the colonial army and volunteers.[16]

By September 1792 French negotiators such as Léger Félicité Sonthonax attempted to crush the rebellion. In Sonthonax's case, he commissioned and promoted free blacks while appointing some to administrative jobs. Social tensions increased nonetheless, even as international events once more involved the island's inhabitants. On January 21, 1793, the French national convention executed King Louis XVI, provoking war with England and Spain. These countries held Caribbean possessions, and a Continental war spread to Saint-Domingue. Spanish colonial leaders secretly supplied French slaves with weapons and commissioned former members of the slave armies. One individual who became a Spanish officer was the freed man Toussaint Louverture, born in Haut-du-Cap in 1746. He would prove to be one of Haiti's greatest generals.[17]

Meanwhile, the British navy arrived to intercept French ships traveling to the Caribbean. In the midst of this mayhem, France sent a new governor to the colony, Thomas François Galbaud du Fort. Many whites supported him, a planter's son, rather than Sonthonax, who had aligned with free blacks. Sonthonax arrested Galbaud for undermining his authority, sparking an armed uprising in Le Cap by Galbaud's supporters.

Needing troops, Sonthonax offered amnesty to rebel forces if they fought his adversaries. Several thousand rebellious slaves agreed. A bloodbath ensued in Le Cap, forcing several thousand whites and their slaves to flee to North America. On July 11, 1793, with Le Cap quelled, Sonthonax offered freedom to all who fought for France. The proposition was expanded in September 1793, when British troops from Jamaica landed at Môle Saint-Nicolas at the invitation of counterrevolutionary colonists. Local whites greeted the British soldiers as liberators, and the French Eighty-Seventh Regiment joined them. The combined force spread into western and southern Saint-Domingue as, on February 4, 1794, the French national convention ended slavery in all French territories. After several years of fighting, Saint-Domingue's slaves were both free and French citizens, although racial divisions persisted.[18]

In 1795 the Second Treaty of Basel ceded two-thirds of Hispaniola to France. Spanish troops, however, lingered temporarily because tens of thousands of British troops occupied portions of the newly French colony. French forces could not occupy the entire island without removing the lethal but weakened British, who were suffering from the "black vomit," their term for yellow fever.

Toussaint Louverture played a key role in the convoluted situation. In 1796, now a French officer, Louverture assumed command of twelve demibrigades with about fifteen hundred black soldiers in each. As part of three corps of infantry, the demibrigades attacked the British simultaneously in the north, east, and south. While some of his staff officers were white, all of Louverture's generals and most of his lower-ranking commanders were black or mulatto.[19]

In May 1797 France officially designated Louverture as general in chief of the Armies of Saint-Domingue. He proved up to the task, pushing his army aggressively against the debilitated British force. By 1798 his military skill was evident, for he confined the British military presence to Port-au-Prince, Grande-Anse, and Môle Saint-Nicolas. The British army departed the next year, leaving Louverture free to occupy the entire island by 1801.

The 1801 Saint-Domingue army was impressive by any standard. Louverture commanded a personal protection force of eighteen hundred "Honour Guards," establishing a precedent that continued into modern Haiti, with various national leaders hiring personal protectors. He oversaw three subordinate division commanders: the northern division under Gen. Henry Christophe, with 4,800 troops; the south and west commanded by Gen. Jean-Jacques Dessalines, with 11,650 men; and the east (former Spanish territory) occupied by Gen. Augustin Clerveaux with 4,200 soldiers. In addition to infantry, the army had engineers, artillery, and cavalry, as well as gendarmes. The forces were trained in the French manner and wore French-style uniforms. In total, the Saint-Domingue army comprised a skilled land force of 20,650 troops, at a time when the U.S. Army numbered about 4,100 officers and enlisted men.[20]

Louverture's force became known as the Republican Army of Saint-Domingue. Individual soldier armament varied from sidearms and sabers to modern French muskets, as well as over sixty thousand abandoned British weapons and thirty thousand U.S. government-provided muskets and ammunition in 1800. The significant amount of arms allowed the standing Republican Army to create a reserve, the Garde Coloniale, which formed on July 30, 1801. Reserve manpower was supplied by mandate; every male from age fourteen to fifty-five served in the standing army or reserve. Louverture directed the wealthier reservists to drill four times a year, resplendent in their intricate French uniforms while bearing arms. His policy served several purposes, one being that Haitians accepted the concept of the armed citizen. It also demonstrated a well-armed and capable force to impress domestic and foreign observers. Moreover, precision drill movements in extravagant uniforms conveyed military service as a means to attain social uplift and prestige.[21]

Revolution and the Creation of Hayti (Haiti)

By 1801 Louverture's abilities to lead, organize, and manage Saint-Domingue had not escaped the attention of Napoleon Bonaparte. While the island was quieter than it had been in years, Napoleon was concerned that Louverture had created a military dictatorship similar to his own. Indeed, by July the colonial leader proclaimed himself governor general for life, and the island operated under the Constitution of 1801. Thus a colony of France existed with a supreme, lifelong ruler but not as a republic with shared power, a precedent that would haunt Haiti for decades.[22]

Haiti was to soon experience yet another military incursion. Fearing Louverture would seek independence, Napoleon readied French forces for deployment under the command of his brother-in-law, Gen. Charles Victor Emmanuel Leclerc. The Vicomte de Rochambeau was made second in command. After the French consulted the British and Spanish governments and found that they also desired Louverture to be vanquished, a joint Franco-Spanish fleet carried twenty thousand French troops to the Caribbean island. On February 3, 1802, the force landed at Samaná on the north shore of Saint-Domingue. Leclerc's force spread through the entire island, driving General Christophe's division out of Le Cap. Leclerc carried a letter from Napoleon calling for Louverture's surrender, and an additional eight thousand French troops further communicated that directive when they arrived on February 15. The entire French army now assaulted the island's western portion. Some black troops resisted but about half joined the French.[23]

Leclerc soon requested two thousand men per month to ensure mission success. But resistance continued despite his having trapped both Dessalines and Christophe in the north. In March 1802 France and Britain ended the French Revolutionary Wars with the Treaty of Amiens, allowing Napoleon to send more troops to the French colony.

In April, still unable to force black leaders' capitulation, Leclerc offered Louverture retention of his title, staff, and army in exchange for retirement at a site of his choosing. Louverture accepted, as did Dessalines. Dessalines, however, soon blamed Louverture for not throwing out the French and broke ties with him, vowing to finish the job later. Louverture's trust in Leclerc eventually proved his undoing, for he was arrested, imprisoned, and expelled to France along with his family and servants. On April 7, 1803, Louverture died of pneumonia while imprisoned in the Alps.[24]

Louverture's departure brought a general but ephemeral peace to the island. June 1 saw fourteen battalions of black colonial troops join French demibrigades and the island fell under French control once again. But French domination quickly unraveled as news reached the island that Napoleon had reinstated slavery in Guadeloupe. Sensing that they were next, numerous black Haitians fled to the mountains to join insurgent bands. Meanwhile, many black officers deserted the French army.

In early October the island witnessed a general uprising as disease and murder swept across the land. The French army lost nearly 160 men per day to fever; overall losses were catastrophic. One unit had 85 men fit for duty with 107 in hospital out of an authorized strength of 1,395. The rest were dead. There were so many deaths among whites and blacks from disease and killings that Leclerc wrote Napoleon that the only solution was to eradicate every black man and woman while sparing children aged twelve years and under.[25]

Mid-October witnessed Dessalines and Christophe leaving the French army to form another black and mulatto force united by one purpose: to expel the French. In early November Leclerc expired from yellow fever but not before recommending to Napoleon that Rochambeau assume command. Rochambeau soon requested additional troops, with some arriving in December. In the interim, Rochambeau undertook a policy of savagery, exterminating men and women while importing Cuban hunting dogs trained to eat human flesh.[26]

By March 1803 about nine thousand French troops remained

alive, most having succumbed to yellow fever or combat operations. A pro-French national guard composed of local men was
organized to augment the depleted French units, and a desper-
ate offensive began in April. The attack failed, partially due to
many starving French troops having sold their weapons for food.

Compounding the situation was that on April 7, 1803, upwards of
thirty-five thousand black laborers went on a rampage in Grande-
Anse, burning settlements and killing whites. Meanwhile, Napoleon had reluctantly concluded that his dream of a resurgent French
empire in North America was over. Cutting his losses, he decided
to sell Louisiana to the surprised but pleased American government under President Thomas Jefferson. Without Saint-Domingue's
wealth, Louisiana with its key port of New Orleans became less
important strategically to France and thus was jettisoned.

For his part, Dessalines consolidated power by executing rebel
leaders who refused his authority, a practice that would continue
well into Haiti's future. In May he succeeded in merging the many
factions into one force. Taking a French tricolor flag, he ripped it
apart and had the red and blue portions sewn into what became
Haiti's flag. The two colors symbolized blacks and mulattos in a
country without whites. He also made everyone present swear
allegiance to him, a continuation of Louverture's practice of consolidating power within one individual.

With dwindling numbers and Napoleon's withdrawal of support, the French army's position became untenable. In August the
French abandoned Jérémie in the south. On November 17 Rochambeau surrendered to Dessalines after being defeated at the Battle
of Vertières and promising to withdraw French troops within ten
days. Soon thereafter, Dessalines and eight thousand men occupied Le Cap and renamed it Cap-Haïtien. Of the one hundred
thousand European soldiers (French, British, and mercenaries)
and sailors who fought in ten years of war, only eight thousand
escaped to the eastern portion of the island in December 1803.

Military Power and Creating Haiti

On January 1, 1804, Dessalines declared a new, independent country, "Hayti," based on the original Taino name. Dessalines and Christophe signed a new constitution, thereby disbanding Saint-Domingue forever. Though the country was independent, the Haitian citizenry feared foreign invasion. French troops remained in the eastern part of Hispaniola and French civilians lived throughout the island. France pressured England, Spain, and the United States to isolate Haiti commercially and diplomatically, arguing that a black republic was a threat to the plantation system and slaveholders.[27]

Although Dessalines promised the remaining French residents in Haiti protection, he soon ordered and participated in their slaughter. From January to February 1804, gangs of blacks and mulattoes, most of them former slaves, tracked down and butchered four thousand white men, women, and children while burning homes and stealing property. Haitians came to understand the power of mob violence early on in their history, a circumstance that did not escape their educated elites then and later.

On September 22 Dessalines proclaimed himself Emperor Jacques I and commander in chief of the army. A coronation ceremony on October 6 formalized his title. He had created a country through military power but that alone could not ease the racial divisions within it. Tensions still existed among people who identified themselves by degrees of skin tone, as well as being island-born or born in Africa.

The second Haitian constitution, ratified May 20, 1805, created an empire, not a republic. Militarily, only the emperor could make peace or war, engage in political intercourse, and form treaties. The document attempted to reconcile the country's various factions racially and ethnically by proclaiming all Haitians black. Slavery was permanently abolished. All Haitians were free and equal with inalienable rights to landownership and the sanctity of the home. Whites, however, were not allowed to own land. Yet, Haiti remained a segmented, pluralistic society where people who lived side by side remained well aware of their racial and social status divisions.[28]

Given Haiti's long history of military power and its effect on

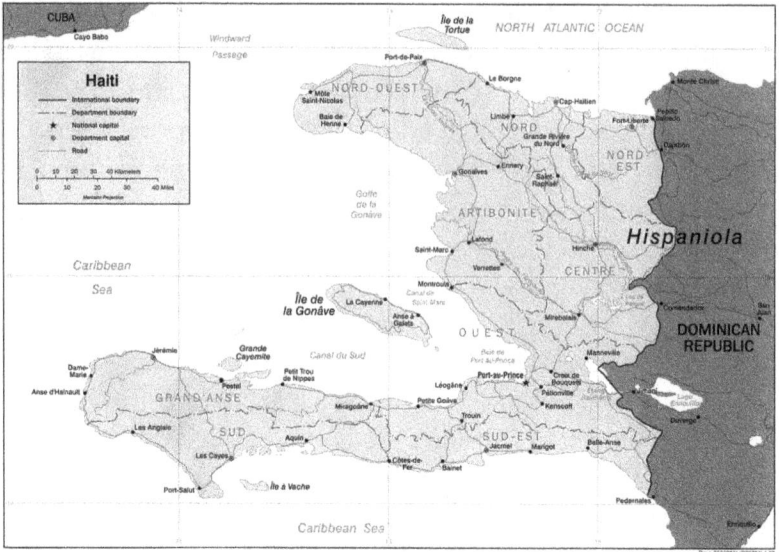

2. Modern Haiti, showing regional areas. Courtesy of the University of Texas Libraries, the University of Texas at Austin.

society, it was no surprise that the army's role permeated the 1805 Constitution. Haiti's leading generals shunned the American government model, in which Revolutionary War veterans such as George Washington gave up power and limited the army's and navy's role in society. With no strong civilian figure to lead them, Haiti's constitutional framers applied what they knew best: military authority. Articles 15–17 divided the country into six military divisions with a general in charge of each for administration and oversight. The six generals were independent of each other and corresponded directly with the emperor or a general in chief of the army, if one was appointed by "His Majesty." Article 38 mandated division and brigade generals to compose the Council of State, thus making military figures key advisors to the emperor. Article 4 denoted that the military was obedient to the state, not the people. Militarization extended to each Haitian male, for Article 9 noted that "no person is worthy of being a Haitian who is not a good father, good son, a good husband, and especially a good soldier." Not only were military leaders the adhesive that held society together but every male was expected to take up arms when needed. In mid-1806 a revised document established a bicameral government under an elected president, but this provision was revoked in 1816 to appoint presidents for life.[29]

Dessalines's imperial power grated on two Haitian generals, Christophe and Alexandre Pétion, who desired state authority for themselves. On October 17, 1806, Dessalines was assassinated and Haiti plunged into civil war. Christophe took over the north. He built a fortress in Cap-Haïtien and was elected president in 1807, serving in that capacity until 1811, when he proclaimed himself King Henry I. The north became a kingdom. Pétion, a mulatto, occupied the south and Port-au-Prince as president for life under a French-styled republic. After Pétion's death in 1818, Christophe failed to spread his influence across the country. He suffered a stroke in 1820 and ended his life by firing a silver bullet from a pistol into his brain.

The civil war lasted from 1806 until 1820. It marked the beginning of near-continuous political instability, social inequality, blatant racism, and savage violence. Without a common foe, the Haitian military fragmented into mostly unpaid militia groups. Many officers shunned their constitutional authority and seized local power over the people. At play was fear of the mob, a situation that many military leaders had witnessed or participated in during the war for liberation. Between 1806 and 1879 approximately sixty-nine government uprisings occurred, each one backed by various military factions who fought for whoever paid them.

Military Power and Island Reunification

Although Haiti was independent, its government was not powerful enough to quell the independence-mindedness of Spanish-descendant residents in the east. In 1808 Santo Domingo's *criollos* revolted against French rule when Napoleon invaded Spain. Spain reestablished colonial authority in July 1809, a clear security threat to fledgling Haiti. In 1822 Haitian president Jean-Pierre Boyer invaded Santo Domingo to unify the island. Thus began a twenty-two-year occupation that created lasting animosity between Haitians and Dominicans. Dominican and Roman Catholic Church property was taken and redistributed, while Haitian troops often procured whatever they wanted without payment.[30]

While sporadic resistance had existed throughout the occupation, Juan Pablo Duarte was able to form a secret but viable effort against the Haitians in 1839. In 1843 opportunity presented itself when Boyer was overthrown and his successor, President Charles Rivière-Hérard, was busy consolidating political power. In February 1844 Dominican rebels defeated Haitian troops and declared independence. Santo Domingo again became a Spanish colony in 1861 but then won a war of restoration (1863–65) against Spain.[31]

Foreign Interests

Haiti's recurrent bloody coups and foreign intrigue badgered U.S. presidential administrations. Fearful of potential slave uprisings in the United States and of French diplomatic influence, the American government under President Thomas Jefferson refused to recognize Haiti's independence. Formal trade between the two countries ended in 1806, although U.S. ships entered Haitian ports, but not vice versa. In 1825, in defiance of President James Monroe's famous 1823 declaration regarding the Western Hemisphere, fourteen French warships blockaded Haiti's capital, Port-au-Prince. The fleet's commander demanded 150 million gold francs (later reduced to 90 million) in exchange for recognizing the former colony's independence. Although President Andrew Jackson considered annexing Haiti to expand U.S. power in the Caribbean, fear of the island's people inspiring a slave revolt prevented the U.S. government from taking action.

Following the Emancipation Proclamation in 1863, President Abraham Lincoln directed that an embassy be established in Port-au-Prince under consular minister Frederick Douglass. Haiti's recognition was followed by open trade for the first time, and the U.S. government considering establishing naval bases in both Haiti and Santo Domingo. Although the bases failed to materialize, nine years later, in 1871, President Ulysses S. Grant nearly sent troops to Hispaniola when the Haitian government armed Santo Dominican rebels as the U.S. government pondered Dominican annex-ation. In 1891 President Benjamin Harrison authorized American troops to occupy the U.S.-claimed island of Navassa, west of Haiti. This was but one of nineteen U.S. government–authorized naval incursions against Haiti that occurred between 1857 and 1913.[32]

Haiti's splintered military was dangerous internally but ane-mic regarding outside threats. Lacking a potent navy of their own, Haiti's creaky governments were in no position to oppose foreign military interventions by sea. For its part, the Haitian "army" of the late nineteenth century was no real obstacle for an organized land invasion, given its estimated strength of about ten thousand loosely associated men operating under hundreds of general offi-cers. Public concern over security caused opportunistic civilian paramilitary groups to form. Mercenary *cacos*, roughly eleven criminal bands named for a red-plumed bird of prey, operated in Haiti's lawless mountainous northern interior. They participated in coups when not involved in crime or fighting Haitian soldiers. Another group, the *piquets*, were black peasants named for the pikes that they brandished. Operating in southern Haiti, they despised mulatto rule and, in 1844, rebelled in order to appoint a black pres-ident to power, giving rise to Faustin Soulouque. Elected president in 1847, he appointed himself Faustin I, Haiti's second emperor. To eliminate opposition, he organized a secret police force, the Zinglins, which he unleashed on any black leader who dared speak out against him. Faustin's rule, perhaps the second most cruel in Haitian history, served as the model for Haiti's most brutal dic-tatorship a century later, under François "Papa Doc" Duvalier.[33]

Internally dysfunctional, Haiti also suffered from foreign intrigue that involved military power. In the late nineteenth cen-tury, Germany, along with Britain and France, claimed Haitian financial interests as a result of unpaid loans. The 1897 Lüders Affair, a legal dispute between Haiti and Germany over depor-tation of the Haitian-born German national Emile Lüders, led to two German warships arriving in Port-au-Prince harbor. To avoid war or at least occupation, the Haitian government paid an indemnity to Lüders. Although there were but two hundred Germans living in Haiti at the time, they controlled 90 percent of foreign trade through the Hamburg-Amerika shipping line. Unlike many German communities in the Caribbean that held little sway with the fatherland, Haitian Germans exercised sufficient economic clout to entertain talk of a permanent German naval base in Port-au-Prince.[34]

In truth, much of Haiti's inability to pay its military stemmed from financial debt to foreign powers. This was true in 1898, when 50 percent of Haiti's revenue went to compensate France alone. By 1910, 80 percent of all revenue went to reduce foreign liability. Financially unstable, Haiti's leaders often imposed coercive labor laws to squeeze every drop of wealth possible from the masses. This practice in turn led to six presidential coups from 1911 to 1915, many of them backed by Haitian military factions. From 1910 to 1915, with civil unrest and economic instability potentially fomenting revolution or further foreign military mischief, the U.S. government encouraged American banks to obtain control of Haiti's debt. The liability totaled $21.5 million, $2 million owed to Germany alone.

In August 1914, with World War I commencing in Europe, President Thomas W. (Woodrow) Wilson worried about a strategic threat to the newly opened Panama Canal if British and German fleets clashed off the U.S. coast. A key canal access route crossed the Atlantic from Europe into the Windward Passage off Haiti's seaboard, prompting the U.S. Navy to make plans to invade the island as a precautionary measure against foreign encroachment. Plans turned into reality after yet another bloody Haitian coup in July 1915. Wilson soon approved a limited military intervention under Rear Adm. William B. Caperton to restore civil order. On November 11, 1915, Wilson's administration forced the Haitian government to accept American management. The short-lived military foray to restore order turned into a nineteen-year occupation, Haiti's first by foreign troops since independence.[35]

By exploiting Haitian domestic turmoil under the guise of stabilization, Wilson had gained control over Haitian domestic and international affairs. He now used American military power to crush several uprisings. Meanwhile, the Haitian army of 308 generals and nine thousand troops was disbanded, replaced by the Gendarmerie d'Haïti, a national police force. This unit was commanded by U.S. Marines and naval personnel, who trained Haitian members for numerous missions, including public safety and fighting *cacos*. In 1928 the force was renamed the Garde d'Haïti.

U.S. forces dabbled in nation building by constructing roads, bridges, wells, schools, and hospitals but failed to train Haitians to maintain them. Although American marines occupied Haiti during the Wilson, Warren G. Harding, John C. (Calvin) Coolidge, and Herbert C. Hoover administrations, the enterprise also failed to remedy Haitian social issues and exacerbated economic ones. The American experiment in infusing democracy by military intervention and instilling a sense of civic responsibility in the Garde ended under President Franklin D. Roosevelt during the Great Depression in 1934. In 1940 the U.S. Marine Corps (USMC) published its military "lessons learned" in its *Small Wars Manual*, an impressive work that has remained relevant for understanding the vagaries of military interventions.[36]

Ten years later, Haiti was again a dysfunctional state lacking the means to check government power. During World War II and the Cold War, the American government supported Haitian presidents and often vicious dictators who professed anticommunist rhetoric and kept order through foreign aid and intimidation. Haiti's political and social structure had unraveled rapidly when American military forces departed in 1934, undermining government and constabulary force relationships. After yet another Haitian coup in 1946 brought Léon Dumarsais Estimé to power and Col. Paul E. "Bon Papa" Magloire later assumed the presidency by force in 1950, the Garde returned to being a political weapon instead of a national security force. Magloire ruled as dictator until the military deposed him in 1956.

The Army Redux

Haiti's most ruthless dictator, François "Papa Doc" Duvalier, turned militarization into a debased art form. Upon assuming office in 1957, Duvalier found the armed forces in disarray. Internal divisions existed over race and generational views as well as intricate political ties. The aging leadership of the Garde d'Haïti was solidly entrenched while frustrated newly commissioned officers craved more authority.

In late 1958 Duvalier retired the older officers and promoted younger ones. Wary of the historical role of the Haitian army in making or terminating governments, he created the Garde Présidentielle, an elite force led by loyal officers who reported directly to him. He also disbanded the Garde d'Haïti as a holdover from the U.S. occupation, reorganizing and renaming it the Forces Armées d'Haïti (Armed Forces of Haiti; Haitian army), or FAD'H. The seven thousand members of the FAD'H included the army, a small navy, a tiny air force, a coast guard of a few vessels, and about six companies of Port-au-Prince police. The army, the oldest service, dating to 1804, was dominant politically. To offset the army's political influence, Duvalier established the Cagoulards (hooded men), allegedly to augment the Garde Présidentielle. The Cagoulards were known for wearing *cagoules* (balaclavas) to hide their identity. They later became the Milice Civile. To ensure loyalty, the estimated ten thousand members were drawn from the slums and provided with weapons and status. Most were deliberately unpaid. As streetwise individuals, they lived off of extortion and racketeering. Their propensity for violence and secrecy inspired the moniker "Tontons Macoutes" (Uncle Knapsack, or bogeymen), referring to a Haitian folkloric figure who stole children and ate them. Many members were also vodun leaders who were held in awe by the people. Their supernatural aura was enhanced by their dress: straw hats, dark sunglasses that hid their eyes, blue denim shirts, firearms, and machetes. People who opposed them were often hung, burned alive, or simply disappeared. After 1962 the Tontons Macoutes became formally known as the Milice de Volontaires de la Sécurité Nationale (Militia of National Security Volunteers, or VSN). The VSN acted as a secret police force that monitored Haitian society and particularly the uprising-prone rural areas. They gathered information and analyzed intelligence while reporting directly to Duvalier.[37]

Gradually the armed forces lost government influence to Duvalier's private thugs. In 1961 Duvalier closed down the U.S. Marine Corps–founded Haitian military academy out of fear that educated officers would resist him. In 1963 he also expelled the U.S. military training mission that he had invited in 1959 (the same year as Fidel Castro's successful Cuban Revolution), fearing American instructors would pass on their foreign values to Haitian students, who would then object to his restructuring efforts.

Resistance occurred nonetheless and Duvalier was swift to act. He eliminated or exiled anyone who opposed him. While the VSN and the army cooperated on internal security matters, Duvalier fomented suspicion among the groups to limit their power and influence. When several bombs detonated near the presidential palace in 1967, nineteen officers were executed as a warning to others. In 1970 Haiti's coast guard staged a mutiny and fled to Guantánamo, Cuba, seeking U.S. protection.

After François Duvalier's death in Port-au-Prince on April 21, 1971, his son, Jean-Claude "Baby Doc" Duvalier, came to power. Jean-Claude sought to realign the FAD'H and the VSN to rein in their activities and to receive U.S. funding. With U.S. backing, Duvalier created the Léopards, an educated and highly trained internal counterinsurgency unit known by their leopard-spotted uniforms. They were designed to act as an independent force that "bridged" the disputatious FAD'H and VSN. The Léopards grew in power and influence under Duvalier but eventually suffered decline once he left office. They were disbanded in 1989, but not before having trained a future Haitian general, Raoul Cédras.[38]

Duvalier also reopened the military academy in 1972, seeking a way to reprofessionalize and modernize the FAD'H. Yet despite his military initiatives, the army was never the political force it had been for generations. While it prevented several coups from succeeding, it ultimately failed to prevent Duvalier's political demise. Growing public discontent and VSN brutality gave impetus to a populist uprising and riots that undermined his regime. In February 1986 U.S. president Ronald W. Reagan's administration let matters run their course and Baby Doc Duvalier fled to France.

Several military coups later, president of Haiti Lt. Gen. Prosper Avril handed over his office under international pressure to Supreme Court justice Ertha Pascal-Trouillot. An interim government formed, followed by the first free presidential elections in Haiti's history, on December 16, 1990. Jean-Bertrand Aristide, a defrocked Roman Catholic priest who had promoted class warfare from the pulpit, garnered 67 percent of the vote.[39]

Aristide, upon assuming office on February 7, 1991, enjoyed international support. His election had been recognized by the UN, the Organization of American States (OAS), and the Caribbean Community (CARICOM). The election was a democratic one, a Haitian first, and offered hope for the future. Many Haitians believed that they would be able to erase centuries of internal strife and the more recent horrors of François Duvalier and his son, Jean-Claude. They also hoped that the subsequent five years of political instability under five different regimes could be left behind, giving rise to an era of social justice.

Considered by Haiti's elites to be a Marxist, Aristide used his Lavalas political party to undertake aggressive and unachievable social reforms. After surviving a failed coup attempt but one month into office, he called Haiti's elite "bourgeoisie thieves," threatening legal action. On September 27, after returning from the UN, Aristide gave his "Père Lebrun" speech, allegedly prodding his followers to burn opponents alive by "necklacing" them with fiery diesel-fuel-filled tires around their necks unless his reforms were realized. While debate over Aristide's actual words continues, some of his backers did carry tires in the streets, while his leftist speechifying terrified many Haitians. His supporters quickly acted; known Aristide opponent Sylvio Claude was necklaced in Les Cayes on September 29. That same day, FAD'H commander in chief Lt. Gen. Raoul Cédras, along with his cohorts the army general and chief of staff Philippe Biamby and the chief of the national police Col. Joseph-Michel François, deposed Aristide.

Approximately 20 Haitians were killed and 120 wounded during the takeover. The Haitian president fled to Venezuela on October 1, 1991, and later to the United States.[40]

Military and police power, with its recurrent interference in the lives of citizens, had been imprinted on Haitian culture over several centuries and played a key role in the purging of Haiti's president by a military coup. While the violent removal of political figures was nothing new to the island nation, removing the first democratically elected head of state through military force was something else. That action, combined with thousands of Aristide supporters soon suffering arrest, murder, torture, and rape under the junta's wrath, would not only garner international attention but prod the United Nations and others into taking action.

2

Preventive Diplomacy and Military Intervention

"The overall thing was we were going in to do these humanitarian type things. The high vis[ibility] medical and construction type things, obviously nonlethal. We were to do that to sort of pave the way for Aristide coming in and to show that hey, this is a good deal. Look what this guy is bringing back to the country."

—Lt. Col. Phillip J. Baker Jr., U.S. Army (Ret.)

Preventive diplomacy using military power can require time to reach an agreement to act. From October 1991 through October 1993, UN, OAS, and U.S. government leaders deliberated over the removal of Haiti's first democratically elected president, Jean-Bertrand Aristide, and what to do about it. Meanwhile, Haitian army commander in chief Lt. Gen. Raoul Cédras and his junta members seized control of the country. Cédras, a U.S.-educated officer and former member of Jean-Claude "Baby Doc" Duvalier's Léopard Corps, exercised military and paramilitary power to take revenge on Aristide's supporters. He also "played" the international community to his advantage. Preventive diplomacy calls for seeking a peaceful solution before using military force. Haiti serves as a specific illustration of what happened to people in uniform while nonviolent solutions were pursued.

Aristide's Departure and Initial Planning

Two days after Aristide's removal on September 30, 1991, the OAS met with the deposed president. They developed a resolution that demanded his immediate reinstatement, recommended sanctions, and organized a delegation to negotiate his return. On October 4 mediators arrived in Haiti and met with members of the FAD'H and others. Discussions ended abruptly when Cédras ordered the mission out of the country on October 7.[1]

Meanwhile, Aristide was busy drumming up support for his cause. He addressed the UN Security Council and, on October 3, UN secretary-general Javier Pérez de Cuéllar supported the OAS, condemned the coup perpetrators, and called for Aristide's return to office. The U.S. government was also far from idle. Office of the Secretary of Defense directives to the Joint Chiefs of Staff (JCS) reached U.S. Atlantic Command (USACOM) in Norfolk, Virginia. As Department of State bureaucrats worked the issue, USACOM military planners prepared a contingency plan to evacuate American citizens using U.S. Marines from Guantánamo Bay, Cuba, if the Haitian situation worsened. The American army's contingency force headquarters, the Eighteenth Airborne Corps at Fort Bragg, North Carolina, designated the Eighty-Second Airborne Division to prepare for actions in Haiti. The directive involved updating a preexisting army plan developed in the 1980s, which called for a noncombatant evacuation of U.S. and designated civilians if the country became unstable. Several variants addressed changing circumstances in Haiti, with each one estimated to take about ten days and involve thousands of troops.[2]

On October 11, 1991, the UN General Assembly adopted Resolution 46/7, condemning the junta and calling for Aristide's restoration to office. Boutros Boutros-Ghali's preventive diplomacy report to the Security Council on June 17, 1992, concerning the potential future use of military intervention to make, maintain, or keep peace also did nothing to convince the junta to vacate office. A UN-OAS delegation to Port-au-Prince in August met with Haiti's junta leaders over four days but failed to reach an agreement. On November 24, 1992, the General Assembly adopted Resolution 47/20, which again demanded Aristide's return but added that the secretary-general should take "necessary measures" in cooperation with the OAS to end the Haitian crisis.[3]

The UN and OAS secretary-generals also appointed Dante Caputo, former minister for foreign affairs of Argentina, as a special envoy for Haiti. U.S. military plans were postponed with the promise that negotiations might be more focused and productive through a single UN negotiator.

In December 1992 Caputo met with Aristide in Washington DC and then traveled to Haiti to meet with leaders there. Meanwhile, Aristide wrote letters to the UN and the OAS to keep his concerns at the forefront. After further diplomatic meetings at Port-au-Prince in mid-January, both Cédras and Acting Prime Minister Marc L. Bazin accepted an international civilian mission to Haiti to resolve the crisis. The UN approved the mission on January 18, 1993, one that would be shared cooperatively with the OAS.[4]

The Creation of MICIVIH

On February 9, 1993, the International Civilian Mission in Haiti (MICIVIH) came into being. Agreed to by the UN, OAS, Aristide, Cédras, and others, the UN mission was designed to "verify respect for human rights as laid down in the Haitian Constitution and in the international instruments to which Haiti was a party, in particular, the International Covenant on Civil and Political Rights and the American Convention on Human Rights." MICIVIH members were allowed to access any Haitian place or establishment and to interview anyone without hindrance in order to ensure that Haiti's junta was not committing human rights violations. On February 13, 1993, before the mission was officially approved, an advance team and survey party arrived in Haiti to prepare for a follow-on UN multinational group. Forty civilian observers arrived the next day and they combined efforts with OAS members who had been in country since September 1992.[5]

Professor Bryant Freeman, then director of the Haitian Studies Institute, University of Kansas, was in Port-au-Prince working as an observer for Pax Christi, a global Catholic human rights organization, when the advanced party arrived. A member of the multinational group sought out Freeman to "join the UN team as an instructor" due to his knowledge of Haitian Créole and culture. He agreed and became "a regular instructor when more and more people started coming in. Eventually there were up to 240 observ-

ers for the UN from something like twenty-five, thirty-five different countries." He noted that all the observers "spoke fluent French
and were to learn Créole. A few Americans from the Peace Corps
were in the group and they already spoke good Créole." Freeman
and two others "gave a three-week course on Haitian history, politics, and Haitian Créole, so as to train the observers coming in and
before they were sent out to the field in one of fourteen bases."[6]

The UN component ultimately numbered about 200 personnel, of which 133 were human rights observers. Additional individuals came from the OAS. MICIVIH headquarters was located
within Port-au-Prince and operated under a joint UN/OAS head of
mission who reported to Caputo. Following training under Freeman's team, observer deployment to the provinces began on March
5, 1993. By the end of March, MICIVIH members were located
throughout Haiti within each of the country's then nine administrative departments.

Additional International Pressure

Caputo met with Haitian junta leaders while MICIVIH personnel
moved throughout Haiti. He stressed that Aristide's return was
paramount, as were the appointment of a legitimate prime minister and resolving issues of amnesty for junta members. Despite
bringing significant international pressure to bear, Caputo failed to
convince the junta to give up power. Given the obstreperous nature
of the junta members, the OAS recommended to the UN that an
embargo be placed on arms and petroleum products. Petroleum
was a significant matter; Haiti's electrical power came primarily
from diesel generators. Without diesel, the country would suffer
a severe blackout. On June 16, UN Security Council Resolution
(UNSCR) 841 was passed, thereby imposing the OAS-recommended
arms and oil embargo. Sanctions were delayed until June 23, 1993,
giving the junta time to reconsider its position.[7]

Despite UN and OAS pressure, events in Haiti became increasingly horrific. Freeman reported that MICIVIH and the embargo
further infuriated the junta leaders, who had allowed a UN-OAS
presence only because "Cédras thought that he could gain favor

and official acceptance by the rest of the world if he allowed more observers in." Junta thugs, however, continued to viciously target Aristide supporters. Throughout the summer of 1993 Freeman observed the violence firsthand. He recalled, "One or two bodies were deposited on our doorstep each week, the road that is leading to our headquarters, with their face hacked off. It was some poor person who was at the wrong place at the wrong time just to show that they [the junta] did not want the foreign presence there."[8]

The Governors Island Accord

Despite ongoing junta brutality toward Aristide supporters, UN and OAS pressure held out a glimmer of hope for a peaceful end to the crisis. On June 21, 1993, Cédras notified Caputo of his willingness to begin a conversation with Aristide. Representatives of both parties met at Governors Island, New York, and reached an agreement on July 3. Aristide "was to appoint a new Commander-in-Chief to replace Lieutenant-General Cédras, who would take early retirement." This would open the way for the exiled president to return to Haiti on October 30, 1993. Cédras wanted amnesty and military assistance to "professionalize the Haitian military." He also requested that a prime minister be confirmed and a new police force established. The UN and OAS would act as mediators. All sanctions would be lifted once Aristide was reconfirmed. The Governors Island Accord, as it became known, was signed without Cédras and Aristide present but was considered to be a peace-seeking "good faith" arrangement.[9]

The accord also allowed UN personnel to enter Haiti to assist in "modernizing the armed forces and establishing the new police force." But what "professionalization" actually meant was left up to the UN secretary-general and the government of Haiti to determine. No agreement had been reached over that issue when additional talks were held on July 14, 1993. Two days later the New York Pact was signed, an arrangement calling for a six-month peaceful transition period including guarantees "for human rights and fundamental freedoms and to refrain from any action that might lead to violence or disrupt the transition to democracy."[10]

Cédras, however, was not motivated by civic virtue in signing the documents. A former Léopard Corps member under Baby Doc Duvalier and a U.S. military–trained cold warrior, the junta leader was not about to have his country run by a Marxist. Given his background, he surely viewed himself as a Haitian nationalist and patriot. An educated, astute individual, he was undoubtedly cognizant of the UN's preventive diplomacy concept and expected that peaceful means would be pursued before armed military intervention. Regardless, he was far more interested in stalling for time to perhaps gain international legitimacy and to lift sanctions. Those motives became evident after weeks of dialogue in the Haitian Parliament to ratify Aristide's appointment of Robert Malval as prime minister–designate on August 25, 1993. The UN immediately suspended the embargo and unfroze Haitian bank funds, which was what Cédras wanted. However, Cédras's sincerity remained questionable regarding Aristide, and the UN did not trust him. On August 27 UNSCR 861 was passed, stipulating that the sanctions would be reinstated if the Governors Island Accord was violated.

On August 25, 1993, the UN secretary-general recommended that a UN mission be sent to Haiti under the Governors Island Accord provisions. A UNMIH totaling 567 civilian police monitors, sixty military trainers, and a military construction unit was proposed. It would remain in Haiti for six months during the Haitian government transition period. Caputo would head the mission while also being in charge of MICIVIH.

Caputo and his UN forces would have to deal with the Haitian army (FAD'H) and the police, two separate but associated entities. In truth, the FAD'H acted as both. Creating a new police force per the Governors Island Accord would require UN civilian police monitors, who could vet FAD'H members to remove criminals and thugs while monitoring ongoing activities, advising, and ensuring that Haitian law was enforced. Modernizing the military would require military training teams. The teams would train FAD'H members of all ranks in nonlethal skills such as "disaster relief, search and rescue, and surveillance of borders and coastal waters. The military construction unit would work with the Haitian military in such areas as conversion of certain military facilities to civilian use and renovation of medical facilities."[11]

On August 31, 1993, UNSCR 862 approved an advance team of twenty-five U.S. military trainers and forty Canadian policemen to be sent to Haiti. Led by Caputo, the team arrived on September 8, 1993. While Haitians cheered their arrival, Caputo immediately observed that things were amiss. Aristide's allies and the junta supporters were alienated and anxious. Widespread human rights violations, murder, and violence were normal occurrences. As a civilian group, MICIVIH was unable to prevent such matters from occurring. A military intervention force was needed to show resolve and establish a more robust presence. Caputo called for deploying the remaining UNMIH forces.

The USS *Harlan County* Affair

Three weeks later, on September 23, 1993, UNSCR 867 authorized UNMIH to deploy for six months with an extended mandate of seventy-five days, if required. Meanwhile, the UN Security Council called on Haiti's various factions to cease using violence as "a means of political expression," an accepted Haitian cultural value for centuries. Not surprisingly, the plea went unheeded.[12]

Deliberations over peaceful solutions to Haiti's problems continued but military planning languished. In early August the potential for the creation of UNMIH reinvigorated the process. Planning for the deployment of an international police and military force trickled downward from the UN to the U.S. government. Through the JCS, USACOM was alerted to plan the mission and to execute it on order.

As a multiservice command and control headquarters, USACOM controlled no troops of its own. Its staff officers therefore tapped into units such as the U.S. Army's Training and Doctrine Command (TRADOC) to find qualified personnel. One such individual was Lt. Col. Phillip J. Baker Jr., U.S. Army, a military history instructor at the U.S. Army Command and General Staff College, Fort Leavenworth, Kansas. On August 18, as talks were ongoing in the Haitian Parliament over the appointment of Robert Malval, Baker was teaching military history to CGSC students. That afternoon, Baker's director, Col. Richard Swain, informed him that he was to join a military taskforce headed for Haiti. Baker was chosen because "he was the only person [within his department] with staff experience at the division level." He might be deployed for 179 days to one year and was told to "go home, figure out what you are going to tell your wife, come on back in the morning, and tell us what you have been working on to make sure you have it covered."[13]

Baker had less time than imagined, for he found himself flying out the next morning for Fort Monroe, Virginia, and an impromptu meeting with Brig. Gen. Carl Ernst at TRADOC headquarters. Ernst told Baker that "he [Baker] was not going to change the course of events of 200 years in that country [Haiti]. You are going there for your experience [and] to put out brush fires, whatever you can, and you will know it when you see it when it is bad." Not quite sure of what he specifically was tasked to do, Baker was transported to USACOM headquarters a few miles away.[14]

Baker soon discovered that he was to join UNMIH, a headquarters with two major Haiti assistance components, the first being a police unit commanded by Supt. Jean-Jacques Lemay of the Canadian Mounted Police. The second was a multiservice, multinational military force commanded by Col. James G. "Gregg" Pulley, U.S. Army Special Forces (SF). The commander of the U.S. Seventh Special Forces Group (Airborne) at Fort Bragg, North Carolina, Pulley had recently been in Port-au-Prince before the UNMIH advanced party. There he earned his Haitian-designated nickname of Colonel Poulet (chicken) due to his being overly cautious. He also spent considerable time shuttling back and forth to Norfolk, Virginia, for meetings. Although Aristide and Cédras had guaranteed that the *blancs* (whites) would be safe, Pulley correctly reported that Haiti was a dangerous place. Members of the Office of the Secretary of Defense and the Department of State's Working Group for

Haiti shared his views. Neither U.S. government department had any enthusiasm for the mission. Caputo and others, however, did not share Pulley's opinion.[15]

Baker's initial meeting with Pulley found the colonel exuding confidence nonetheless, for he told Baker, "Listen; here is what we are going to do. We are going to separate the police from the military because they are all kind of one big organization now. Our job is to go in, separate those two forces and then concentrate on professionalizing the Haitian army." Baker asked, "What does that mean?" Pulley said, "Well, that is a little tricky as to what it means but we are going to train them to be what we think a good army ought to be." Baker was told that he was to train the Haitian army general staff, recalling Pulley's words: "We need a special person for that, as we will have a Special Forces battalion train the lower echelons but we have no one in Special Forces capable of training the general headquarters staff. That is why we went to TRADOC and the staff college for someone with the requisite rank and perhaps experience."[16]

Armed with a better understanding of his mission, Baker met with the operations officer, "a marine lieutenant colonel who quite honestly was the most abrasive person I have ever met in my life." He told Baker, who twenty-four hours earlier had been teaching graduate-level students, to come up with "a mission statement, a plan of action, and a concept for how I was going to professionalize the Haitian army staff. So I sat down in a small room, there was thirty people running around and maybe twenty chairs. Rank had no bearing. There was supply people in there, logisticians, there were admin people in there all trying to get a grip on the situation."[17]

Baker spent hours looking for documents that "might give me a good idea [of what to do] because vocally I could not get that from anybody. Everyone was running around like a chicken with their head cut off." Fortunately, he located a 1990 report from U.S. trainers in Haiti. "I sat there and read a mission analysis on the Haitian army. It was very detailed and it gave all sorts of ideas of what ought to be done. I was like gee; this was what I was being told to do. This [report] was done in 1990 and here it was 1993. I started getting the sense that we were reinventing the wheel here." Still, Baker was able to put together a plan that satisfied the operations officer.[18]

The mission clarified as time passed. Baker recalled, "We were to just get people to Haiti and what we were going to do there is nation assistance, nation building, two terms used often and interchangeably. We are going to send some medical folks in there and we are going to send some construction people, high visibility, you know inoculate people and also fix things. Then people like me and the Special Forces would spend time training the Haitian army." To Baker, the operation was a UN and U.S. political show of force using the military.[19]

Baker noted, "Colonel Pulley wanted to see a binder full of lesson plans." But Baker had little time to go over such matters, for

> the six weeks I was there [in Norfolk] I personally saw Pulley twice. He was being yanked either to the State Department, to the UN, and he was doing all that high-level stuff and leaving the staff to do its thing. When he did come back he would talk to the marine operations officer and the air force lieutenant colonel they had as the deputy. That little cell would do a lot of things but the rest of us were pretty much out of the loop.

By the end of September 1993, two U.S. Navy tank landing ships, the USS *Harlan County* and USS *Fairfax County*, embarked 218 members (193 Americans and 25 Canadians) of what was now designated the Joint Task Force Haiti Assistance Group (JTF HAG). Baker, the senior U.S. Army officer under Pulley, was appointed commander of embarked troops on the USS *Harlan County*, a task that required spending "the rest of the day and most of the night coming up with the troop list." After departing Little Creek, Virginia, the ship took eight days to reach Roosevelt Roads, Puerto Rico. The USS *Fairfax County* remained at Little Creek and was scheduled to follow on October 16. Upon arrival, Baker found that a USACOM staff officer had phoned about "a certain Special Forces Sergeant First Class Smith" whose commander at Fort

2. Port-au-Prince harbor docks, September 1994. Source: Department of Defense.

Bragg, North Carolina, said was aboard ship but who was not on the joint task force (JTF) roster. Baker replied that the list had been checked several times and "if Smith is not on that list he is not on this ship." Instructed to check anyway, Baker went looking for the sergeant. He soon found him. "I felt like strangling him," said Baker. Apparently the fairly senior noncommissioned officer came aboard late at night in Virginia and neither he nor anyone else had reported his presence to Baker for over a week. After notifying USACOM officials that he had indeed found the sergeant and that he was well, Baker thought, "This could be a funny story but God forbid something had happened to this young man. He might have jumped overboard or fell overboard in the middle of the night and washed up along the North Carolina coast. Wouldn't that be an embarrassing story for the army?"[20]

With Pulley already in Haiti with fifty Americans, Baker queried the staff about their intentions upon arrival. Each answered that he or she would consult with Colonel Pulley. To Baker, "the boss" was busy enough with larger issues. So he directed the staff members to come up with their own plans, "at least something. If all else fails start doing something that you know needs to be done. Do not sit there and wait for someone to tell you what to do." Baker was "watching noncommissioned and commissioned officers from all branches of the service, we had Canadians, army, navy, air force, and marine corps personnel in that room, male and female. The female captain who was my executive officer was a civil affairs person. She was able to say to the Seabees who had never been to Haiti that you are going to repair this particular school. We had maps because the Special Forces had them at the appropriate scale. It was good sharing information."[21]

Although Baker and his shipmates thought that their stay in Puerto Rico would be but a few hours, the uss *Harlan County*'s departure was delayed. Baker heard rumors that it was "for some political reasons. They just said stay there awhile until we get some other things in place, high-level political things that the un and the State Department were working on." Indeed, unbeknownst to those who were about to execute preventive diplomacy, negotiations were occurring over two potential "showstoppers," the status of mission agreement between the government of Haiti and the un and the U.S. rules of engagement. Although neither document had been finalized, the rules of engagement had nothing to do with the Haitian junta's permission to enter Haiti or not. The mission agreement was crucial, however, for it involved multiple parties and specified the un military force parameters and the Haitian authorities' responsibilities. Haitian representatives had signed the agreement but the document nonetheless languished in the Pentagon awaiting a legal review. State Department involvement soon forced the issue, the document was signed, and the uss *Harlan County* proceeded to Haiti.[22]

As the ship's propellers churned the Caribbean waters once again, circumstances arose that further complicated the mission. Members of the Clinton administration had equated Haiti with Somalia, a un and U.S. intervention that had commenced in 1991 under President George H.W. Bush. On October 3, 1993, with preparations for entering Haiti ongoing, eighteen U.S. Army

Rangers were killed, seventy-five wounded, and a helicopter pilot taken prisoner in Mogadishu, Somalia. Televised images of dead Americans being dragged through the streets shocked the president and the nation. Soon thereafter, on October 9, CNN reported a Pentagon announcement that American troops would leave Haiti if attacked. Perhaps the announcement was meant as a signal to the junta that the Governors Island Accord would be void if things tuned violent. Cédras, however, sensed opportunity.

Cédras understood international events and the effectiveness of media attention. He certainly viewed Somalia's effect on the U.S. government as a mechanism to prevent the USS *Harlan County* from docking. Following the Clinton administration's tepid public announcement, the junta leader informed his staff members what Pentagon officials had allegedly said. He also reached out to the recently organized Front pour l'Avancement et le Progrès Haitien (Front for the Advancement and Progress of Haiti; FRAPH), an anti-Aristide group founded by Emmanuel "Toto" Constant, a CIA operative. Constant's organization was told to begin anti-U.S. demonstrations immediately so as to sway U.S. opinion and to further target Aristide supporters. The FRAPH would ultimately kill four thousand Haitians but for now planned a riot at the Port-au-Prince docks, one large and intimidating enough to ensure ample media coverage. The Clinton administration's expressed fear of military casualties, the so-called Somalia Syndrome, not only emboldened Cédras but also would affect U.S. military policy in future military interventions such as Bosnia.[23]

Aboard the USS *Harlan County*, the ship's captain, Cdr. Marvin E. Butcher Jr., U.S. Navy, was kept abreast of the Haitian situation via radio from Pulley in Haiti and satellite communications from USACOM in Virginia. Butcher informed Baker of various ongoing activities. "We were under the assumption that proved false that it was going to be a permissive environment. In other words, they were going to let us in and they were happy to see us there," Baker explained. Having painted their vehicles white with a simple black "UN" on the sides, the force members "were all getting ready to put on our blue berets. We had a little thing in that room that night [before entering Port-au-Prince harbor] on how to wear a blue beret and okay does everyone have their UN patches on, let's get ready to put on the big show. We thought there was going to be a ticker tape parade and all that," a completely different view than what U.S. government officials were thinking in Washington DC.[24]

At 2:00 a.m. on October 11, the USS *Harlan County* arrived at Port-au-Prince harbor to find the entrance clogged with ships anchored purposefully near the reefs. At 5:00 a.m., after the ship had negotiated the obstacles, Baker saw that "the captain docked about a mile out and waited for instructions as to which pier to pull into. We had radio communication with a U.S. Coast Guardsman who said that there was a whole bunch of people at the docks. The gate to the harbor from the town side was locked and the harbormaster said everyone is on strike." This information contradicted the fact that the same U.S. Coast Guard officer, who worked at the U.S. embassy, had arranged for a pier the previous Friday. Instead, an old Cuban freighter was anchored at that location.[25]

Without a pier to dock at, Butcher launched a small watercraft to have a look for himself. He and an SF major came within fifty feet of the pier, which was patrolled by Haitian police but no one else. Meanwhile, the U.S. Coast Guard officer whom Butcher had communicated with also reached the pier. He soon informed Butcher that he was leaving due to hearing gunfire. Butcher also heard shots fired and at about 7:00 a.m. witnessed a mob of people entering the harbor area through the now open gates. At that point Butcher turned his small craft around and returned to his ship. He then ordered all unnecessary personnel to remain below deck. An assortment of Haitian "bum boats," small craft used for menial tasks, surrounded his vessel but kept their distance. A few of them flew the flag of the Tontons Macoutes, the infamous secret hit squad from the Duvalier era. When Butcher ordered the ship's machine guns manned, however, the bum boats dispersed.[26]

Butcher had spotted a small mob of some forty Haitians, each "being paid one U.S. dollar a day." They were accompanied by liquor carts that they liberally accessed. Drunk, they shouted anti-American epithets such as "Remember Somalia!" and periodically fired weapons into the air while waving machetes. Upon hearing of the situation and shunning Pulley's advice, Nikki Huddleston, the U.S. chargé d'affairs, arrived in her armor-protected sedan. She attempted to find the port authority but several mob members struck her car with ax handles. Embassy spokesman Stanley Shrager was bullied. Frustrated but unharmed, Huddleston left after about one hour. Pulley reached the scene to witness two corpses being tossed from a bus. News cameras recorded the spectacle. Still, Pulley believed the mob to be disorganized and more nuisance than threat.[27]

Butcher, however, followed U.S. Navy regulations and secured his vessel, for he was responsible for ship, crew, and passenger safety until docking. After it docked Pulley would take command of the UN landing troops, but not until then. Butcher, while in communication with Pulley, was also talking with officers at USACOM headquarters, who in turn were in contact with the JCS. JCS officers were communicating with the UN, the White House, the State Department, and the secretary of defense. To be sure, officials at each layer of bureaucracy held their own perceptions of ground truth, which complicated things. Still, Butcher was the ship's commander and his on-the-scene assessment mattered most. Although Pulley repeatedly told Butcher "not to worry about the demonstrations and to land the troops," Baker heard Butcher reply, "No, it doesn't look friendly to me and I have further indications that things could get ugly if we tried to pull in. We are a humanitarian mission. We are not geared to force our way in." He did offer to land a party of armed U.S. Marines to intimidate the crowd, but armed force was contrary to the UN agreement and thus denied.[28]

In the late morning several Haitian police boats patrolled near the USS *Harlan County* without incident. Butcher ordered several small watercraft to circle the ship during the night to watch for swimmers planning mischief. The evening passed in relative quiet. At one point several automobiles drove onto the docks and shone their headlights on the ship to blind the onboard night vision devices. The attempt failed. Butcher's crew soon spotted trucks moving personnel dockside along with what appeared to be two v-150 armored personnel carriers armed with 90mm guns. To Butcher, the situation was no longer permissive but at least semi-permissive or even hostile.

At dawn Butcher ordered morning colors raised and the U.S. national anthem blared over the ship's loudspeakers. Meanwhile, UN and U.S. officials scrambled to find a peaceful solution to the standoff. Pulley used his assets to survey a beach north of Port-au-Prince for an over-the-shore landing. But Butcher responded that no landing could take place without U.S. Navy SEALs having looked the site over themselves. Since none were readily available, Butcher determined that landing craft would work best and the dock should be used for that purpose. Pulley agreed and both men waited for orders.

A few hours later the U.S. embassy contacted Butcher and told him to recover his two landing craft, which were patrolling around the ship. Butcher refused. A few minutes later Adm. Paul D. Miller, commander in chief (CINC) of USACOM and the Atlantic Fleet, called the ship's captain and asked if he could move the two craft closer to his vessel. While Butcher considered this request, two Haitian Montauk motorized vessels carrying twin machine guns left Admiral Killick Haitian Naval Base to the south. The passengers represented Haitian navy, army, and police forces. The guns were manned. As the boats sped toward the American vessel, Butcher ordered his own machine guns to be armed and snipers placed topside. He then notified the crew that they were to open fire if the Haitians touched the machine-gun triggers. The Haitians seemed to take notice, reduced speed, and circled but did not shoot. Butcher, who believed that the Haitians were monitoring his unsecure communications, called the U.S. embassy and informed them of the situation. He also relayed that if any Haitian boat came within one thousand yards of his ship he would blow it out of the water. Soon thereafter the Haitian vessels departed, only to return two hours later, although they remained a respectable twenty-five hundred yards distant.[29]

At about 2:00 p.m. Butcher called his Norfolk, Virginia, headquarters with his situation assessment. He reported that there was military equipment hidden on the docks. The ship's berth remained blocked. While the circumstances ashore might improve, the armed Haitian boat threat was significant and at night could lead to provocation or potential violence. Therefore, in his judgment as the commander in charge, the situation was no longer permissive and he was leaving. While naval officers conferred in Norfolk and Washington DC, Butcher said he was weighing anchor. After thirty-five minutes and conferring with the White House and other parties, U.S. Navy officials notified Butcher that they supported his decision. Baker put it this way: "Butcher was the man on the scene and they said, Look, you are the boss, you are the commander on the scene, you decide what to do."[30]

The Camel's Back

On October 12, 1993, news reporters' cameras captured the USS *Harlan County* leaving Port-au-Prince for Guantánamo Bay, Cuba. After ten days in Cuba, the ship steamed to Virginia and JTF HAG stood down. Although the ship had safely returned to home port, the ramifications of its having left Haiti were both immediate and politically calamitous. The Cédras regime and the FRAPH had achieved the first rebuff of a U.S. naval vessel in Haitian history. They had also successfully played and discredited the UN Security Council, the OAS, and the Clinton administration, all of which now appeared weak. For Professor Bryant Freeman, who watched from the UN staff offices in Haiti's Hôtel Montana, the vessel's departure was dumbfounding. Freeman recalled, "It was soon after lunch and I happened to be on the balcony of the hotel. Standing on my left by chance happened to be Dante Caputo. He was just as astounded as [I was] to see the *Harlan County* leaving. Here was a ship with two hundred Americans and some fifty Canadians, all armed, who were cowed by a small group of fifty or sixty hoodlums. We were frankly horrified."[31]

In Haiti, the emboldened junta was quick to act. On October 14 Haitian minister of justice Guy Mallory, a staunch proponent of social reform, was murdered in broad daylight. Freeman reported, "Our phone lines were cut. Our water was cut at the headquarters.

Another nearby building where we housed some of our trainees was machine gunned. No one was hurt but the threat was definitely there." That night Freeman was informed that the observer team was leaving, along with all remaining UN and OAS personnel. "Our head of mission, Colin Granderson, said you have two choices. One is to leave on a chartered plane in two hours with one small suitcase to the Dominican Republic. The other choice is leave at 5:00 a.m. tomorrow morning on a chartered plane for the Dominican Republic. There is no third choice, don't argue with me. So that is what we did. When we left there were Haitians crying and saying you are our only hope." UNMIH, MICIVIH, and other international agencies followed Freeman's departure in October 1993. The UN Security Council resumed its embargo.[32]

The *Harlan County* incident proved to be the straw that broke the camel's back in a series of attempts to execute preventive diplomacy peacefully. As UN and OAS members pondered their next move just days after the *Harlan County*'s departure, embarrassed U.S. government officials once again ordered intensive military planning to storm Haiti. For Cédras and his junta, the astonishing victory over international power at the Port-au-Prince docks would be short-lived. In the meantime, however, many Haitians lived in fear of their lives.

3

Planning a Military Intervention

"The problem with the Haiti planning was it was so tightly held that a lot of people who needed to be involved could not be involved until almost right before execution. We could not get the information down to the people who would be executing it on the ground."

—COL. MARK D. BOYATT, commander, Third Special Forces Group (Airborne)

After the October 11–12, 1993 USS *Harlan County* incident, U.S. military planning commenced in earnest. However, the "wait and see" realities of continued preventive diplomacy actions taken by the UN and others seeking a peaceful resolution to Haiti's woes forced planners to adjust to ever-changing circumstances. An initial U.S. military plan eventually produced two intervention options, a hostile peacemaking invasion and a permissive peacekeeping scenario. Both were to be followed by peacebuilding. A third, semipermissive option was later added to account for additional uncertain social conditions in Haiti. The three plans assumed that a military force would remove the Haitian junta immediately, either by their death, capture, or exile. The invasion was to be executed under UN Chapter VII on the night of September 18–19, 1994, but a last-minute peace agreement caused it to be aborted. Amid the resulting chaos, a semipermissive fourth military plan emerged within hours to address cooperating with the junta members, who would remain in power for nearly one month.

Retribution

Haitian lieutenant general Raoul Cédras's surprising triumph at the Port-au-Prince docks in October 1993 had not only turned away the USS *Harlan County* but embarrassed world leaders. Repercussions included most MICIVIH members leaving the country on October 13, along with the UNMIH advanced party. Three days later the UN Security Council sought retribution by reestablishing an arms and oil embargo on Haiti under Resolution 875. On October 30, 1993, after the deadline had passed for President Jean-Bertrand Aristide to return, the Security Council condemned Cédras and his cronies for unfulfilled obligations under the Governors Island Accord.

For U.S. military forces, UN embargo responsibility fell to Rear Adm. Charles J. Abbott, U.S. Navy, and JTF 120, a navy-heavy task force headquartered aboard the USS *Nassau*. The force consisted of a commander, a staff, a special marine air/ground task force, an SF planning cell, and various ships. Its mission was to perform maritime interdiction of vessels potentially carrying banned items such as fuel to Haiti. It also had the authority to track, board, and divert commercial shipping departing from or headed to the island nation.

The embargo was intended to immobilize Haiti's limited transportation system and diesel generator–dependent power grid by denying fuel to businesses owned by Haiti's wealthy elites. In theory, the "suffering" upper class would pressure the junta into stepping down and allowing Aristide's return. The UN was careful to avoid stopping the flow of humanitarian aid so as to convince the Haitian people that the embargo was targeting the wealthy, not them. Whether or not the Haitian people understood that nuance was another matter, for the embargo destroyed Haiti's teetering economy.

UN Resolution 875 had also confirmed that the Security Council was "prepared to consider further necessary measures to ensure full compliance" with resolutions pertaining to Haiti. Due to the junta's obstreperous behavior and the USS *Harlan County* incident, "further necessary measures" could mean anything from verbal posturing to an all-out invasion. The worst-case scenario was an assault, which would most likely involve U.S. airpower and sea-born assets, at least. To avoid being caught off-guard by a UN military intervention, Maj. Gen. Michael C. Byron, USMC, the senior plans officer at USACOM in Norfolk, Virginia, proactively formed a highly classified planning group code named Jade Green. This group of individuals "started planning in earnest for a forced entry into Haiti" under the daily supervision of Capt. Timothy E. "Spike" Prendergast, U.S. Navy, and later under Col. John Langdon, USMC. The plan was classified Secret at the time and designated Dragon's Blood. No UN military officers were involved; the planning was purely a U.S. effort.[1]

The planning team scrutinized existing documents for Caribbean-area contingencies and found several, with the most recent dated 1988. According to Lt. Col. Edward Donnelly, U.S. Army, a USACOM plans officer, the Jade Green cell "went through them [plans], decided that an Army-based plan for military operations in Haiti was best for the circumstances for a forced entry [invasion] into Haiti and then they went back and reviewed the supporting plans for that document." There were five supporting plans, none of them perfect for the current Haitian situation. At some point in November 1993, Dragon's Blood was modified and redesignated Operations Plan (OPLAN) 2370, signifying that the initial concept was approved by Adm. Paul D. Miller, USACOM's CINC.[2]

In November the planners determined that combat was less likely as UN negotiations continued and any involvement would probably be an "operation other than war" (OOTW) or what the UN might consider peacemaking under Chapter VI, using military strength to assist diplomats in forcing a resolution of the crisis. Under prevailing American military doctrine, an OOTW required military assets but also the involvement of several branches of the U.S. government and the National Security Council (NSC). The NSC contained multiple levels of bureaucratic subordinate government agencies with members having specific expertise in crises or potential crises.[3]

Soon after Byron formed the Jade Green cell, the planners met with the JCS's and USACOM's multiservice representatives. Donnelly recalled, "[We] discussed what it was that we thought were

U.S. national objectives for Haiti; what it was we thought we were supposed to be doing, and how we go about doing it." But it became apparent to those present that the UN and the U.S. government were attempting a peaceful settlement; thus the fewer individuals who knew about a possible military intervention the better.

To keep things mum, it was decided to place the plan in a "compartment," a term for keeping a tight lid on a highly classified endeavor. According to Maj. Robert Shaw, SF, a compartment is "a small group of people with some sort of special access. All that does is limit the amount of people knowing about the specific crisis or the plan you might be working on. It is done for security reasons, mainly. Again, it was very important to do at this time because we thought it was the President's wish to settle this diplomatically." Byron was not pleased with the decision, for, according to Donnelly, "he suggested to the JCS that we not develop it in the compartment because it was an OOTW. We knew an OOTW would have a lot of U.S. government interagency involvement and we needed to bring it out of the compartment in order to freely discuss it. And they could still keep it classified." Interagency discourse was particularly important given Presidential Review Directive (PRD) NSC-13 of February 15, 1993, which addressed the U.S. government's preparedness to support UN peace operations. The JCS staff did not agree with Byron; it was JCS chairman Gen. John Shalikashvili's decision "not to allow the plan out of the compartment. So they continued planning OPLAN 2370 in the compartment." In truth, the plan was so tightly held that fewer than ten JCS officers were aware of it, along with a handful of USACOM personnel.[4]

While compartmentalization helped to maintain clandestineness, it also complicated planning for military interventions. Planning requires many experts, and when plans are compartmented, as Shaw related, "it is really difficult. You are trying to get answers to your questions but you need to expand the circle of the ring larger and larger and bring in other people into this. If you try to do it in a vacuum you probably won't have all the answers and you will have more assumptions later in your planning. Well, for a good plan you need to strike a balance knowing that your assumptions are correct." Having but a few people involved "became a problem because some of the required people weren't let into the circle. So you had people on the outside of the circle making some assumptions and people inside the circle making assumptions and you lose the clear exchange of ideas and information. It makes the planning process much harder to accomplish." Shaw's point surfaced when USACOM planners briefed the JCS and requested that the force commander who would lead the potential intervention be brought into the planning. The request was denied, for security reasons.[5]

Jade Green officers worked feverously over the Christmas and New Year's holidays. On January 6, 1994, USACOM representatives returned to Washington DC and briefed Gen. John J. "Jack" Sheehan, U.S. Army, the JCS director for operations. Speaking for Shalikashvili, Sheehan shifted away from an OOTW and ordered planners to target Port-au-Prince with a large invasion force. He also directed that an area in Haiti be designated for returning migrants who had fled their home island primarily by sea. That requirement addressed growing NSC staffer concerns over increased numbers of Haitians fleeing to Florida, where they posed an economic and social inconvenience as well as a political predicament. The Haitian boat migration clearly "was a national security issue." On the other hand, the shift to a large invasion force meant that OPLAN 2370 was now to focus more on combat and occupation under Chapter VII of the UN Charter rather than an OOTW under Chapter VI or even a limited strike on critical FAD'H headquarters buildings and communications nodes.[6]

Sheehan's directive also meant focusing effort on the UN's concept of postconflict peacebuilding, with the "conflict" being an invasion to remove the junta by force and the postconflict being peacebuilding afterward. In Boutros Boutros-Ghali terms, taken from his 1992 Security Council report, peacemaking might be viewed as armed conflict (eradicating the junta and its supporters by force). Peacebuilding implied disarming warring factions (Haiti's military and paramilitary groups), destruction of weapons (military and civilian-owned arms and arms caches), repatriating refugees (Haitian migrants), advisory and training support for security personnel (vetting and rebuilding the Haitian National Police), monitoring elections (securing voting sites), advancing efforts to protect human rights (security forces for stability, police monitors, and UN observers), reforming or strengthening governmental institutions (Haiti's judicial system in particular), and promoting processes of political participation (registering voters, printing ballots, and other tasks).[7]

Even without the classified compartment restrictions, planning a large military intervention is complex and requires intervention commander and staff participation. On January 7, 1994, the JCS justifiably caved to USACOM requests and the compartment broadened. USACOM notified Lt. Gen. Henry H. "Hugh" Shelton, the commanding general of the U.S. Army's Eighteenth Airborne Corps at Fort Bragg, North Carolina, that he had been designated as the JTF commander for a potential Haiti invasion. Shelton received a mission statement to assist in his initial planning, and his headquarters was designated JTF 180. USACOM staff officers had now separated responsibility for the Haiti plan. They would examine strategic and some operational military issues regarding an invasion but they left most of the operational and tactical details to Shelton and selected members of his headquarters.

JTF 180 Planning

As the nation's primary strategic-level military staff, the JCS soon issued an alert order to USACOM and JTF 180, the document that notified a unit for possible deployment. Shelton now officially knew that he was to plan a forced entry or combat operation. Meanwhile, U.S. Army officers deputy corps commander Brig. Gen. Frank Akers, chief of staff Col. Daniel McNeill, and plans officer Maj. William B. Garrett III traveled to Norfolk and became part of the Jade Green planning team. Maj. Kevin C. M. Benson was the Eighteenth Airborne Corps's chief of plans within the operations section. According to Benson, "It was the first time in my life when I had actually read a highly classified JCS alert order directing the initiation of planning." Benson was also let into the compartment, along with Col. Robert Barfield, the corps' operations officer, and Maj. Steven Sifers, an Eighty-Second Airborne Division operations planner. Oddly enough, the Eighteenth Airborne Corps intelligence officer was not part of the compartment initially. Benson found that situation to be "incredibly frustrating and incredibly stupid but those were the restrictions given to us."[8]

Benson and Garrett were not allowed to work alongside anyone outside of the compartment, so they were physically separated from the staff. "Garrett and I were literally locked into a closet," said Benson. "We moved supplies out of a supply closet and we locked ourselves in this closet because we had to begin the initial mission analysis for the corps commander. We had about a week or ten days or a two-week period from the receipt of the alert order until the time that General Shelton had to go to Admiral Miller at USACOM and give his initial concept briefing on how he was going to conduct the forcible entry into Haiti to lay the conditions for Aristide's return." The pressure exerted on the two officers was tremendous; they set aside their personal lives, including time spent at home with their families. "Burke [Garrett] and I worked countless hours. Our wives brought us changes of clothes. Because it was so classified and compartmented that the rest of the planners, even though they knew pretty much what we were doing, could not know the specifics. But they were supportive. They would make us coffee and brought us food and stuff but it was a mole's existence for a while, it really was."[9]

Benson was fortunate in that the JCS document "was the best-written piece of paper I have ever seen. It was unmistakable as to what we were to do in terms of giving us a boost to begin designing a campaign." Benson and Garrett looked upon the mission as "a campaign more akin to Operation Overlord [the Normandy invasion] in 1944." Their guidance from Akers was to "think of it not just as the front end of a forcible entry that might last only eighteen hours. This was going to be a campaign because we were going to set the conditions for the restoration of democracy or the return of a democratically elected president and we had to find

3. Port-au-Prince airport tarmac after the intervention commenced. Source: Department of Defense.

out what those conditions were." To be sure, this meant "a very short but violent and intense forcible entry and then with transitions. Think through the scope of the problem of getting gunfighters in and then withdrawing gunfighters and replacing them like a relief in place with other troops who weren't coming in with a gunfighter mind-set who were there to conduct stabilization operations." For Benson, "this involved thinking about so-called 'black' special operations forces, those doing the front-end violent stuff, to 'white' special operations forces, the Green Berets who would spread throughout the entire country to help keep a lid on the situation. We were even thinking about UN forces and what that would entail. We thought about coordinating with the navy and the air force and [even] asked, What are the Cubans going to do?" What eventually developed was a campaign that considered "combat operations, a relief in place from combat operations to stability forces, extended stabilization including psychological operations, civil affairs, and civil-military operations, to a handover to UN forces.[10]

While preventive diplomacy and military intervention are broad-brush ideas, Benson thought about more tangible matters such as "a concept of operation or at least a presentation of our concept for review, approval, and guidance from Admiral Miller. Potentially we figured we were going to go from USACOM to the NSC and the National Command Authorities [NCA; by law, President William J. Clinton and Secretary of Defense Leslie Aspin] so we really had to devote our thoughts to that."[11]

Within a few days a plan emerged for securing the country of Haiti and removing its junta by force. For Benson, U.S. troops would "focus our operations on specific leaders that were the 'center of gravity' in our estimation, as well as population centers. Our understanding of the threat, I can't really say the enemy but the threat, was how the people received their information through the grapevine. There weren't many functioning radio stations at the time due to a lack of power. Those that worked were just in Port-au-Prince itself. The telecommunications system didn't work that well but word was spread by mouth and radio when it worked and this was how things got out." Benson believed that once the invasion occurred, word would spread quickly from the large population centers into the rural areas. Maj. David Schroder, an SF officer who had been admitted into the compartment, told Benson,

> What we had to do was get out into the populace and establish a presence in the hinterlands, the [Central] plateau region, the Artibonite Valley below the ridge of [the Central] mountains. So we decided that we had to consider two options. The first was that the invasion would come very quickly. So we could only use the forces available, which really was the Eighty-Second Airborne Division. One of the campaign options was a very large parachute assault at the airfield in Cap-Haïtien and then taking control of the city. The other [assault] was right at Port-au-Prince itself going at focused objectives such as Camp D'Application where we knew that the heavy weapons companies of the FAD'H had their equipment.[12]

The second option was "a link-up operation with special operating forces that were going right into Port-au-Prince itself." Benson described both options as "ostentatious, fill the sky with parachutes. But the Eighty-Second Airborne Division assault while important was really a supporting effort for what was to come. We also felt that it would be a magnet for the press, dramatic parachutes in the sky, AC130 gunships circling above, [aircraft] carriers in the water." While this would be an impressive display of American military power, the main thrust of the first twelve to eighteen hours was "a joint special operations task force of all the [Army] Rangers and [Navy] SEALS and Joint Special Operations Command and those kinds of guys going in with focused objectives to attack the leadership, which we felt would unhinge." The FRAPH was also a target. "We really thought they were too disorganized, mostly thugs. So they weren't going to be a big threat." But Benson also knew that certain individuals might prove to be stalwart junta supporters. In that case, "they might be dissuaded if we went right in after Cédras, Biamby, and François. So they were the main effort or the main attack of the campaign."[13]

If there is any argument to be made for military intervention planning to consider the targeted country's history and what the people think about military authority, then Haiti is a prime example. The planners had U.S. Marines available, if needed. Benson believed,

> We could use a Marine Expeditionary Unit in Cap-Haïtien and then focus more of our effort with the Eighty-Second in Port-au-Prince. But we were reluctant to use marines because of the history of the corps in the [previous] Haitian campaign [1915-34]. We went back to our history books and read a lot about that trying to recall lessons learned. We were reluctant to use marines because they weren't going to help us when the invasion information spread around. We felt the political folks, the Haitian right-wingers, might use them to inflame the populace. That didn't happen. But we did not know that it wouldn't. So that is why we felt that if something was going to break quickly it would just be an all-army show for ground forces.[14]

Meanwhile, the UN had also been active. On January 26

MICIVIH executive director Colin Granderson returned to Port-au-Prince in a fact-gathering role under Chapter VI. By the end of the month, twenty-two UN and OAS observers were in country. MICIVIH reported increased violence in Haiti since their departure, including numerous murders and human rights violations. Executions, suspicious deaths, and disappearances plagued the country, along with appalling mutilations. MICIVIH members reported that most of these actions were attributable to the FAD'H or the FRAPH. Other violent acts included retribution killings by armed civilians (*attachés*), who often acted independently.[15]

JTF 180 planners were aware of Haiti's domestic situation and worked even harder, believing that the execute order would come any day. But after one month and no order to execute forthcoming, Pentagon officials decided to upgrade OPLAN 2370 to Top Secret, for the purpose of keeping matters even more closely held. But that decision further complicated matters. Top Secret status required individuals to have a special background investigation, and not all pertinent personnel had one. About the same time, Benson remembered, "We added Eighty-Second Airborne Division planner Maj. [Anthony] 'Tony' Tata, the assistant division commanders, division commander Maj. Gen. William M. 'Mike' Steele, and his operations officer." In June 1994 Lt. Col. Gordon Bonham replaced Benson, who was reassigned to the Second Armored Cavalry Regiment (Light). After more refinements, a draft plan emerged with a list of forces to be made available if the mission was executed. At this point even more key leaders were brought into the compartment and a planning meeting was held at Fort Bragg. Still, no one discussed the plan outside of the circle of authorized individuals.[16]

The invasion plan, conceived of and modified over several months, had now reached maturity. Given its magnitude and complexity, it serves as an example of what is required to plan a military intervention. Invading Haiti as a peacemaking operation under the UN's Chapter VII meant removing the junta, neutralizing the FAD'H and Haitian National Police, protecting U.S. citizens and property, extending protection to designated third-country foreign nationals, protecting designated Haitians' interests and property, conducting a noncombatant evacuation operation if needed, restoring civil order and disarming thugs, establishing essential services, setting the conditions for the return of Aristide, and reestablishing the legitimate government of Haiti. Due to the mission's scope, JTF 180 required an area of operations that encompassed all of Haiti plus the island of Great Inagua. Since naval support was necessary, the Caribbean Sea west and southwest of Haiti, along with naval bases at Roosevelt Roads, Puerto Rico, and Guantánamo Bay, Cuba, were included. The bases would serve as logistical and force-staging areas.

By April 1994 Eighteenth Airborne Corps intelligence section staff officers joined the compartment. It was known that Haiti's military had about eight thousand troops, half of which had official duties. Upwards of four thousand men were organized into companies of about 160 to 180 soldiers each, primarily in Port-au-Prince but also small garrisons throughout the country. There were also about one thousand Haitian policemen and numerous groups of armed thugs at varying strength. The intelligence officers quickly tapped into various national and military assets that identified nine police companies and eight FAD'H companies by exact location in Port-au-Prince. Moreover, the intelligence effort uncovered thirty-three additional FAD'H company locations in Haiti, as well as three other police companies. Various intelligence sources reported on the government center in the capital, Port-au-Prince International Airport security, and the threat posed by the heavy weapons company with its V-150 armored cars located at Camp D'Application.[17]

Operationally, the mission was envisioned to take twenty-four days. Four days were needed to alert the force, activate JTF 180, establish support bases, and preposition certain assets. Three more days were necessary to conduct a simultaneous strike on Haiti using airborne, airpower, and amphibious assaults to destroy the FAD'H and Haitian police, secure key facilities, kill or capture junta members and supporters, restore civil order, and begin rebuilding Haitian forces. Special operations forces would strike designated targets while SF spread out into the hinterlands. Several more days were involved in establishing contact with Haitian leaders deemed to be legitimate by the interventionists and Aristide. Additionally, civil-military operations would commence and the Haitian National Police would be reorganized while being given short-term training. Preparations were then to be completed for force handover; the UN was expected to assume responsibility for Haiti, but no agreement had yet been reached over that issue.[18]

Rehearsing an Invasion

In early 1994 UNMIH, the UN force created in August 1993, saw its mandate period nearing completion. Given the political conditions in Haiti, UN members initially believed that continuing the mandate made little sense. But an extension might allow the UN field headquarters to activate and deploy faster if circumstances in Haiti changed. Thus the UN Security Council passed Resolution 905 on March 23, 1994, extending UNMIH's mandate but only until June 30, 1994. The resolution also requested that the secretary-general make specific recommendations on the composition of UNMIH's forces and the scope of its activities per UNSCR 867 in 1993.

With UNMIH extended, U.S. forces now rehearsed the invasion plan during a multiservice exercise called Agile Provider at Camp Lejeune, North Carolina. Military officers practiced the mission using computers and worked through the nuances of handing over the operation to another headquarters. Numerous logistical and transportation details were also clarified.

Political and Military Planning

While the UN membership was still seeking a peaceful solution to the Haitian situation, portions of the U.S. military were proactively preparing to invade the island. After U.S. secretary of defense Aspin resigned his post, Secretary William J. Perry received briefings and provided additional input to the planning effort. USACOM officers operating at the strategic and operational levels now prepared a political/military implementation plan (POL/MIL plan) over the summer of 1994.

Having left most of the peacemaking details to JTF 180, USACOM staffers worked with national-level agencies to address high-level postconflict peacebuilding. The POL/MIL document included the political and military end state and defined criteria for military success. It also incorporated supporting plans that covered peacebuilding activities such as a weapons buyback program and international police monitors. The key portion, however, specified the responsibilities for the U.S. government and various agencies in supplying assets, funding, and resources if an invasion occurred either by UN or U.S. approval. Lt. Col. Edward Donnelly, U.S. Army, at USACOM recalled, "Department of State had responsibility for planning, fielding, and orchestrating international police monitors." He added, "We did most of the work at the strategic level and a little bit of the work at the operational level. Most of our interagency work was done within the context of the NSC system through interagency working groups [IWGs] and an executive committee [EXCOM] chaired by Richard A. Clarke, [chairman, Counterterrorism Security Group]. The EXCOM and IWG reviewed the POL/MIL plan, modified and codified it, and then let us work through the details with the various agencies."[19]

Given that undersecretaries from the applicable departments and agencies were part of the IWG, military planners assumed that they would inform their appropriate department secretary as well. It was also assumed that each agency would do what it had agreed to do in gathering the resources and funding necessary to execute their assigned tasks. That proved not to be the case in all instances.[20]

Sending Signals

While the UN Security Council was seeking a peaceful resolution, its body also considered a military intervention to restore Haitian democracy, as evidenced by UNMIH's mandate extension. At this point U.S. officials decided to integrate UN representatives into portions of the peacemaking planning. In late May, U.S. diplomats and key military commanders informed the UN that if an invasion was to occur, it would require a ten-day advance warning to execute it. Assembling aircraft, updating intelligence reports, and marshaling the forces and logistics for a large-scale military intervention took about two weeks. In June U.S. officials also decided that the plan should include postconflict details regarding mission handover to the UN and specifically UNMIH. The 1993 Somalia debacle in Mogadishu had convinced U.S. government bureaucrats that multinational force operations were challenging and often confusing due to diverse doctrine or the lack thereof, as well as language and military terminology disparities. Multinational invasion planning, however, was not normal for UN operations at the time and required surrogate military headquarters such as those of the United States to do much of the work.[21]

June also saw the creation of what became JTF-160, a naval task force formed to interdict Haitian migrants fleeing their country by boat. The task force patrolled the Caribbean to find migrants and take them to sites outside the United States, such as Guantánamo Bay, Cuba. There they were interviewed to determine if they were economic or political refugees. Political refugees could be admitted into the United States, while economic ones were returned to Haiti.

On June 2 the U.S. government also announced the deployment of U.S. troops to the Dominican Republic border to close gaps in the UN embargo. Embargos tend to make smuggling a lucrative business, particularly when large quantities of diesel fuel are required for thirsty Haitian power generators. Much of that fuel came from the Dominican Republic, albeit watered down with urine to increase the amount and maximize profit. The military observers, primarily from Fort Lewis, Washington, became known as the Multinational Observers Group. The group had originally been designated a technical assistance team, with the advance party headquartering aboard the USS *Wasp* and then conducting a border survey June 4–5. The main body trained at Fort Benning, Georgia, and eventually became multinational, with the United States, Canada, Argentina, and Caribbean nations participating.

They deployed on September 11 and immediately patrolled the border area, reporting violations to co-located Dominican military and police units. However, increased tensions between the UN and Haiti caused the force to be withdrawn to Santo Domingo on September 17, where it remained until the twenty-sixth, one week after Haiti was invaded.[22]

A number of critical announcements in June signaled that an invasion of Haiti was imminent. On June 7 the OAS called for a multinational peacekeeping force to assist the Haitian government once the junta stepped down. Although there were no indications that Cédras and his partners were leaving anytime soon, the UN Security Council nonetheless revealed plans to use UNMIH as a post-junta assistance force. The same day, the U.S. government provided evidence that Colombian drug lords had an established link with the FAD'H. A similar situation between drug cartels and the Panamanian military had previously contributed to the 1989 U.S. invasion of Panama under Operation Just Cause. In Haiti the drug connection with Colombia led to increased U.S. sanctions and a financial freeze on all Haitian-owned assets within the United States, less those belonging to Aristide and his followers. Later, on June 24 and in line with UN preventive diplomacy constructs, the Clinton administration announced that UNMIH would contain twelve thousand to fourteen thousand troops, of which three thousand would be U.S. troops. The troops would be combat soldiers in a peacekeeping role under Chapter VI of the UN Charter but nonetheless would be heavily armed and capable of doing more if necessary, an indicator that the use of force might also be under Chapter VII.[23]

The UN Security Council, the OAS, and the U.S. government were signaling that the junta's control of Haiti was about to end. But also at play was the Clinton administration's growing concern over Haitian migrants seeking asylum in the United States. During the last week of June, U.S. ships intercepted two thousand Haitians at sea, bringing the total to about twenty thousand in 1994 alone. As the numbers increased, politicians in Washington DC and Florida increasingly perceived the flood of humanity as a national security threat. Immigrant Haitians were considered a destabilizing factor socially and politically, as well as a financial burden. Extensive media coverage ensured that the American public was fixated on the issue and emotions were enflamed. President Clinton, who had initially rejected his predecessor's policy of not allowing Haitians into the United States, now changed his mind. On June 29 his administration stopped granting asylum to Haitians, although Cubans continued to enjoy that privilege if they could make it to U.S. soil, a policy that smacked of racial prejudice.[24]

The Haitian refugee question affected potential American military activity toward the junta as well. The appalling image of impoverished Haitians in rickety watercraft that leaked and often sank, with catastrophic results, was hard for many Americans and their elected officials to stomach. Political pressure increased upon the federal government to act. The numbers of refugees and their desperation to escape their homeland also indicated that social conditions in Haiti had worsened due to the embargo and not the junta's predatory policies alone. American lives in Haiti might also be threatened. With that in mind, the Clinton administration ordered the USS *Inchon*, with two thousand U.S. Marines aboard, into the Caribbean to evacuate American citizens, if ordered. USA-COM created a Haiti Response Cell that was manned twenty-four hours a day. As far as the U.S. military was concerned, something was about to happen regarding Haiti and it would occur sooner rather than later.

The Development of OPLAN 2380

In July 1994 U.S. military authorities continued to believe that the compartmented and highly classified peacemaking plan, OPLAN 2370, would be executed momentarily. A select group of U.S. government agency representatives knew of the POL/MIL postconflict peacebuilding plan but knew nothing about the peacemaking invasion plan. But as Haitians continued to flee their island home, it became apparent to military leaders and civilian government officials that numerous federal agencies and the government of the state of Florida were involved in Haiti, directly or not. That conclusion necessitated more civilian involvement in military planning but without revealing the highly classified details of OPLAN 2370. Thus, due to the necessity of more civilian involvement, a second plan emerged, OPLAN 2380.

Boutros Boutros-Ghali's 1992 report did not articulate that preventive diplomacy might mean having two military options, one coercive and the other peaceful, occur simultaneously. But military commands explore multiple options in addressing uncertainty, and such was the case with Haiti. A peaceful entry option was first discussed on May 20, 1994, during Exercise Agile Provider. Under U.S. multiservice doctrine of the time, entering a sovereign nation was described as hostile, semipermissive, or permissive. Whereas OPLAN 2370 was a hostile invasion, OPLAN 2380 was permissive; planners skeptically assumed Cédras would agree to Aristide's return and thus make an invasion irrelevant. Still, if no cooperation was forthcoming, OPLAN 2370 would be executed. Both plans, however, competed for forces and funding, as well as requiring a great investment in time and intellectual effort.

OPLAN 2380 was a humanitarian assistance plan in line with UN peacekeeping under Chapter VI. It shared many of the same forces as the combat option but was a permissive-force entry. It did not involve other military assets designed for covert infiltration and target destruction that required a high-level security classification. Thus it was a Secret document and government agencies whose employees held that level of clearance could now participate in planning. Key organizations such as the State Department's International Criminal Investigation and Training Program (ICI-TAP), as well as the Immigration and Naturalization Service, the Bureau of Alcohol, Tobacco, and Firearms, and the U.S. Agency for International Development (USAID) could now participate in postconflict peacebuilding, in this case the postconflict period being marked by the end of Cédras and Aristide's dispute. Military planners in Norfolk hosted several meetings in June and July 1994 that involved government agencies. By the end of July Admiral Miller had two plans available to him, the most likely

2370 invasion plan and the less likely OPLAN 2380, code named Maintain Democracy.[25]

In mid-July, as UN, OAS, and U.S. leaders were hopeful of a peaceful solution to Haiti's woes, Cédras ordered the UN and OAS human rights monitors out of Haiti. In response, the USS *Mount Whitney*, a naval command and control ship, was ordered to the Haitian area of operations. U.S. Marines conducted an evacuation mission rehearsal on Great Inagua Island in the Bahamas, seventy miles north of the Haitian coast. U.S. ambassador to the UN Madeline Albright revealed that eleven nations had pledged to provide supporting troops once the junta had been removed. For its part, the UN leadership reaffirmed that a fifteen-thousand-man peacekeeping force would be placed in Haiti after Aristide returned. Radio Democracy began broadcasts to Haiti to prepare the population for an invasion. Although the Clinton administration announced that no such mission was possible until September, the U.S. State Department announced a forthcoming $1 billion aid package over the next five years. On July 25 the UN finalized details for a multinational force (MNF), but the junta seemed undeterred, organizing an anti-American protest in observance of the anniversary of the 1915 U.S. occupation and beginning plans to elect a president in November.

On July 29 Admiral Miller and his USACOM staff made a critical decision that demonstrates the unintended consequences that can occur when planning interventions. Haiti's junta proved so obstinate that the UN was considering an invasion. Simultaneously pouring over the infinitesimal details of a peacemaking invasion plus a peacekeeping operation consumed Admiral Miller, especially given his other duties. To ease his burden, Miller directed his staff to notify the U.S. Tenth Mountain Division (Light) headquarters at Fort Drum, New York, that they would be designated JTF 190 and would take over OPLAN 2380.

Miller's decision to pass the peacekeeping option that was based on Cédras's assumed cooperation to a U.S. Army division was significant and seemingly feasible. Military doctrine writers had endorsed a U.S. Army division headquarters as fully capable of planning and executing multiservice operations, but only when other services' representatives augmented the staff. As it turned out, JTF 190 did not receive adequate multiservice reinforcement during planning. The JTF was ad hoc. Some augmentees arrived at Fort Drum, stayed a few days with their army counterparts in New York, and then returned to their own headquarters in other states. Some Tenth Mountain officers communicated with other service experts only by secure telephone lines or fax. Many key division personnel flailed themselves into exhaustion by working eighteen-hour days or more seven days a week, plus traveling around the country. Moreover, when matters seemed settled, the plan often changed, thus unraveling hours or days of detailed work.

In truth, the division-based JTF was a terrible idea. A multiservice headquarters such as USACOM contained senior and well-experienced personnel; most officers were War College–equivalent or Command and Staff College graduates. The Tenth Mountain staff, however, had fewer graduates of those institutions and far more junior personnel assigned to it. While they were dedicated professionals with a "can-do" attitude, most lacked the requisite staff skills necessary for joint force decision making and execution. Nearly all of the junior officers were unaware of non-army doctrine and other services' terminology and jargon. Most were unfamiliar with the military software and computerized equipment that made joint force planning and execution possible. Most significant, however, was that few soldiers in the division had any actual experience in permissive peacekeeping operations, although about 40 percent of them had seen combat in Somalia. Still, the commanding general, Maj. Gen. David C. Meade was confident that forming JTF 190 under his supervision was appropriate, saying, "[It] was doggone smart of them [USACOM] to come up with the idea that there might be another end [noncombat] to that spectrum there and that we might not want to have the whole Eighty-Second Airborne jumping out of the sky on top of Haiti for all kinds of obvious reasons." His point was well taken, for OPLAN

4. USS *Eisenhower* with Tenth Aviation Brigade, Tenth Mountain Division (Light), helicopters, September 1994. Source: Department of Defense.

2380 permitted low-level interagency planning that the compartmented plan could not.[26]

On July 30, as military intervention planning continued, the UN Security Council passed UNSCR 940. After months of unsuccessful preventive diplomacy, the UN authorized the U.S. government to militarily intervene in Haiti to remove the Haitian junta. The UN leadership envisioned that an American-led multinational force would conduct a peacemaking operation under Chapter VII, not Chapter VI, invading Haiti to remove the junta alive or dead while disarming the FAD'H, police, and various thugs. The force would also take control of the government until Aristide returned, while postconflict peacebuilding efforts retrained the army and police and attended to other matters, such as supporting Haiti's government. At some point UNMIH would assume mission handover from the U.S.-led MNF under Chapter VI and would remain until Haiti's government was functional. Given Haiti's political and economic history and cultural views of military power, this was a tall order, to be sure.[27]

Meanwhile, although the UN had authorized coercive force, its membership still used preventive diplomacy to find a peaceful end to the crisis. This approach was in line with UN preventive diplomacy theory, but military commanders and planners nonetheless continued to grapple with planning two different interventions in secrecy. Yet security was not as tight as some imagined. At Fort Bragg, Maj. Kristin B. Vlahos-Schafer, U.S. Army Military Intelligence, recalled that the plan details were closely held but "the Eighty-Second Airborne had been conducting pretty extensive planning and I didn't think operational security was that great. Pretty much the post [Fort Bragg personnel and families] knew this was going to happen. They just didn't know when."[28]

Col. James M. Dubik, commander of the Second Brigade, Tenth Mountain Division (Light) at Fort Drum, New York, experienced the planning chaos firsthand. "Okay, the planning process, let me put it kindly, it was dynamic and there were lots of variables in it," he recalled. "First off, we had no clue as to how things were going to develop politically. If you remember the political events leading up to it all, that was one of the dynamics working. The other dynamic was whether or not we were going to execute an invasion or not an invasion. Our plan changed at least daily and sometimes more frequent than that."[29]

Much of the division-level planning concerned available aircraft, for if a combat invasion was executed instead of a peace operation, then, as Dubik put it,

> lots of aircraft would be dedicated to them and lesser amounts to us. So then you have to have a contingency for that. Well, then if there was not going to be an invasion, what part of the invasion force was going to participate and how many aircraft are they going to need? All those permutations were incredibly complex and caused the division to not have the classic military decision-making system. It was deliberate planning in that we were not at war but we might as well have been at war, as we were changing the situation on the "battlefield" every single day. I would go into briefings [at Fort Drum] and sometimes find out that major por-

tions of my mission were changing or could change. The mental flexibility was a big, big deal.[30]

The concern over available aircraft to support two competing and diverse options led to a compromise and a historical first, U.S. Army troops postured on an aircraft carrier to be inserted into a country via helicopter. The division's Tenth Aviation Brigade "practiced this on the USS *Theodore Roosevelt* off the Virginia Capes in the summer" and later, as forces moved toward Haiti, the First Brigade embarked aboard the USS *Dwight D. Eisenhower*.[31]

Moving toward Invasion

In the summer of 1994, the U.S. military was now planning for two entry options into Haiti. Simultaneously, JTF 160 was interdicting Haitians at sea and diverting them to Guantánamo Bay, Cuba. Complicating matters was Cuban leader Fidel Castro's decision in July to flood the shores of Florida with Cuban refugees, which soon consumed the U.S. government's attention. About fifteen thousand Cubans took to the Gulf of Mexico beginning on August 13 and attempted the ninety-mile crossing only to be intercepted by U.S. naval vessels. On August 17 another five hundred Cubans were intercepted, along with five hundred more per day for the next forty-eight hours. With U.S. Navy and Coast Guard personnel working feverishly to locate, pick-up, and transport the Cubans to Guantánamo in what became the Balsero (rafter) Crisis, President Clinton reversed twenty-eight years of U.S. policy and stopped granting Cuban refugees asylum, thus giving them status equal to that of Haitian refugees. The human tide did not stop, however, for 1,770 Cubans were interdicted on August 27. On September 9, 1994, the U.S. and Cuban governments reached an agreement under which twenty thousand Cubans would receive visas to enter the United States each year. When the refugee flow ended on September 13, a total of 30,879 Cubans had been intercepted, the equivalent of a small U.S. city. Clinton, however, treated Haitians no differently. The double standard was apparent to those who cared to see it.[32]

Despite years of extensive UN, OAS, U.S. government, and military planning involving Haiti, the Balsero Crisis demonstrated where actual priorities lay. The plight of fleeing Cubans shifted the American press spotlight despite it having been fixated on Haiti for months. In truth, the political power and influence of Cuban Americans far outweighed the pressure exercised through Aristide's lobbying Congress, Haitian Americans voicing outrage, and members of the Congressional Black Caucus joining them. It took the August 27, 1994, assassination of Father Jean-Marie Vincent, Aristide's close friend in Haiti, to shift media and U.S. government concern away from Cuba and back to Haiti. The brutal murder induced many Washington DC officials to believe that further discussions with Cédras were futile.

Meanwhile, diplomatic discussions were underway to ensure that Caribbean nations joined the effort to present a multinational front against Cédras. USACOM's Major General Byron visited Port Royal, Jamaica, in July and met with various countries' representatives. After a pitch on how the UN was squeezing the junta and the need for regional solidarity, seven CARICOM nations offered up a total of 266 soldiers for training in Puerto Rico. As USACOM's Lt. Col. Christopher J. Olson, U.S. Army, noted, CARICOM participation was essential to tell Cédras, "Yes, we are coming and we've got your neighbors against you. See, they came to our training area in Puerto Rico and we're training them to come take you down and you know, ready or not, here we come."[33]

Coordination of CARICOM forces fell to Olson, who had just graduated from the U.S. Army War College. Upon arrival in Norfolk, Olson went through clearance procedures, became part of the OPLAN 2370 compartment, and was then told he was responsible for multinational force participation. Assembling the CARICOM contingent on short notice meant "you basically had eighteen- to twenty-hour days and some days, like you can see my desk still has a poncho liner somewhere, I just slept in the back room. You know they'd ask you questions and you do what you had to do." Olson coordinated multinational force training through USACOM's special operations command representatives. They reported that participants would need "equipment, parts, trucks, forklifts, engineering equipment, refrigerators, generators, TA-50 [canteens, pistol belts, and small packs], and rations. But most people had their own weapons, although some used former-Soviet ammunition. We had nine days to design and make a CARICOM shoulder patch depicting the seven nations around here."[34]

Olson discovered that outfitting CARICOM in a common uniform was problematic. "It sounds kind of stupid but we even provided underwear. They would come with their foreign uniform and they would throw it down and we would put it into a box and give it back to them. We provided boots, a lot of size 7 boots, and we had to figure out which depots to get this from." U.S. government supply clerks did not share Olson's sense of urgency. American equipment was designed to "fit a U.S. Marine guy but these CARICOM country guys were wide, short, and deep," so finding properly fitting uniforms was problematic. Olson also "established a twenty-one-day training program and it was focused on modules we'd done in the past about peacekeeping. And we started talking with the Tenth Mountain Division and asked them that we have this battalion-sized element and where do you envision them? And they would give us guidance like we want them to guard the Port-au-Prince airport or the harbor or Cap-Haïtien."

On August 30, with CARICOM forces now training in Puerto Rico, the UN again failed to convince Cédras to leave office. The following day, all American family dependents were evacuated from Guantánamo Bay, Cuba, which would become a staging base for the Haiti invasion. Secretary of Defense William Perry authorized the deployment of forces to the Haiti area of operations for posturing purposes while Admiral Miller activated both JTF 180 and JTF 190. Army forces from the First Brigade, Tenth Mountain Division (Light) began loading aboard the USS *Eisenhower* in Norfolk, Virginia. JTF 120, the naval task force in the Caribbean enforcing the embargo, became JTF 185, the naval component for the hostile entry option. Command and staff members of JTF 180 boarded the USS *Mount Whitney*. The USNS *Comfort*, a floating hospital, deployed to support about twenty thousand troops from numerous countries.

POL/MIL Hitch

As military force pre-positioning was underway, final coordination conferences took place at different government and military commands. The meetings covered last-minute details to ensure that all was in readiness for the anticipated U.S. presidential decision to invade Haiti.

On September 11, at National Defense University in Washington DC, the government-approved POL/MIL plan underwent a "back-briefing" where NSA representatives explained how they would execute their assigned responsibilities. By necessity, OPLAN 2370 and the peacemaking invasion came out of the compartment for the first time. Whereas government officials are notorious for leaking information, the Top Secret plan had been held so tightly that many government officials in attendance were completely unaware of it.

After explaining to those present that the U.S. government's EXCOM had approved the invasion plan weeks before, USACOM's Major General Byron asked each agency representative who had been in the compartment to explain what he or she was doing to support the plan, which was surely to be executed. According to Lieutenant Colonel Donnelly, "This was a rehearsal for them. Okay, when we do this, you're supposed to do this and that. Of course, they were like I don't think we can do it that fast. But you have been shaking your heads saying yes, yes you can. So now you have to do it because planes are moving, people are moving, the execution checklist is counting down, West Coast stuff is moving to the East Coast and East Coast stuff is loading up."[35]

The strategic-level POL/MIL plan placed responsibility squarely on the State Department for planning, fielding, and orchestrating the International Police Monitors (IPMs), the force that would enter Haiti to evaluate, guide, and train the new Haitian police. But much of the planning for the IPMs actually fell to the Department of Justice (DOJ). Byron was initially taken aback by DOJ representatives rendering oversimplifications in response to his specific questions. Donnelly recalled that Byron was obviously irritated, "at which point he put it right to Ms. [Jamie S.] Gorelick, the deputy attorney general of the U.S., who represented the DOJ. He said, What is your plan? She said she did not have one. And right then and there the mission passed to Department of Defense and USACOM." Donnelly ran from the room, grabbed a secure telephone, and called USACOM to report that the DOJ had dropped the ball and "boned us."[36]

In Norfolk, Virginia, Lt. Col. Phil Idiart, U.S. Army, was at his desk when he first heard Donnelly's report. Idiart, as with the staff in general, was miffed but not overly surprised. He was stunned, however, when notified to take over planning the IPM mission, a formidable last-minute task. "I was told," he said, "to receive the IPMs, to form them into an organization, deploy them to a training base, train them, and then deploy them onward to Haiti." While the State Department and DOJ had had months to facilitate this action, Idiart had two days to come up with a concept of operations. "I was given some very specific guidance," he recalled, "and within a nonstop thirty-six-hour period a concept was produced." No one within the headquarters "had prior knowledge or experience of how to do this job. It was an aggregate sum of the knowledge and foresight of a lot of individuals."[37]

Idiart took advantage of SF units having a training facility to train CARICOM at Camp Santiago, Puerto Rico. The camp would now house and train the IPM. To its credit, the Department of State offered assistance through Robert B. Gifford of the Office of Policy Planning and Coordination, International Narcotics and Law and Anti-Crime Enforcement Affairs. His knowledge proved valuable, for, as it turned out, he had previously conducted some IPM planning within his office. Idiart also coordinated with Joseph G. Sullivan of ICITAP within the now embarrassed DOJ. Idiart reported, "Sullivan was a contract employee acting on behalf of ICITAP. One of the products that we took was their program of instruction, which is a forty-hour program on how to train police monitors. The IPM vetted and trained Haitians for an Interim Public Security Force

[IPSF]," which replaced the current Haitian National Police and formed the basis for a new national police force.[38]

The IPM's main purpose

> was to oversee the new interim police organ of the restored government of Haiti. There were legal issues of what we could do with police forces. As it turned out, ICITAP actually conducted most of the training certification for the IPSF. But the next issue was what do these IPM individuals look like? A decision was made that each would wear their country's specific police uniform and that they had a choice of either coming with a sidearm or we would provide one. We were interested in a common caliber. Our message to the world outlined IPM uniform requirements, medical conditions, immunizations, what personal belongings to bring, and weapon; if 9mm or caliber .45 we could provide ammunition. Also we would provide a pistol belt, canteen and cover, and first aid kit. Headgear was provided by the State Department and was a yellow baseball cap embossed with "IPM."[39]

Unbeknownst to Idiart, State Department officials, and others not attuned to Haiti's history, yellow was the official building color of the FAD'H. The Haitian people, however, did not overlook this gaffe when forming their initial opinion of the IPM.

The next problem to be solved was providing the IPM with vehicles and leadership. "It was decided that there was a surplus of commercial utility cargo vehicles, a military version of a three-quarter-ton K5 Chevy Blazer, that we supplied by need," Idiart explained. "We also needed an IPM commander. That turned out to be former City of New York Police Commissioner [Raymond W.] 'Ray' Kelly. He arrived late in the process but we were fortunate to find a USMC Reserve colonel by the name of [Richard] Rosser who had prior law enforcement experience. He was designated the deputy commander with the mission to deploy the IPM to Camp Santiago, build up the headquarters, begin to receive the policemen, and then deploy to the island to be the advanced party for the rest of the IPM when they arrived." Within one week, Idiart had accomplished what the Departments of State and Justice had failed to do over several months.[40]

Meanwhile, another crucial decision was made that is indicative of what can happen during preventive diplomacy and military interventions. Lieutenant General Shelton, the designated JTF 180 commander, merged the combat option and the peacekeeping option into a third option, OPLAN 2375. His reasoning was based on continued UN deliberations to find a peaceful solution to the crisis, Department of Defense messages, and intelligence reports. The UN and U.S. government had approved a peacemaking operation under Chapter VII to invade Haiti and everyone expected that to occur. But UN preventive diplomacy efforts might still succeed, so a Department of Defense message stated that the U.S. government considered OPLAN 2380 as viable for continued planning, most likely under Chapter VI. This meant that although UNSCR 940 had been passed, no UN or U.S. executive decision had yet been made to execute it. Reports indicated that some Haitian factions might not appreciate a peaceful U.S. military intervention, regardless of Cédras's approval. Thus OPLAN 2375 became a "bridge" between the first two options, accounting for a semipermissive environment in which the junta would allow forces into the country as Cédras stepped down but recalcitrant factions might resist anyway and have to be violently eradicated. In other words, the "in-between" plan was more an improvised UN Charter Chapter VI+ operation and more akin to an OOTW.

A Convoluted Invasion

At 9:00 p.m. on September 15, 1994, President Clinton spoke to the American people in a televised event scripted for domestic and foreign consumption. He noted that Cédras was an oppressive tyrant and a threat to the United States. More importantly, he stated that an attack was imminent, but "our mission in Haiti, as it was in Panama and Grenada, will be limited and specific. Our plan to remove the dictators will follow two phases. First, it will remove dictators from power and restore Haiti's legitimate, democratically elected government. We will train a civilian-controlled Haitian security force that will protect the people rather than repress them. During this period, police monitors from all around the world will work with the authorities to maximize basic security and civil order and minimize retribution."[41]

Clinton had summarized the crux of the three military intervention options, as well as announcing that two aircraft carriers were headed toward Haiti. The next morning he notified key leaders of his intent to invade the island on September 19. The Tenth Mountain's Major General Meade reported, "I'm standing on the *Mount Whitney* now ready to take orders and do what it is that the circumstance . . . that the team wants done." Meade was directed to have his First Brigade aboard the USS *Eisenhower* readied as a reserve for JTF 180.[42]

In Haiti, Cédras heard from spies he had placed outside Pope Air Force Base near Fort Bragg, North Carolina, that the Eighty-Second Airborne Division was readying for a major operation. The junta leader panicked. He had met Jimmy Carter years before and now called the former U.S. president at his personal number and requested assistance. Carter contacted Clinton, who agreed to send a delegation to Haiti on September 17. Carter would be joined by former JCS chairman Gen. Colin Powell, U.S. Army, and Senate Armed Services Committee head Senator Sam Nunn of Georgia. While the team hastily went to Haiti and met with Cédras, Biamby, and François, the U.S. military moved warships off the Haitian coast and the invasion countdown continued. Frantic negotiations continued into September 18. But with no agreement reached, U.S. secretary of defense Perry signed the execute order to invade Haiti under OPLAN 2370.

Soon thereafter, sixteen C-130 aircraft carrying several hundred paratroopers lifted off from Fort Bragg and headed toward Haiti. Army Rangers loaded aircraft at Fort Stewart, Georgia, and prepared for liftoff in two hours. Other special operations forces deployed by sea and air. Admiral Miller, hearing that an agreement might be reached with the junta, was in a predicament, for operational commanders reported that additional paratroopers were loaded and ready for takeoff. But Miller ordered the troops to wait. Meanwhile, aircraft already airborne had limited fuel and had to drop their soldiers by midnight or abort the mission. In total, there were sixty-two aircraft in the air with more readied for departure, some with troops, several for air traffic control and communications, and others with combat ordnance ready to strike designated targets. In addition, U.S. Marines were afloat off the city of Cap-Haïtien. Two thousand U.S. Army Rangers along with special operations aircraft and First Special Forces Group (Airborne) soldiers were aboard the USS *America* preparing to lift off.

Aboard the USS *Mount Whitney*, the situation was tense and exhilarating. American service personnel had trained for war for years and now they were to experience it firsthand. But the Haitian American Maj. Anthony "Tony" Ladouceur was not totally convinced. Ladouceur, a Medical Service Corps officer, had been brought into the operation due to his knowledge of Haitian Créole. As Haitian cultural advisor to the JTF 180 commander, he arrived aboard the *Mount Whitney*

> around 10:00 a.m. on 18 September. I remembered the first time I saw General Shelton and I shook his hand. He said, "How are you, Tony?" and asked me, "What is going to happen?" I said, "Sir, the Haitians are going to wait until the last minute and then they are going to give up." I remember sitting on the *Mount Whitney* and everyone was excited and watching General Powell, President Carter, and some of the negotiating team on TV and also seeing that the Eighty-Second was on its way. I was thinking, man, I could have been in that plane jumping with those guys. But the general asked me again, "What is going to happen?" And I said, "They are going to give up." And that is exactly what happened.[43]

Miller learned that Carter and Cédras had reached an arrangement through the intervention of Haitian president Emile Jonassaint. Under the Carter-Jonassaint agreement, the junta would remain in place for the moment and be protected from harm but must depart on October 15. A multinational force would enter Haiti permissively to secure the country immediately and prepare for Aristide's return. Soon thereafter, President Clinton terminated OPLAN 2370, the peacemaking option. In the most chaotic military invasion in U.S. history, nearly one hundred military aircraft turned around twenty minutes before striking targets. Hundreds of embarked and unbelieving combat paratroopers who had prepared for combat for months returned to Fort Bragg to join thousands of their comrades, who were angry, disappointed, and even relieved over what had promised to be the largest U.S. Army airborne combat insertion since World War II. Thousands of invasion troops around the United States and in the Caribbean along with their ships and aircraft stood down.[44]

With the invasion cancelled, Admiral Miller reassessed the situation. The remaining peacekeeping OPLAN 2380 and the semipermissive OPLAN 2375 had anticipated that a multinational force might see Cédras and his cohorts remain for a few days but not several weeks. Moreover, U.S. ambassador William Swing wanted troops on the ground, and fast. This meant establishing a robust military presence immediately while simultaneously taking control of the FAD'H and Haitian National Police facilities. It would also mean securing the country quickly to prevent Haitian-on-Haitian violence.

In the wee hours of September 19, military planners sat in stunned silence aboard the USS *Mount Whitney*, for months of planning and increased adrenaline had instantly vaporized. Preventive diplomacy had worked in preventing a war but had now unleashed planning chaos. Radios and telephones blared with commanders demanding to know what had just happened. Frenzied planners sprang into action to pour over the three existing plans and find anything that remotely matched the new reality. No one knew how the Haitian government, its military and paramilitary forces, and the Haitian people would respond to a "helpful" foreign military intervention that had not destroyed the regime as everyone anticipated. Thus it was assumed that Haiti was a semipermissive environment or a Chapter VI+ option similar to but not quite OPLAN 2375 and OPLAN 2380.

5. U.S. Army troops securing Port-au-Prince International Airport. Source: Department of Defense.

In a matter of hours, OPLAN 2380+ came together from a white-board sketch drawn two days before on a whim. The new plan drew on available forces from OPLANS 2370 and 2380 and concepts taken from OPLAN 2375. Since the Eighty-Second Airborne had returned to Fort Bragg, the Tenth Mountain became the force of choice. In a few hours, it would enter Haiti along with SF and support troops as a U.S. peacekeeping force trained for war.

Although the planners had assumed Haiti to be a Chapter VI+ semipermissive situation when creating OPLAN 2380+, UNSCR 940 and its Chapter VII mandate remained in place and U.S. troops entered the country under that authority. Meanwhile, UN, OAS, and U.S. government civilians applauded the Carter team for averting a potentially bloody affair. The near-use of an invasion had accomplished what UN preventive diplomacy had sought for years: a peaceful solution. However, for the military men and women on the ground, the military intervention had just become far more complicated.

4

Conducting a Military Intervention

"There were different perceptions about how to go about conducting the mission that really had to be worked out on the ground."

—MAJ. GEN. DAVID C. MEADE, commanding general, Tenth Mountain Division (Light)

On the night of September 18, 1994, the U.S. government initiated a peacemaking military invasion of Haiti under the authority of UNSCR 940 and Chapter VII of the UN Charter. The objective was to crush the junta and assist in postconflict peacebuilding. But a U.S.-led preventive diplomacy mission achieved peace minutes before the incursion. While lives were spared, Haiti was not the postconflict state that had been imagined. American military troops attempted to mentally shift from a peacemaking to a peacekeeping approach overnight, even as Haiti's junta remained in power and continued to prey on those who challenged the regime. The state of affairs on the ground was no longer hostile in a warlike sense but instead semipermissive and extremely confusing. No one had envisioned multinational troops cooperating with the junta for weeks, a perplexing situation for Haitians and interventionists alike. As intervention forces entered the country, few of them understood how Haitians had historically viewed military power, which caused operational friction among soldiers and the populace. Time was also a factor; U.S. government political realities limited the American military presence to six months in order to avoid casualties and "mission creep." Still, the multinational force stabilized Haiti sufficiently enough to realize mission handover to UN troops before leaving in late March 1995.

D-Day

D-Day, the commencement of the military intervention in Haiti, was the morning of September 19, 1994. At approximately 9:00 a.m., about two thousand members of the First Brigade, Tenth Mountain Division (Light), lifted off in waves of helicopters from the USS *Eisenhower* to perform the first air assault from an aircraft carrier in American history. Dressed in combat gear and armed with loaded weapons, the soldiers disembarked at Port-au-Prince airport, dropped on the tarmac, and established a perimeter. SF members of Task Force Black had previously secured the airfield

Conventionally trained troops such as the Tenth Mountain and their unconventional SF counterparts have different missions. The two rarely operate together, as a matter of routine. The lack of familiarity with each other's culture caused immediate friction at the Port-au-Prince airport. On the scene was Brig. Gen. George Close, the Tenth's deputy commanding general and commander of the ad hoc unit Task Force Mountain. Outfitted in helmet and body armor, he chided the Green Berets for having removed their protective gear and donning soft caps and sunglasses. Although Close had no command authority over the SF, he also castigated them for practicing their French with Haitians through the airport fence. Capt. Horacio Schwalm, SF, was flabbergasted. "We just got chewed out for talking to Haitians. For us that was like telling a race car driver to go slow. That is what we do, we talk to people. And that pretty much set the tone. And this is no small dramatic event in a country that doesn't have any electricity or running water." Right from the beginning, it was clear that conventional and unconventional forces had divergent views of what constituted force protection and mission accomplishment during a military intervention.[1]

In 1993 the army's key doctrinal manual, Field Manual 100-5, *Operations*, had stressed that senior leaders must build trust and teamwork as well as maintain a unity of effort in an OOTW. Because of Clinton and Carter, Haiti had suddenly become an OOTW. But doctrine means little if individuals in responsible positions do not comprehend it or remain wedded to their beliefs as to how things should be done. Maj. Gen. David C. Meade, the Tenth Mountain's commanding general and MNF commander, held the view that the special operators "were driving me nuts; but they did a great job." Maj. Robert Shaw, SF, stated, "It is a commander's prerogative to protect his force and do what he thinks is right. But in some cases too much of it doesn't send a clear message that you are trying to come here in a peaceful manner and settle things and calm things down. As you can imagine, it is hard to tell someone to be nice, quiet, and calm when you are holding a weapon and he is not."[2]

The adage that a unit takes on the personality of its commander rang true in Haiti. Meade's demanding temperament permeated the Tenth Mountain. Maj. Michael Hoyt, an Eighteenth Airborne Corps chaplain from Fort Bragg, North Carolina, was skilled in human dynamics. He had observed the general and his unit

on two other occasions prior to Haiti. There were wonderful people in the Tenth Mountain Division. Some of them I had worked with before. It wasn't a matter of having inferior people or guys that didn't know their job. But the "command climate" up there at Fort Drum [New York] was really oppressive. It was not pretty; guys were not happy. It was not the place to be on the block. It is hard enough to be at Fort Drum just by itself [due to its isolated location]. So, General Meade brought his command climate with him. It didn't get any better when they went to Haiti.[3]

Meade's toughness aside, he was justifiably upset with some SF soldiers. He recalled, "[SF] guys took a truck and three of them went downtown, got a bottle of whiskey, drank the bottle of whiskey, and stayed downtown all night so that the SF guys had to report to the MNF headquarters that three guys had gone. Gone! And they didn't know where. I called the USACOM J3 [Rear Adm. Thomas] "Tom" Fargo at home [in Norfolk, Virginia] at 7:00 p.m. and reported it. They could have been ambushed and who the hell knows what went on." This was not the only

6. Tenth Mountain Division (Light) soldiers observe the daily street life of Port-au-Prince. Haiti's congested urban areas posed numerous challenges to surveillance and movement. Source: Department of Defense.

incident involving SF soldiers, for Meade continued, "I don't go for the fact that we weren't supposed to be drinking in town up at Cap-Haïtien and they [SF] just decided to have some beer. They write their own regulations. I don't go for the fact that one of their sergeants major stole a pump and generator from the Brown and Root contractors so they could put water into their swimming pool. Now those are the kinds of hijinks that those guys get involved in." Meade added, "I don't approve of any of that. It is kind of like having a sensitive kid. You got one kid and you tell him to clean up his room or whatever and okay. You tell the other kid and it is a disaster. He can't and he doesn't want you to tell him anything. And they do not take kindly to outsiders. They want to be, they are, special. So, well, Dave Meade had some problems with special operations guys and the answer is: yes! But they were at the top of my hit parade in terms of per-

formance." Meade's agitation with some SF operatives continued for several months.[4]

Part of the disconnection between all parties (conventional
troops, SF, and the junta) emanated from what each understood
stability to mean. According to U.S. Army operational doctrine of
the time, the use of military force to create stability meant "to maintain or reestablish a safe and secure environment, provide essential
governmental services, emergency infrastructure reconstruction,
and humanitarian relief." For the Tenth Mountain and similarly
organized combat-focused units, stability meant maintaining civil
order forcefully, creating steadiness in daily life through security, setting the conditions for President Jean-Bertrand Aristide's
return, protecting U.S. citizens and designated third-party foreign
nationals and property, confiscating weapons, and offering support to Haiti's legitimate government upon reestablishment. For
SF, experts in more subtle unconventional warfare approaches
and military assistance, it meant securing Port-au-Prince airport
and other urban targets, which included FAD'H installations and
police garrisons. Once that was accomplished, they went into the
hinterlands to calm the area and work alongside the people to build
strong ties with Haiti's rural citizens. But perhaps Raoul Cédras
saw things differently. The country was stable because he was
alive and remained in power, his intention since the 1991 coup.
He had cheated death and spared his country's destruction. He
and his cronies still controlled Haiti, for their enemies had much
to fear but their friends were safe.[5]

But Col. Mark D. Boyatt, SF, disagreed with Cédras, for Americans do not see federal or state military power on their streets
every day. About four thousand of the eight thousand FAD'H and
one thousand Haitian police controlled the country, along with
hundreds of paramilitary force and armed criminal gang members. To Boyatt, armed force in general had made Haiti "anything
but stable. Everything depended upon the FAD'H, from electricity
to water; the whole instrument of governing a town. There were
Cédras appointees, FAD'H appointees, FRAPH influences, armed
thugs, and attachés. Everything was focused upon the military as

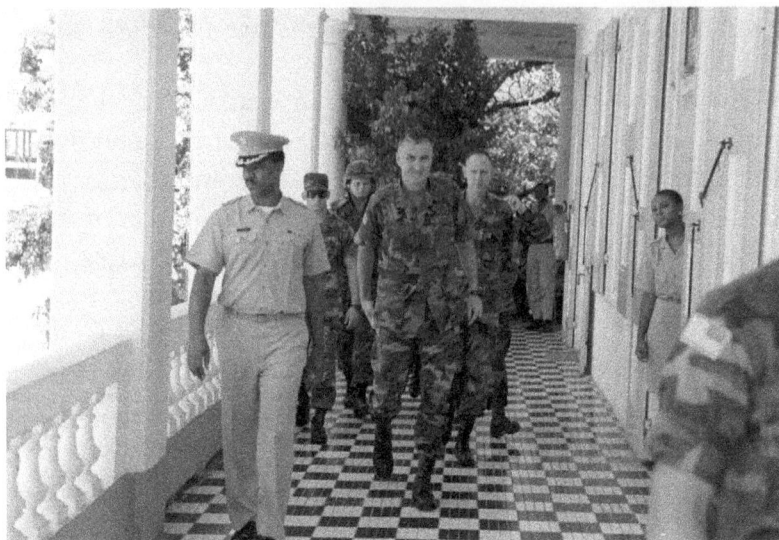

7. Lt. Gen. Henry H. "Hugh" Shelton arrives for a meeting with Raoul Cédras wearing a maroon beret. The six-foot five-inch Shelton intimidated the junta leader into cooperating with military intervention instructions, although not all Haitian forces complied. Source: Department of Defense.

the instrument of a predatory state that sucked everything out of the people and funneled it to Port-au-Prince with little coming back except basic survival. Couple that with 97 percent of the people living in poverty and 3 percent in total luxury."[6]

Boyatt summarized the complexity of an intervening force attempting to impose its will on various armed forces and a civilian populace of 7.7 million in an area about equal to West Virginia.

Eventually, you had twenty thousand U.S. soldiers basically in Port-au-Prince or somewhere around that number controlling about 1.5 to 1.7 million Haitians. You had another brigade-size element [about eighteen hundred troops of the twenty thousand soldiers] in Cap-Haïtien controlling a couple hundred thousand people. Then you had a total of twelve hundred SF and psychological operations [PSYOP] soldiers together controlling the other 95

8. USMC troops aboard amphibious assault vehicles enter Cap-Haïtien on September 20, 1994, for the first time since the 1915–34 U.S. occupation. Source: Department of Defense.

percent of Haiti and they are scattered around the country. So you wound up with a SF A Team with a PSYOP attachment, maybe a linguist, so a total of twelve to fifteen guys, controlling two thousand square miles, 250,000 people, eight to eleven towns of ten thousand to fifty thousand each. Basically the entire civil infrastructure had broken and there was no police. There was nothing.[7]

While former president Jimmy Carter's negotiating team had convinced Haiti's junta leaders to capitulate at the last minute, some pundits believed it was years of international pressure and the embargo that swayed Cédras most. But the intervening forces soon discovered reality. Episcopal minister Rev. Willard S. Squires Jr. and his wife, Margaret, lived in Port-au-Prince from November 1993 until October 1996. From their perspective, "some Haitians did not even know that there was an embargo or what that even meant. We never got any negative feedback from the Haitians about the embargo." For Colonel Boyatt, the embargo had not perturbed the wealthy, for

> they got stuff, all they wanted, across the border from the Dominican Republic in boats. Some boats can come in that country anywhere. It had no effect on the rich at all, the people they were trying to affect. It completely destroyed the nation's infrastructure for the poor. They no longer had roads to move their crops for commerce or marketing or sale. They no longer had water pipes that transmitted water. They had to rely on pumps of which the FAD'H controlled and even disabled some so they could sell the people water. The electrical system was totally controlled by the central government and all revenues from electricity that worked went back to it. So you couple that with the political infrastructure being Cédras-appointed, the mayors, judges, the whole court system being [junta] appointees [who] either fled, left, or tried to negotiate but were not vetted by the people. There were no police because the police were the FAD'H.

As U.S. Army transportation officer Capt. Doni Colon ascertained upon his arrival in country, "This place is in trouble."[8]

For returning Haitian Americans such as U.S. Air Force master sergeant and psychological operations expert Eddison Andre, the Haiti he remembered leaving for New York City as a boy of eleven was gone. "When I first got here in September 1994, I got here at night and couldn't see much of anything," he recalled. "But in the morning the sun broke through the mountains and I saw it. It was devastating, devastating for me to see it. Haiti normally has a strong, earthy smell, very warm, kind of like when you go to Hawaii. But it wasn't there. That was the first thing. After that, it was poor, it was desolate. It was . . . just . . ." His voice trailed off. At least in Andre's case, he still had relatives in Haiti. He appreciated that there were "visitation policies for families to come and visit soldiers."[9]

Gaining control of Haiti's dysfunction began with JTF 180 commander Lt. Gen. Henry H. "Hugh" Shelton departing the USS *Eisen-*

9. JTF 190/MNF headquarters within the Port-au-Prince Light Industrial Complex. Temperatures could exceed one hundred degrees in the building, taking a toll on personnel and electronic equipment. Source: Department of Defense.

hower via helicopter for a 10:00 a.m. office meeting with Cédras. Maj. Anthony "Tony" Ladouceur, Shelton's Haitian American cultural advisor and translator, was to accompany him. Instead, Shelton left on a different aircraft because, as Ladouceur recalled, "It was total chaos. Everybody wanted to get in that bird [helicopter] to be with the general." Ladouceur forced his way onto a different aircraft and arrived at Port-au-Prince airport before Shelton. "I remember they had several Haitian generals there," said Ladouceur, "and General Meade was already on the ground talking to them. And then Shelton's helicopter landed."[10]

The chaotic events that transpired after the invasion was canceled and how the various actors perceived the security situation were reflected in their personal appearance at the airfield. The Haitian military officers wore summer khaki uniforms and sunglasses. U.S. ambassador William Swing and embassy representatives sported suits. Swing's military aide wore a summer uniform with sunglasses and highly shined shoes. Shelton "was wearing a [maroon] beret" and a pressed battle dress uniform but without protective body armor or a weapon. Major General Meade wore a Kevlar helmet and body armor and carried a sidearm because "my people in Haiti were in [combat] uniform and squared away because not only did you want them to look like a fighting force but you want them to be a fighting force and be in the mind-set of a fighting force." Boyatt wore a soft cap, noting that the differences in uniform "came down to culture. I guess it has something to do with the comfort level of the commanders. The Tenth Mountain Division was totally in line with a military tactical environment." In truth, it also had much to do with home-station training and trust, for conventional troops are taught to obey orders while unconventional soldiers are selected for their ability to innovate without direct supervision.[11]

After arriving in Port-au-Prince, Shelton met with Cédras and other junta leaders. He was brief and to the point. The JTF 180 commander emphasized that the multinational forces were deadly serious. Full cooperation was expected. His troops would be visible and prolific, imposing by nature but reassuring in purpose. Cédras promised cooperation.

Still, for all the months of planning before the incursion, confusion clouded the initial stage of the operation. No military plan had anticipated that an American general officer would negotiate with the junta instead of directing its members' death or capture and crushing their forces. Thrust into the role of diplomat but not a military governor, Shelton issued rational but firm directives to Cédras. Pragmatically speaking, the flow of intervention forces into Haiti was not rapid enough to secure the country while removing the FAD'H, which was the only functioning public institution within Haiti. Leaving the Haitian army in power provisionally was a necessary evil; many Haitian soldiers refused to surrender their sidearms and batons. When the issue was not pressed, the Haitian people thought the U.S. military and the junta were in cahoots. To counter that view, Shelton forced Cédras to turn over command of Haitian armed forces to Maj. Gen. Jean-Claude Duperval, who placed vetted Aristide supporters in positions of authority. Still, the use of "trusted" FAD'H members as agents of public safety while American troops interacted with them created ill feelings among Haitians and intervention forces alike.[12]

While army Tenth Mountain and SF units moved into Haiti's capital, U.S. Marines arrived in Cap-Haïtien. The situation reminded many of them of the 1915–34 U.S. occupation. Many Haitians stared at them and vice versa. Aggressive patrolling commenced immediately as the marines awaited mission handover to the Second Brigade Combat Team (BCT), Tenth Mountain Division (Light), scheduled for D+5. Although most Haitians were glad to see American marines, local stakeholders resented their presence. A sense of apprehension hung over the city.

In Port-au-Prince, the Tenth Mountain's headquarters (soon to be referred to as JTF 190/MNF) contracted for an abandoned warehouse as its operational hub and troop billet location. Known as the Light Industrial Complex (LIC), the place was infested with vermin, garbage, and indescribable filth. Maj. Kristen B. Vlahos-Schafer, Military Intelligence, recollected, "It was mostly open bay. No place to go to the bathroom. That was also where everyone slept. There weren't even cots so you were just kind of on the floor. It was difficult to locate water points initially." Maj. Jeffrey Miser, the executive officer for the 524th Corps Support Battalion, remembered, "Tarantulas were around quite a bit. You would step on them in the dark. Mice, a lot of mice. You would hear them overhead." Maj. Peter J. Cafaro, a satellite communications officer borrowed from U.S. Army Space and Missile Defense Command, remarked, "There were 500 troops living in those warehouses. There was dust and bird crap and all kinds of nasty things running around." The refuse was so bad that Captain Colon reported, "When we first arrived we were told that the dust you are breathing happens to be human waste."[13]

Disposing of human urine and feces was no small matter for a force of twenty thousand soldiers. For Col. Jonathan S. Thompson, commander of the Twentieth Engineer Brigade, that task fell squarely on his unit. When planning for the invasion, Thompson recalled, "Everyone had been looking at it for so long that everyone sort of presumed that it was always crying wolf and there was no need to prestock and prepare for the actual event. There was something basically wrong with the philosophy of the plan. We submitted a list of requirements but that was too costly. If it's a hostile invasion there isn't going to be a contractor on the ground to set up port-a-potties, much less service them."[14]

When the peaceful military intervention occurred instead of an invasion, Thompson was livid.

> We did not have the basic services that are required for simple sanitation and life support. What it boils down to is you can feed ten thousand guys three meals a day and then their body processes it. Even if they only process a pound of waste each, which would be unusual, it's a lot of urine too. You gotta do something with it. Every day you are in country the number of people mounts and ten-thousand-plus pounds of shit you gotta do something with. And we had no one to blame but ourselves. At D+25 we still briefed the commanding general at the JTF on the status of what we call SSTs or "shit-sucking trucks," the truck deadline [breakdown] rate was monitored daily. It's absolutely ridiculous.[15]

SF troops in Port-au-Prince were no better off. Colonel Boyatt's soldiers inhabited the Dessalines Barracks dispensary, a FAD'H-occupied facility built by U.S. Marines in 1921. Joint occupancy meant increased stress; many FAD'H members contemplated shooting the Americans, while others offered help. Crammed into two rooms, the U.S. troops found the floors strewn with syringes, condoms, medicine, plastic panties, feces, urine, and a garbage pile that contained human remains. It was here that they slept, cooked, ate, and used the restroom without piped-in water, which the FAD'H had opportunely turned off.[16]

While America's military men and women endured spartan living conditions initially, U.S. government–contracted civilians received extraordinary consideration. IPMs led by former New York City police commissioner Raymond W. Kelly had trained at Camp Santiago, Puerto Rico, where, according to Lt. Col. Phil Idiart, U.S. Army, at USACOM, they were briefed on Haiti's grim living conditions. In addition to other equipment, the IPMs "were issued mosquito netting, cots, and sleeping bags." However, when the advance party of twenty-five IPMs arrived in Haiti, "they faced the actual austere conditions of the country. They were taken to a warehouse totally in non-air-conditioned, cramped conditions. They were all shocked."[17]

Idiart remembered, "DynCorp [a civilian government contractor], acting on behalf of the State Department, immediately and resourcefully offered to contract hotels. Unfortunately, [USMC] Col. [Richard C.] Rosser, the new Haiti police commissioner working with Kelly, did not intercede [to order the IPMs into tents]. In the best interest of diplomacy, he was fearful that if we offend an IPM the donor nation may say that I am going home. So we allowed an expectation that all IPMs would be accommodated in hotels."[18]

Rosser's informal agreement resulted in adverse mission consequences. Idiart noted,

When Mr. Kelly saw this and the second body of twenty-five IPMs were brought in and went to hotels, he concurred with this. Now the expectation became hotels. However, the economy of Haiti following our intervention was just attempting to become restored. A number of other agencies [such as the UN] were in hotels so room spaces were at a premium. So we did not deploy IPMs until hotel rooms became available. We had thirty nations and 850 IPMs. Where we had a very deliberate IPM deployment schedule based upon when you completed training, now it was Commissioner Kelly using call forwarding based upon an open hotel room. This backlogged IPMs in Puerto Rico as they completed training and put great pressure on USTRANSCOM [U.S. Transportation Command], who needed thirty-six hours to confirm flights. Kelly gave a 'GO' or 'NO GO' six hours out or less, so we were constantly making adjustments. The sidebar is that this also placed an [unexpected] expense burden on the State Department because the agreement was that we [Department of Defense; DOD] would provide equipment and training but State would provide IPM accommodations[, which had been planned as tents].[19]

The IPM deployment was to take only a few weeks, beginning in September. But it now stretched into November over hotel rooms. Kelly and Rosser's diplomatic decision to place personal comfort ahead of mission accomplishment meant fewer IPMs on the ground initially. This also signified that there were fewer IPMs available to check for human rights violations. But diplomacy and cultural issues mattered. As Idiart acknowledged, "The hotel room decision was also based upon Haitian interpreters being DynCorp employees who were envisioned to be in hotels. But you could not have an interpreter in a hotel while a Jordanian or Argentinian IPM is living on a cot. Unfortunately, this created first- and second-class citizens because Haitian American U.S. Army reservist interpreters were not living in hotels. There was a lot of cultural sensitivity that had some very significant impacts throughout the operation."[20]

IPM accommodations aside, the LIC was where many U.S. forces were housed and worked in decrepit conditions for weeks. The Tenth's leadership soon barricaded it and was immediately accused of having a "bunker mentality," a perceived aversion toward engaging the population. While the barriers were necessary for security and protecting access to classified material within the LIC, Major General Meade also explained his decision this way: "It gives the impression to potential antagonists that these guys are serious."[21]

In truth, Operation Uphold Democracy was a UN peacebuilding operation overlaid with the Tenth Mountain Division (Light)'s warlike mind-set. This view had carried over from the division's 1993 combat operations in Somalia. Pre–Haiti intervention training at Fort Drum, New York, consisted of live-fire weapon exercises including the use of field artillery, although the artillery did not deploy. Major Cafaro noticed: "This unit had been to Somalia, a lot of them [about 40 percent]." Somalia practices carried over to Haiti in that "the rule was unless two vehicles would go in convoy you couldn't leave the base and at times it was three vehicles.

It just depended upon the unit." Major Miser also thought that the Somalia experience had carried over to Haiti. "Maybe since we just left Somalia and had lost soldiers there," he recalled,

> and a lot of people have said to me that you went to Haiti for a humanitarian mission loaded for bear. But maybe our chain of command did not want to risk taking things for granted. When we first got there we had flak jackets on for the first two weeks. Then the flak jackets came off when in camp but you had your Kevlar helmet and LBE [load-bearing equipment]. Eventually that went to soft cap and no LBE but we always carried a weapon inside the wire. Outside the wire you had [live] rounds. And you better have two vehicles; one for protection and it was a general order.

The carrying of ammunition outside the LIC was not universal, however. Cafaro noticed that one Signal Corps U.S. Army captain who had been ordered to deploy from Fort Huachuca, Arizona, "had no ammunition for his M-16 rifle. That is a hard thing for a person to realize that they are giving you a rifle for a purpose but all you can do is display it."[22]

JTF190/MNF's prudent approach resulted in no American soldiers being killed initially. But while U.S. Marines patrolled Cap-Haïtien straightaway and around the clock, the Tenth Mountain did not do so in Port-au-Prince at night over fear of reprisals by various Haitian groups. Without U.S. soldiers on the streets, criminals preyed on the people. Major Vlahos-Schafer observed that, before deployment, "I was under the opinion that there was going to be resistance and not necessarily a formal resistance but guerrilla attacks. In fact the commanding general of the Tenth Mountain did not allow any movement at night because of his fears of that. This caused some problems because that allowed dissident elements to basically terrorize the population at night because we wouldn't go out."[23]

Dr. Bryant Freeman, the director of the Institute of Haitian Studies at the University of Kansas, was working for the UN at the time. He also noticed that the Tenth was not patrolling Port-au-Prince aggressively at night, which confused and angered him and Haitians. "Oh man, I was so mad," he said. But Freeman also noted that most of the citizens' anger was directed at former U.S. president Jimmy Carter.

> There was graffiti on the walls in town in Créole that said, "Carter is the agent for rapists, torturers, and murderers." We moved in and were in an impossible situation of having to cooperate with the people we should have been putting down. Carter thought he secured this big victory. And here was the Tenth Mountain Division from New York State in hot [combat] uniforms avoiding contact because of two words: no casualties. So when there is no contact, there is very little chance of casualties. The population would have felt encouraged if they had some more contact with the American troops when they first arrived. My observation was that there was minimal contact. In the first U.S. presence in Haiti, 1915–34, there was enormous contact. Many of the marines learned to speak Créole, got out, got around the population, but this is not the case at all in 1994–95.

The Squireses held similar views as Freeman, describing U.S. military contact with Haitians as "minimal, although we were glad to see them." Willard Squires added, "The first American to approach me was a Haitian American staff sergeant who had been in the U.S. a number of years. He asked me if I was an Episcopal priest because his father was one."[24]

Of course, the lengthy occupation by the U. S. Marines in the early twentieth century allowed for more opportunity to engage the population, learn the language, and earn public trust. Yet in 1994 there were counterintelligence reports coming in to JTF 190/ MNF from field agents with pro-American Haitian contacts. The agents related that pro-Cédras groups were taking vengeance on Haitians who cooperated with Americans. Vlahos-Schafer elaborated: "There was a big problem with General Meade's concern about force protection and not getting the U.S. soldiers out there. It allowed the forces that the Haitian people were reporting [about] to the counterintelligence guys to continue to terrorize the people. The people who actually reported on them were at risk. Fortu-

10. Camp D'Application FAD'H V-150 vehicles equipped with 90mm guns. The vehicles posed a significant threat to the USS *Harlan County* and lightly armed intervening ground forces. Source: Department of Defense.

nately, at about the two-week period, the Tenth Mountain Division started patrolling. General Meade lifted the night restrictions and started to take care of some of these problems of lawlessness, especially at night, and retribution attacks where we were really getting the bad guys."[25]

The hesitancy to patrol Port-au-Prince at night had its advocates and opponents. Meade explained what he called the fire department analogy":

The fire captain says to get those guys out of the basement and get them out right now. He doesn't know if the roof is going to fall in but he is experienced [enough] to know that the roof could fall in and there is no reason to take that risk at all. They'll get the fire, they'll get at it a different way. So if you make the wrong call on force protection including the gear of the soldiers but also the mind-set of caution that goes with it, you can be aggressive and be cautious and alert at the same time. If you go in there unprepared and they shoot your ass, you're stupid, you know?

Boyatt, however, disagreed: "The conventional forces had very little interface with the Haitian people. They perceived the Haitians as a threat, as opposed to what I think, that they were an asset or something to work with." Regardless of viewpoint, Maj. Clayton Cobb, a psychological operations officer, was quick to point out that at JTF 180, "Lieutenant General Shelton's [personal] approach was no body armor, no LBE when he would meet with people, and that kind of placed him on equal terms rather than this knight in armor."[26]

D+1

On September 20, twenty-four hours into the intervention, most Haitians went about their business as the multinational force slowly gained control of their country. Curiosity nonetheless overcame several hundred locals who strolled to Port-au-Prince harbor to watch the U.S. ships offload cargo. Television crews tagged along to broadcast live video. Many Haitians were watching the activity and celebrating, when a group of FAD'H members appeared and began to beat them. Camera crews broadcast the horror on live television. One man was killed. The well-armed, shocked Americans showed incredible restraint and stood by, following orders that the FAD'H were in charge of public order and not to interfere with Haitian-on-Haitian violence. But U.S. military discipline also drew vilification. Freeman remarked,

> The [American] troops were horrified by what they saw, the way the Haitian army was treating the people. The Haitian army did not get the word when we first went in and what the American population and U.S. government saw on television was nothing unusual. It was just what the Haitian army had been doing all along: clubbing people, beating people, in arbitrary fashion. There were people simply watching tanks [actually Bradley fighting vehicles] and large equipment coming off the large supply ships at the dock, which was an extremely interesting thing to see. They hadn't seen such things in their life. So they were simply gathering around watching these things quite peacefully. The Haitian army decided they

should not be there. They suddenly arrived and without warning began clubbing people. There was a lemonade salesman who happened to be in the wrong place at the wrong time and he was clubbed to death in front of American TV. This changed the orders greatly. We were horrified but the American population doesn't realize that this is nothing unusual.[27]

The White House immediately responded with new rules of engagement that hurriedly flowed down the military chain of command. According to Major General Meade, "That's when we talked, General Shelton and I talked and so I called Cédras on the phone. I said that I was coming to see him and then that's the afternoon that I went to see Cédras by myself with my interpreter. And I told him to knock that stuff off. I really believe in my own mind that Cédras had no idea that incident had happened; the Haitians are not that good at command and control. The people [FAD'H] at the port responded as they would have twenty-four hours earlier."[28]

Whether or not Cédras knew of the incident is unknown. Yet he had held sway over Haiti's people for three years and his military had carried out well-entrenched policies. Indeed, the junta's militarism was so effective in controlling society that American leaders had hotly debated the role of the intervening force in preventing Haitian-on-Haitian violence long before the intervention occurred. Now those who had won the argument for noninterference watched as the results of their oratorical victory unfolded on television. Major General Meade recalled the fallout as, "Yeah, the [new] guidance was you're not prohibited from intervening in that kind of thing, when you see it happen, get in there." For the moment, however, many observers continued to believe that JTF 190/MNF remained hesitant in stabilizing a very bad societal situation.[29]

D+2

By September 21, about ten thousand U.S. troops were ashore and more continued to arrive each hour. JTF 190/MNF was soon reinforced by one company of the Third Battalion, Fifteenth Infantry

(Mechanized), a Bradley-equipped heavy unit from Fort Stewart, Georgia, that deployed via ship and aircraft assets. Although the unit was to reinforce the Eighty-Second Airborne Division under OPLAN 2370, its involvement remained necessary under OPLAN 2380+, given that Camp D'Application, a FAD'H encampment of 250 soldiers, had ten artillery pieces (75mm and 105mm howitzers) and twenty-one V-150 armored fighting vehicles that had not yet been seized.

Capt. John C. Valledor, the Bradley commander, had prepared his unit since September 10 for the Haiti mission. "We did a couple of map exercises and then some small unit training lanes with possible missions. Many of the commanders had been in Somalia so we trained on how to establish a roadblock, a checkpoint, and how to react to crowds and how to properly employ a Bradley in a mountain environment and in crowd situations." With rumors swirling that Haiti was about to be invaded, Valledor's training "was all flavored by Somalia. The initial impression was Haiti was a worst-case scenario so we went back to our last operation, which was Somalia, and the experts in the battalion who had been there, which was a benefit." Not everyone saw it that way; one battalion officer thought the training was useful for an invasion but not for what actually occurred in Haiti.[30]

Valledor's company was to have spearheaded the initial portion of a full battalion deployment, which did not materialize. Fortunately, his force was heavily augmented by additional units. His unit was temporarily redesignated Task Force Victory after the Twenty-Fourth Infantry Division motto, "Victory Division." "I was 'plused up' with soldiers from my sister companies to 100 percent strength," Valledor explained. "I received two additional sniper teams with Somalia experience. The day before departing for Haiti I received a counterintelligence team, a medical facility with a woman lieutenant medical specialist, welders and iron for [vehicle] body armor, and other logistics people. My company grew from 105 to 220 personnel. I also had a captain from the Twenty-Fourth Division's Main Support Battalion who controlled the logisticians and our battalion executive officer, Maj. [William

11. A CARICOM patrol reflects the inherent tension of confronting an agitated Haitian citizen on the streets of Port-au-Prince, although JTF 190/MNF force protection policies had eased when this photograph was taken. Source: Department of Defense.

E.] Dickens, to be a liaison officer to the infantry battalion we were to join in Haiti."

After a preinvasion briefing at Fort Bragg, North Carolina, Valledor's unit arrived in Haiti on D+2.

Basically we landed at Port-au-Prince airport and I met with Brigadier General Close. He gave me an OH-58 helicopter and we did an aerial reconnaissance of Port-au-Prince looking for a staging area for my Bradleys. I looked at the pier but did not find them. I then linked up with Lt. Col. [James L.] Terry, the commander of Second Battalion, Twenty-Second Infantry. I found my Bradleys at the port in one of the biggest snafus that I have ever experienced. There are personnel everywhere unloading all the administrative stuff, the milvans [cargo containers], and they had blocked the pier. Behind all of that admin stuff were my combat Bradleys and maintenance vehicles. We spent half an hour trying to find someone who could open an avenue to get them out. That goat rope then took about two hours. I had to get the vehicles, upload ammunition, and then move out. My concern was I could not respond if needed. I then staged the vehicles in convoy and prepared to move to Port-au-Prince airfield to be part of the Quick Reaction Force.

Although commanders had doubts as to how the Americans would be received by Haitians, Valledor's unit became a spectacle.

The Bradleys were sand-colored and stood out. There were humongous crowds plastered along the fence line right outside the gate and I was concerned how to navigate without running over anybody. When I got the call to move out, the gates opened up and it was just like Moses. The noise and vibration of the vehicles scared the parting crowd. But they were jubilant. The turrets were traversing left and right and that drove the crowd crazy. They loved it. Here we were expecting sniper fire but it was like a pep rally all the way up to the airfield. The media was there. I felt like a Roman conqueror walking into a place; we were on chariots. Then it was back to business, we have a mission to do but it was kind of fun.[31]

Just forty-eight hours into the intervention, other American troops were trying to make life bearable. Major Miser remembered,

When we first got there we didn't have wood floors so it was high grass in the tent. Latrines were a trench dug in the dirt and a canvas cordoned off for privacy. Within a day, we started making latrines out of plywood and used fifty-five-gallon drums cut in half and then we burned the contents. We hired male Haitians to cut the grass with machetes. We had female Haitians who would clean the dining facility, sweep out your area, and dust your desk, except the restricted areas. We had a guard with them the entire time and they were paid in cash at the end of each day. We got an artist who painted unit signs. A Haitian vendor coordinated for port-a-johns and washbasins. We built plywood stands that we could set the round basins in. They had mirrors so you could stand up and shave and wash your face.[32]

12. Soldiers of the First Brigade, Tenth Mountain Division (Light), negotiate the crowded streets of Cap-Haïtien. Source: Department of Defense.

D+3

With the Bradley unit's arrival, the major goal for September 22 was to move into and occupy Camp D'Application. The facility was a priority target but after three days still remained an urgent objective. Under the invasion option, Army Rangers were to have assaulted the camp immediately. But now the task fell to SF. Although the situation was edgy, SF soldiers moved into the area and secured it without incident. Soon thereafter, infantrymen from the Tenth Mountain along with Valledor's fighting vehicles arrived to tow the Haitian combat vehicles to a more secure area. The SF troops welcomed them by "doing the wave." Major General Meade admitted that he was not amused, for this meant that his soldiers had been disrespected by other Americans in front of the FAD'H. Meade admonished Lt. Col. Michael Jones, SF, who then received a similar scolding from his commander, Brig. Gen. Richard A. Potter.[33] The strained relations between the Tenth Mountain and sf soldiers were obvious. In this case, as Maj. Robert Shaw, sf, pointed out, "the light infantry and mechanized troops rolled up to the gate with their helmets and everyone had loaded guns. In fact, the word on the street was that the Tenth had a policy that every operation outside the compound was a combat operation. Well, that is one way to look at it. The special ops at the camp had a different view. They had convinced their adversaries to become more helpful and that lowered the tension. As soon as the Tenth rolled up, the level of tension rose back up again. If the special operations folks had known they were coming, they would have told them that the situation was calm and [to] not roll up with the Bradleys and vehicles. It is not necessary." Meade admitted, "It was a glitch. But when they pulled in with their Bradleys, the crews fell out the back and took up defensive positions on the ground, as they'd been trained to do. And the sf guys were sitting on the berm in their T-shirts and doing the wave for the benefit of the cnn cameras and they derided and made fun of our soldiers. General Shelton had a fit." Regardless, no one was injured and the facility remained secured.[34]

D+4

September 23 saw the arrival of CARICOM, a regional composite force of 266 troops. The force not only demonstrated OAS resolve for Operation Uphold Democracy but served to legitimize the U.S. role in multinational peacekeeping operations. Lt. Col. Chris Olson from USACOM was in charge of assisting CARICOM. "What we were trying to do was show that the seven island countries around here have banded together against the Cédras regime," he explained. "For international appearance, having all the different kinds of flags gave credibility to the U.S. position. Even if you get one platoon of guys, that's another flag. So we can stick it in with the rest so when we show this on TV it's not the U.S., the big, bad U.S., going to kick the shit out of a little island. It's like you've got all these people here who feel the same way you do. So the more flags, the better. But they did not bring a lot of combat power." CARICOM forces reported to JTF 190/MNF and served in numerous locations throughout Haiti during three iterations (CARICOM, CARICOM II, and CARICOM III).[35]

On Saturday evening, September 24, Haitian police near their police station fired on a U.S. Marine Corps patrol in Cap-Haïtien. The marines, who were attempting to negotiate the policemen's surrender, returned overwhelming fire. Ten policemen were killed and one Haitian American translator was wounded. While some decried the marines' action as overly aggressive, Col. James M. Dubik, commander, Second BCT, Tenth Mountain Division (Light), approved: "It was the best thing that could have happened. It was absolutely the best thing. That set the conditions for the success of the mission later. The city [Haitian citizens] would have liked more than ten killed but it was okay because anyone not killed left." The firefight drew media scrutiny and also a visit from Cédras; Shelton wanted him to view the bodies so as to impress upon the junta leader that Americans would defend themselves if fired upon. Major Ladouceur accompanied the group as a translator. Cédras claimed that the Haitian casualties "were not soldiers but we found out they were soldiers. Let me tell you the marines did a job on those boys. I mean they were full of holes. I have never seen so many holes in bodies the way those guys were shot up. The bodies were beginning to smell and people had handkerchiefs over their faces." The Clinton administration supported the young Marine Corps officer who made the decision to return fire.[36]

Things were calmer in Cap-Haïtien, but at a price: the FAD'H departed, leaving Americans to patrol the entire city. U.S. officials soon feared that U.S. troops could end up patrolling all of Haiti's urban centers, a situation that could lead to casualties. Closer U.S. relations with the Haitian military to coordinate activities soon followed, further reinforcing the perception among many that the despised FAD'H and the heavily armed Americans were clones.

On September 25 Colonel Dubik's Second BCT arrived in Cap-Haïtien and assumed mission handover from the Marine Corps. His unit was away from the Tenth Mountain's "flagpole" in Port-au-

Prince, and his division commander gave him the latitude to operate. Smoothing relations after the previous day's firefight became a priority. "I literally went on a little chamber of commerce speaking tour. I talked with every clergy group that I could get ahold of, independent groups, the executive board of the chamber of commerce, the bishop, and all five Lavalas groups. I talked to the school principal group. I went to meetings of youth organizations that were very active and politically astute. I ran a public information campaign, handouts and radio, TV, loudspeakers, and then enlisted certain group members that proved particularly helpful and put them on loudspeakers."[37]

While Dubik went to extraordinary lengths to appear transparent and engage the locals, he held an iron fist within his velvet glove.

> I used force to impose my will on this place. I did it in such a way as to not kill anybody. When I showed up with infantry they moved out in platoon formations with machine guns and SAWs [squad automatic weapons] and they moved into the city. No one was going to screw with them. And that was the mind-set the whole time. We would get reports that someone was going to throw a bomb. So, fine. We go find Person X and knock on their door, surround his house with a platoon, take a military police squad right at his front door and introduce my battalion commander, Lt. Col. So-and-So. We then said, "We have this report that you are thinking about throwing a bomb. Now don't let that happen because we know where you live and we will come and get you."

Many Haitians received similar attention, which had a dramatic effect in reducing incidents in the area.[38]

But Dubik also found himself addressing one of Haiti's major issues, which was unspeakable filth. "I landed on the airfield," he recalled, "and there was literally three piles of a combination of trash and shit, right off the side of the international airport." In Cap-Haïtien, "they leave piles of trash, and garbage, and human waste. We carried out six, five-ton truckloads of decayed animal remains from the butcher shop. Now how many years does it take to accumulate that much remains? The gutters never worked; full of garbage. Along the [Mapou] river that ran through the main city of Cap-Haïtien you could see the routine of adults taking shits, pigs wallowing around and eating the garbage, and kids playing and swimming in the water. I have seen a lot of bad stuff but this was destitute living at its finest."[39]

Over the Wall

The story of Capt. Lawrence P. Rockwood II, U.S. Army, a Tenth Mountain military counterintelligence officer, reveals much about the convoluted nature of military interventions. When Rockwood arrived in Haiti on September 23, 1994, the Tenth Mountain Division (Light) was attempting to gain control of the country. Unbeknownst to his chain of command, Rockwood suffered from depression and was taking Prozac prescribed by a civilian doctor. He also took President Clinton's September 15 speech to heart in believing that "stopping brutal atrocities" was one reason for the military intervention. He did not recall viewing Clinton's September 19 message, when the president stressed that the safety and security of U.S. troops was his first priority, which Major General Meade fully understood.

Rockwood soon became agitated that neither JTF 180 nor his own headquarters had inspected the Haitian national penitentiary, which in his mind was a direct violation of Clinton's orders. Maj. Stephen C. Gomillion, a division counterintelligence officer, recalled that no one seemed interested in inspecting prisons except "him [Rockwood] personally. That is the only thing of any interest I recall anyone doing with prisons whatsoever. He had privy information coming in from various sources but how he interpreted that would be hard to say."[40]

After several more days in Haiti and analyzing more human intelligence source material, Rockwood was convinced that human rights violations were occurring in the prison and they warranted immediate attention. A September 27–28 report from a jail in Les Cayes after a U.S. military weapons search revealed "horrific" conditions there, which Rockwood extrapolated as indicating the possibility of a similar situation in the national prison. Maj. Kris-

13. An American MP executes a crowd control mission in the midst of Haitian protestors. Source: Department of Defense.

ten Vlahos-Schafer recalled that Rockwood, a recent convert to Buddhism, was frustrated, for he was "a pretty sensitive person. But he also had access to our black, white, and gray list, which was our list of bad guys, good guys, and guys we were not sure of."[41] Rockwood believed that the information in such lists and operative field reports justified his opinions. He approached his chain of command, demanding that the commanding general, Major General Meade, do something. His request to broach the subject was denied.[42]

Meade was unaware of Rockwood's pleas. He was concerned over two explosive incidents, the shootings in Cap-Haïtien on September 24 involving U.S. Marines and a September 29 grenade attack on Aristide's followers near the Haitian National Palace in which several people were killed and others wounded. He immediately placed intelligence collection priority on identifying and capturing the culprits. But Rockwood disagreed with Meade's priorities and, on September 30, made a formal complaint to the division's inspector general. For his part, Meade said, "I had never heard of Rockwood nor had anyone said anything like, Jeez, there's this captain with this idea and we think it's kind of not a good idea but you ought to know about it." Meade nonetheless believed himself to be accessible because "I lived in the same building, I mean here's this huge unair-conditioned old building in ninety-five degrees and I live in what used to be the manager's office and I am sweating with the rest of them. The little windows of my office looked right down on the floor of that. We had a briefing most days at 6:00 a.m. and 6:00 p.m. I was sitting in a chair mostly. So someone could have said something or Rockwood could have stopped me and said, 'Hey, I'd like to talk to you.' But I can see why a captain wouldn't do that."[43]

On the night of September 30, Rockwood's anxiety boiled over. He decided to take measures into his own hands. In violation of a Tenth Mountain directive regarding personal security, he went over the wall of the compound without authorization, armed with his M-16 rifle. He eventually arrived at the prison to confront a confused Haitian officer with demands that he be given a full accounting of all prisoners' welfare, although he had no solid evidence of abuse to substantiate his request. He was treated courteously and entered the prison, where he looked around for three hours. It was evening and dark, but he described the place as "open but crowded. I saw crowded cells with what seemed to be military prisoners, peeling paint, a water fountain." An American attaché's arrival soon led to Rockwood being taken into U.S. custody.[44]

On October 1, 1994, it was business as usual for the Tenth Mountain; most soldiers did not know the incident had occurred. That day, with Rockwood now in custody, Col. Michael L. Sullivan, U.S. Army, entered the prison in an unrelated search for a place to house prisoners taken by the multinational force. He reported conditions that were no different than other Haitian prisons suffering from a lack of money in a very poor country. He saw no signs of abuse or torture; several men in the infirmary were ill, but nothing seemed life threatening. After his tour, he recommended to Meade that the UN or some other agency provide relief. He decided not to house his prisoners there.[45]

After a psychological evaluation, Rockwood was sent to Fort Drum. He refused nonjudicial punishment under the Uniform Code of Military Justice and demanded a court-martial. Although former U.S. attorney general Ramsey Clark defended him, he was found guilty of five counts, including conduct unbecoming an officer and failure to report to his place of duty. His appeal was denied and Rockwood was discharged from service. To many Haitians, Rockwood is a hero whose actions will certainly become more myth than fact over time. But to officers such as Vlahos-Schafer, the counterintelligence captain's behavior "is still kind of hard to believe. We have all got our personal convictions. But I think we understand how the chain of command works and what as a U.S. representative on a taskforce like that means and what the boundaries are. This guy was clearly out of them."[46]

Urban and Rural Operations

By mid-October 1994 most of the twenty-thousand-man force had arrived and were conducting daily operations. The junta leaders left the country; Col. Joseph-Michel François fled to the Dominican Republic during the night of October 5. On October 13 Lt. Gen. Raoul Cédras and his family, along with Gen. Philippe Biamby, departed Haiti for Panama on a chartered Boeing 757. Twenty-five retainers and friends went into exile in the United States. Cédras was allowed to rent out three properties in Haiti for personal income and to access $79 million in previously frozen bank accounts. Aristide was reinstated on October 15 to serve out the remaining months of his term. For JTF 190/MNF, conventional military operations followed a pattern of surge, sustain, and reduce operations until January 1995. For Dubik, surge operations occurred when "75 percent of the force was doing something and we did those when Aristide returned or [on] the anniversary of the Haitian Revolution. Sustained operations were what we did twenty-four hours a day and the force was patrolling, etc. Reduced ops occurred once every seven days where we had minimal activity."[47]

Overseeing the military effort was Major General Meade, who

14. The results of Codeine Bob's vehicle search. Source: Department of Defense.

commanded MNF operations until January 1995. His position meant directing the force but also escorting politicians and other interested parties. For those who wanted to visit Haiti for photo opportunities or to see constituents during a military intervention, Meade found that "Haiti is very easy to get to. You can go to your office in Congress in the morning, take the car to Andrews Air Force Base, fly to Haiti, and be there at 10:00 a.m. Take a pretty good tour, have lunch, go up country somewhere, go to a SF outfit, go to an infantry place, go by the headquarters and get a briefing, come back, and be back in Washington by 8:00 p.m."[48]

Despite visitors and high-level commitments requiring Meade to be at his headquarters, he traveled the country periodically. On one visit to the U.S. embassy he talked with the Haitian finance minister and governor of the Bank of Haiti, Leslie Delatour. Delatour told Meade, "I want to remark on your soldiers. Warlike but kind. Your soldiers are big and they have the vest on and they have their helmet and their weapons and they look very alert. At the same time they let the children come and sit in the vehi-

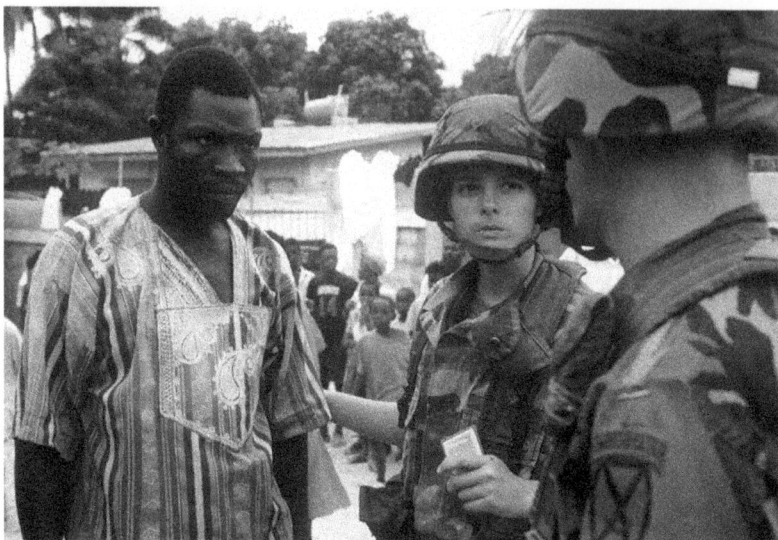

15. A Haitian American translator at work during a weapons sweep. Source: Department of Defense.

cle and pretend to steer it. This is a great surprise to us, that your soldiers can do both kinds of things. I must tell you that our people are very impressed. But I must also tell you that the forces of the FAD'H and the police are scared to death of your soldiers." In response, Meade said, "These are my exact words: They ought to be scared to death of our soldiers. They have good reason to be."[49]

Major General Meade's movements also encompassed the streets of Port-au-Prince. On one occasion just after the Haitian Parliament opened, Meade and his translator were walking along a street when he spotted a crowd of people surrounding a child who was lying on the ground holding his stomach.

> He was barefoot and just had a pair of shorts on and his stomach is [sliced] open and you can look in there. So nobody knows the kid or where he came from. So I said, If we take this kid to the hospital will someone go with him? And my interpreter asked and they said, Yeah. Haitians are nice people and enormously appealing in many ways. So we load the guy in the truck and take him to the hospi-

tal. The doctors looked at him and then they cleaned out whatever is in there and sewed him up. I went over there most every night because you had appendixes being taken out and we had retired guys from Brown and Root Corporation having a heart attack. And a week later the doctors said to come here. They showed me the kid and he's fine and they let him out and away he went.[50]

In Cap-Haïtien, Colonel Dubik held weekly meetings with local leaders. Still, some Haitians tried to take advantage of U.S. forces and their supposed American wealth. Dubik recalled, "The Haitian business guys had this definition of security that it is absolute. I asked them how much money they dedicated to security systems. None. How many of you have a night watchman? None. Do you know how many businesses in the U.S. would go out of business like that? This goes back to liberal education. They had been using the government to pay for that. Well, I am not the government and footing that bill anymore. If you want greater security, then you have to pay for it out of your profits. That is how free enterprise works." Dubik's point did not always register. "I would go to meetings and they would say, My store was broken in. But I drove past your store at 1:00 a.m. and nothing was broken. One guy had his store burnt down. He said that his store was looted. I said, No, I was standing there when the fire started. I think all the windows were locked from the inside. The fire started in your store and I think one of your employees did this. You lost two cans of Crisco and three bags of flour. That is not being looted."[51]

Dubik's view of proactivity also meant not inviting trouble. "From my view," he said,

nobody is going to screw with us. So we put machine guns on flatbed trucks. Nighttime you typically walk around with night vision devices in squads of six, seven, or nine guys. When you turn a corner you have two on one side and five on the other. But in Cap-Haïtien everything was done with platoons [up to forty soldiers], not squads, and at random. We changed our patrol routes regularly, like every two to three days. We altered direction of routes.

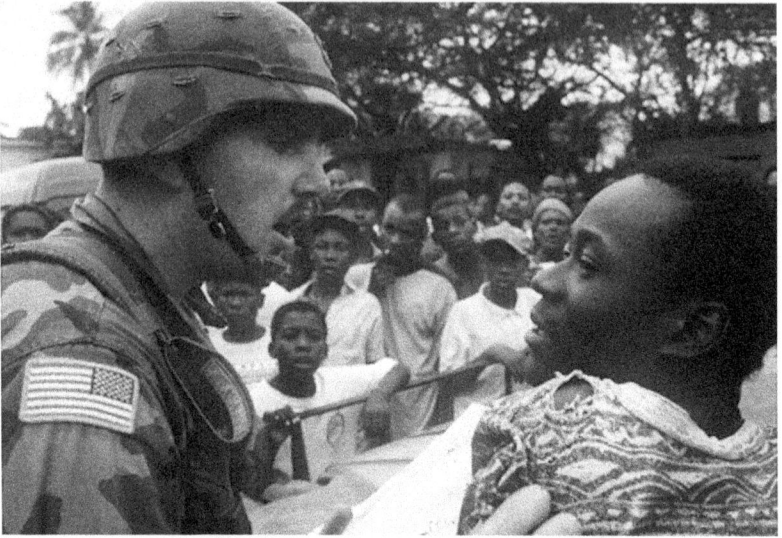

16. A Tenth Mountain Division (Light) soldier interacts with a Haitian citizen. Aggressive behavior reinforced Haitian cultural beliefs that armies exist to intimidate civilians. Source: Department of Defense.

We had static security points and roadblocks that set up randomly day and night. We had no response [from threats].[52]

Army patrols conducted sweeps through neighborhoods looking for weapons caches in what were called "Mountain Strike" operations. Dubik recalled, "We would go into somebody's house looking for weapons and if we did not find any we would leave. We didn't know it but behind us were FAD'H who later accused us of burning the house down. If they thought the people were cooperating with us then the FAD'H executed them. They killed the whole family and burned the house down because *we* had deemed them guilty by our actions. We would be blamed."[53]

Out and About

On September 30 locals reported that a wanted Haitian arms and drug smuggler nicknamed "Codeine Bob" was in Port-au-Prince. The streets were crowded with people. Maj. Chris Hughes recollected,

The number-one hit target in country drove right past the battalion commander of 3–73d Armor from Fort Bragg. An American SF guy yelled, "There he goes! There goes Codeine Bob!" So you had infantry platoons on the street and this guy was in a maroon car with three other people and what do you do? You have a platoon leader stop him. So this platoon leader is running down the road with his M-16 and grenades. What are you going to do when you catch him? Are you going to jump on his vehicle and shoot him or what? I mean here is this infantry lieutenant about one hundred meters behind him running full speed trying to catch him. There were MPs in groups of two monitoring things. So an MP pulls his vehicle up next to the Haitian and got out and pulled out his 9mm pistol. He told him to get out of the car and they arrested him. I mean, it was that simple. Codeine Bob had a case of grenades in the car. He had Uzis and all kinds of automatic weapons. He was going to do something that day but the MP defused the situation.[54]

Gleaning usable information to find people like Codeine Bob often required translators. Some were Haitian Americans serving in the U.S. military; others were contractors. One military intelligence officer remarked, "The first thing that usually pops into my mind with a Haitian translator is trust. How trustworthy is he?" Maj. Tony Ladouceur, a Haitian American, recalled that contracted linguists "didn't know anything and they shove them into an area without thought. You don't put someone into a position where they are going to say something totally wrong because the connotation may be different and they need lots of practice because of the military terminology." Another Haitian American, Lt. Col. Berthony Napoleon, U.S. Army, earned trust on the streets. "The people were the conduit of information in the street," he said, "and I was to find out what was the state of mind of the people, whether they will accept it [the U.S. presence], what is their disposition to the force. I helped to evaluate these issues and sometimes looking at how certain words came across. Translating is a concept because a word can impact upon attitude." A female counterintelligence company commander and her female Haitian American translator figured out that the FAD'H also had an attitude toward women in authority. "A FAD'H guy screamed, 'How dare these females ask me a question and know my language! How dare a woman be in my front room in my domain asking me a question?'" Undeterred, the two Americans discerned that the man was afraid of dogs. "So, you have two women badgering this guy and then an MP [military police] dog comes in and sits down next to him. The guy just choked. So he walked over and moved his private bar away from the wall, opened up a fake partition, opened up a curtain, and we entered his arms room."[55]

Satellite communication and intelligence sites were located around Haiti to access various national assets that might assist Mountain Strike operations. But emplacing in or visiting these sites also provided an opportunity to see how wealthy Haitians lived. Maj. Steve Gomillion "drove up into the mountains because we had a few sites there. The higher you went up you would leave the city and the standard of living would rise. Schools continued to happen and there were businesses. I was amazed at the influence of Western society there. You did not see any real conflict or civil strife occurring there."[56]

But the potential for civil strife was on many U.S. Army leaders' minds, particularly within the Tenth Mountain Division. Division outsider Captain Valledor noticed immediately that daily operations exuded intimidation.

> Everything you do you put the fear of God in the Haitians. We did an operation where my Bradleys supported a roadblock and checkpoint operation in the middle of the night. One of the things we had to do was remove occupants from civilian vehicles so we could search for weapons. One of the battalion commanders I was working for observed that my guys were being nice with the population. They were asking nicely to please step out of the car, step over here while we search it, etc. This commander said, 'If you do that again I am going to replace that squad. I want you to go in there, put the muzzle of the weapon in their face, and convince them that they have no option but to get out of their vehi-

cle. You are here to be aggressive, do you get this?' My soldiers kept wondering why we were being so aggressive. These people are happy to see us but now they fear us. We are here to support democracy. So they were confused. I gave them the party line that your mission is to be aggressive, to show the flag. But it did not make sense.[57]

Command directives calling for aggressive behavior among multinational forces were not universally enforced in Haiti. Although Major General Meade had placed his unit in a combat posture to intimidate troublemakers and protect his troops, not all forces within JTF 190/MNF operated forcefully, and that also impeded operations. Valledor noticed: "The Haitians respect power. That came off right off the bat. One of the things we noticed was that we had a Bangladesh battalion adjacent to us as part of the multinational force. They were not aggressive. They followed their own thing but had more problems because they were friendly. The crowds would prevent them from moving. But when the Tenth Mountain showed up the Haitians knew you don't mess with them. They are going to respond, they are aggressive. Now these other guys [Bangladeshis] are not aggressive so let's go mess with them." But aggression also enhanced mission objectives insofar as being able to operate. Valledor added, "But even more extreme than the Tenth Mountain Division were the Gurkhas. There was a Gurkha detachment in Port-au-Prince. And they were hitting people with their vehicles as they drove through and the Haitians knew that if it was a Gurkha squad they ran right out of the way. So there is a plus and minus to this posture thing, it didn't match the peace-keeping mission if you were aggressive but the Haitians respected power and left you alone to maneuver."[58]

In the rural areas, SF faced their own challenges. They operated using the "hub-and-spoke" method, "key hubs out there on the key cities with Jacmel in the South, Gonaïves in the North." These cities became logistical hubs, "company-sized elements of about 100-105 people each, a B Team company headquarters with eight or nine A Teams" that flowed out of the cities into the sur-

17. The aftermath of Tropical Storm Gordon. Source: Department of Defense.

rounding countryside. Some occupied Haitian FAD'H facilities such as Fort Lamantin, about which 1st Sgt. Louie E. Hough, SF, remarked, "Legends surround this camp and some of the fear of zombies that are here and so forth because of the atrocities that might have transpired." Hough pointed to a building that "was an execution facility supposedly used by the FAD'H and their predecessors. When you walk up to the walls and you look at the bullet holes that are in them, if I was a local, those holes would be just about right from chest to head level. Seated in a chair, that would be a good head shot, the holes are either head high down to chest high. There are mass graves covered with weeds. The locals call this place 'Fort of the Bones' because you would pass through the front gate but never leave."[59]

Colonel Boyatt remembered that his SF troops met no resistance "except in Les Cayes. There was a FAD'H lieutenant colonel as bad as anybody you could imagine. He was basically a sadist. He cut the ear off a guy and made him eat it. He carved his initials in the buttocks of another guy. Terrorized the people. We ran him off. We found forty-two people in a prison cell we thought were dead.

They looked as bad as what you might see in pictures of World War II concentration camps. It was amazing any of them were alive."[60] Haitian medical concerns were something SF could address, but not without overcoming cultural obstacles. As Boyatt related,

A missionary doctor met one of our SF warrant officers outside a village at night. No electricity; cooking fires burning, pitch black. The women were convinced that their children had been cursed by two "witches" and they were all going to die. So the warrant officer walked in the village and broke a chemlight that he had in his pocket. He announced to the village ladies and the witches that he was here to dispel the curse. He went through some motions and incantations and then cut the tip off the chemlight with a knife that was hidden in his hand. In the dark it looked like he cut his fingertip off. He sprinkled the chemical liquid around him, which began to glow a greenish color. He then traced a [glowing] cross on the foreheads of all the children and announced the curse was over. He told the two witches to never try anything like this again or he would suck their souls up through their nose. He spoke this in Haitian Créole, right to the point. The two witches ran off and everyone clapped.[61]

While the witches symbolized Haitian cultural beliefs, they also reflected how important allegory was in Haiti. As Maj. Tony Schwalm related, "One thing about Haitians is that they are very powerful on symbols. The color of the Haitian army garrisons was mustard yellow and one of the first moves we made was to repaint the buildings blue and white." But helping out also caused cultural difficulties.

We got the people and the paint and they repainted but it did not have the effect we expected. The fact that we stood there watching them gave the impression we were muscling in on them. If the people do not agree with what you are doing, you are losing the battle. We were listening and we were so proud of ourselves, only to find that the people construed it as an act of imperialism. So we got T-shirts and put the new Haitian police in them and the people liked that. The Haitian police were as poor as everyone else but had something new to wear besides a khaki uniform. So we were getting feedback and doing symbols.[62]

Listening to the people was what Lieutenant General Shelton described as gathering "street rhythms." Schwalm saw street rhythms as

a vernacular for the cross-cultural communication that we say is one of our strengths within the SF community. For me in Haiti, street rhythms were being open to Haitians, which means you have to change your defensive posture. Outside of Port-au-Prince in the hinterlands we wore soft caps and our LBV [load-bearing vest]. But how can you say it is safe and secure and smile and hold babies while you are in body armor and Kevlar helmets, your weapons at port arms, and you are constantly looking out from behind sunglasses? It is an incongruous signal. You are saying one thing but your body is saying something different.[63]

SF relations with the locals had strengthened by the time Tropical Storm Gordon smashed into Haiti on November 8, 1994, killing an estimated 1,122 Haitians. SF teams were arrayed throughout the countryside in small groups when the storm struck. They now added humanitarian assistance to their ongoing security mission. Schwalm stated,

We had dead Haitians bobbing out in the bay and we are pulling dead kids and dead women out of it. We are giving rides to people that are coming down out of the mountains. It was a huge flash flood and it blew out the banana crop, blew out bridges that had been in place since the 1930s, and these were big ones with concrete and riveted. The roads were out and no way to get to us except by air or boat. We had guys during the flood who tied off a fire hose to the front of a Humvee and then to a Zodiac rubber boat and floated down a street in Jacmel, pulling a Haitian family out of a house as it washed into the sea. We knew these people. We could see fifty dead and rumor was a lot more. But now we had bonds with these folks.

Close ties enabled the SF to help the Haitians with rebuilding, to include "repairing a micro hydroelectric plant, a diesel generator, the water system that we helped chlorinate, the relief packages we brought in, the schools we built." Rebuilding, however, meant bending the overall mission rules about assisting Haitians directly, something that SF soldiers understood how to do.[64]

Transition to the Twenty-Fifth Infantry Division (Light)

None of the four operational plans had envisioned exchanging one unit for another during Operation Uphold Democracy, especially one as large as an infantry division. In truth, OPLAN 2380+ called for JTF 190/MNF's Tenth Mountain to hand over its responsibilities to the UN in March 1995. Regardless, the Twenty-Fifth Infantry Division (Light) from Hawaii replaced the Fort Drum, New York, division on January 14, 1995.

The decision to rotate divisions was made within DOD channels and approved by USACOM. There were many factors at play as to why the unscheduled replacement occurred. A troop rotation after six months to one year is often preplanned, although that had not been the case here. It was also well known that the Tenth had been deployed to Somalia in 1993, where it saw bloody combat and took casualties. It was now overseas once again, this time for six to ten months. Many senior U.S. Army leaders believed that combat soldiers' skills eroded over time when they were involved in peacekeeping operations. Replacing a unit allowed for soldier furloughs followed by intensive training to prepare for future contingencies elsewhere. There was also wear and tear on equipment to consider, as well the strain of family separation at the home station. Moreover, some believed that Haiti was stable enough by December to allow for a large unit rotation in January, one that would replace thousands of soldiers in mid-mission.

In preparation, the Hawaii-based Twenty-Fifth Infantry underwent peace operations training at the Joint Readiness Training Center at Fort Polk, Louisiana. The Center for Army Lessons Learned, an organization in Fort Leavenworth, Kansas, that gathered "lessons learned" from ongoing army missions and published them, provided a country orientation. The division leadership devised twenty Haiti-oriented vignettes so junior leaders could discuss how to handle confrontations. Indeed, nineteen of the twenty training scenarios actually occurred while the unit was deployed to Haiti.[65]

In December 1994 the DOD released an official statement explaining why the Tenth was being replaced early. Department representatives conveyed that it was "a planned rotation of U.S. forces in Haiti to begin this January" and that the "25th Infantry 'Tropic Lightning' task force of approximately 3,500 U.S. soldiers will have the same mission." The U.S. division would "continue support of the democratically-elected government and maintain a secure and stable environment to permit the elements of democracy to continue to develop." The Defense Department also remarked that unit replacement mid-mission was nothing out of the ordinary, for "this rotation represents a normal four to six month deployment schedule most U.S. forces maintain, which allows for training and maintenance of equipment."[66]

While the statement explained that one division was replacing another, it did not shed light on why the preintervention operational plans did not mention it. Nor did it declare that the army's Third Special Forces Group (Airborne) was not being replaced, even though there may have been other Haitian experts within SF. Moreover, the four- to six-month rotation was not fixed DOD policy. In Bosnia, for example, the army's First Armored Division under Implementation Force (IFOR) was deployed for one full year (December 20, 1995,–December 20, 1996) in its peace enforcement operation until it was replaced by the First Infantry Division under Stabilization Force (SFOR).

John R. Ballard, a former member of USACOM's Joint Analysis and Assessment Team in Haiti, witnessed the rotation decision-making process and wrote that it was enacted for three reasons. The first was "to allow the Tenth to rest, [re]cover its personnel and materiel, and restore its level of combat readiness," a decision in line with voguish army thinking that peacekeeping eroded combat skills. Second, the rotation would "provide the Twenty-Fifth Division with much-appreciated experience in a deployment for

18. Twenty-Fifth Infantry Division (Light) patrol break. Note the absence of body armor. Source: Department of Defense.

peace operations." Whether or not soldiers "appreciated" being deployed from Hawaii to Haiti to gain ephemeral experience is disputable. But a contingency mission might also dispel the Twenty-Fifth's unofficial moniker of the "Imperial Army of the Pacific," then a nondeploying division whose real mission appeared to be furthering U.S. government diplomatic and political interests in the Pacific Rim. Ballard's third reason was that the Tenth Mountain was stale. As he put it, "Although the transition would create a short window of vulnerability as the two divisions switched places, the influx of personnel from the 25th would also refresh the spirit of the MNF with vigorous initiatives and approaches."[67]

Regardless of what Ballard imagined, Major General Meade explained his unit's replacement this way:

We had two things to get done in the springtime [of 1995]; one was the transition to UNMIH and the other was the Haitian elections, which were scheduled for June. So if you get the Tenth Mountain Division way on up into this period [June] that at the same time you are trying to make sure the transition to the UN is squared away [April–May] and you are trying to do elections, you have the potential at least during the sixty-day [UN] start-up that you screwed yourself. The Haitian environment cannot stand doing lots of things at the same time. So the decision to move the Tenth Mountain Division officially on January 14 was driven by all of that. I had an excellent relationship with [Maj. Gen.] George Fisher and his staff. We had a ten-day transition period; you could get a second opinion from the Twenty-Fifth on this; I think it went perfectly.

One might also consider that most but not all of the Twenty-Fifth left once the UN took over. A number of former MNF troops remained as UN troops to ensure that the blue berets were becoming "squared away" in handling Haitian security while at the same time preparing to support the Haitian regional elections.[68]

Even as American units were planning to rotate, two issues overshadowed the mission. The first concerned the psychological stress troops encountered due to the confused change of mission and their reaction to Haiti's horrific poverty, filth, and stench. Psychological evaluation teams and chaplains monitored the force, and most personnel adjusted without complications. But the strain proved too much for others. Within a few weeks of intervention ten U.S. soldiers required psychiatric evaluation and were evacuated. Two Tenth Mountain soldiers, Spec. Alejandro Robles, U.S. Army, and Pvt. Geraldo D. Luciano, U.S. Army, committed suicide, on September 27 and October 16, respectively. Lance Corp. Maurice Williams, USMC, also committed suicide, on October 5 aboard the USS *Nashville* while docked in Puerto Rico. The tragedies justifiably drew considerable command and media attention, while a second issue, calming enflamed Haitian passions, continued. In December 1994 rumors spread that a Haitian general had detonated a bomb that killed Aristide. In Port-au-Prince, M. Sgt. Eddison Andre, U.S. Air Force, a Haitian American, and his PSYOP team of six personnel in two Humvees with loudspeakers encountered "a crowd of about two thousand people with bats and bottles and chains in their hands demanding to see the president alive. And my PSYOP team was the first to arrive on the scene. It was truly on the basis of two vehicles and the loudspeakers we had that we were able to calm them, to get them to move on. It could have been a bloodbath, I mean, I was literally fearing a bloodbath."[69]

On January 7, 1995, Meade declared Haiti to be "stable and secure," a necessary prerequisite for UNMIH to assume control of the operation in March. But five days later, the first American death due to hostile fire occurred. On January 12, 1995, a pickup truck ran a checkpoint in Gonaïves. Sgt. 1st Class Gregory Cardott, U.S. Army, was shot dead by a vehicle passenger, a Haitian military officer. An SF soldier, S. Sgt. Tommy Davis, was wounded. A third U.S. soldier arrived and shot the Haitian gunman dead on the spot. The unit rotation continued.[70]

A New Sheriff

Two days later the Twenty-Fifth assumed the Uphold Democracy mission, operating with a staff of four hundred men and women within the LIC. Despite the loss of a soldier forty-eight hours earlier, the transition to new leadership prompted an alteration in JTF 190/MNF's operational philosophy. Captain Valledor, whose Bradley unit had been ordered by the Tenth Mountain Division to conduct aggressive operations, soon found his methods criticized by Maj. Gen. George Fisher and his staff. "The first question I was asked by the Twenty-Fifth leadership was, Why was I conducting presence patrols? Because I had continued with that even when the Tenth left and we were used to it. Then, Why are you driving Bradleys in downtown Port-au-Prince at night? Well, Sir, that is what I have been doing. But the Twenty-Fifth's answer was that we are here to uphold democracy. That [activity] does not portray a peaceful environment. Stop it NOW. So from that point on we did not conduct presence patrols. I basically parked at the airfield and things got boring from that point on."[71]

Major General Fisher's assumption of command had transformed the operational climate virtually overnight. For months, numerous observers had commented on the differences between conventional and unconventional force approaches, with the Tenth Mountain Division being overtly intimidating and the SF more engaging and cautiously relaxed. The JTF 190/MNF troops were now collectively told, "You are not here to scare the population. What you are doing is out of message. It conflicts with the message of the whole mission." Valledor pointed out to Major General Fisher, "Sir, you got to understand that for four months the message was show the flag, be aggressive, and don't let your guard down. Those are the three messages I got and we complied." Referring to Fisher's directives, Valledor added, "Don't get me wrong, the Twenty-Fifth had force protection too as a concern. But they did not go out of their way to be aggressive towards the population and I think the Haitians saw that."[72]

The change in attitude toward Haitians also reflected a growing Haitian National Police force that had been trained by members of the U.S. State Department's ICITAP along with Canadian and U.S. supervisors at Camp D'Application. Because many of the Haitian policemen were vetted ex-FAD'H, over 1,170 IPMs from twenty-four countries had been conducting twenty-four-hour patrols in nine locations since mid-October to keep an eye on them. IPMs often accompanied American military patrols as well but acted independently under the command of former New York City police commissioner Kelly. On January 17, given that the Haitian police were gradually assuming a public security role, President Aristide eliminated the FAD'H and created a border patrol of fifteen hundred vetted, former military members.

But the JTF's attitude shift toward conducting daily operations had little effect on mission tempo, for the pace was unremitting. The Twenty-Fifth Infantry personnel found that their Tenth Mountain counterparts were indeed worn-out. According to Maj. Nancy Nycamp, Military Intelligence, who supported the Twenty-Fifth,

> We found out [at] the end of November 1994 that we would be doing a relief in place with the Tenth Mountain Division. The Tenth Mountain G2 was Lt. Col. Frank Bragg, a great officer who had a staff that was very tired from their numerous deployments. He had a collection management officer that I felt was disadvantaged. He was a brand-new advanced course graduate and had very limited

previous experience as a lieutenant. He had a warrant officer one who was a hard charger but not very experienced and a couple of enlisted personnel. But the biggest challenge for me was the manning of my section. With only nine people the first three weeks [in Haiti], we averaged about three hours of sleep a night just because of the information management, getting it all into place.[73]

Nycamp found that the intelligence community relied heavily on leveraging technology, as opposed to tapping into human sources. Nycamp explained,

I think it is natural to lean away from human sources because it is perceived as not always reliable, which is true. It is only as reliable as the source and it is difficult to cultivate those resources. But we need human sources if for nothing else than force-protection information and because it is cheap. Yeah, it may not be reliable but then you can use it *and* all the sensors to do the analysis. The problem is that the doctrine was written for conventional operations, not military operations other than war, and with conventional you are more concerned about linking a sensor to a shooter [such as field artillery].[74]

Capt. Richard J. "R. J." Muraski Jr., an engineer company commander from Hawaii, arrived in early January to support the Twenty-Fifth. He also discovered that his counterparts were exhausted and wanted to go home. "The unit that we were replacing tried to depart early. That was agreed upon by their commanders. So they were going to leave us high and dry. We did not have our equipment on hand or the capability to assume the mission and they were ready to bug out early. I don't know who made the decision but someone higher stopped that. We informed them [the outgoing unit] they were going to stay the proper number of days and things went smooth."[75]

The Tenth Mountain Division (Light) clearly suffered from mission fatigue, and some would not have selected it for the Haiti contingency when other units were available through the U.S. Army's Forces Command. USACOM's Admiral Miller chose the division to develop OPLAN 2380 because it was an Eighteenth Airborne Corps contingency asset with personnel experienced in deployments, albeit in Somalia, and it was readily deployable as a light division. Although Major General Meade and most of his subordinates were excited and proud to participate in the intervention, the mission did take its toll on the soldiers and their families. Moreover, the last-minute shift in focus from combat to peacekeeping when President Clinton terminated the invasion did not help matters. If the mission had not changed, the Eighty-Second Airborne would have been on the ground first and for several weeks, giving the Tenth more time to make mission adjustments based on on-the-ground feedback instead of being thrown into a very chaotic situation.

JTF 190/MNF was under orders to shun direct assistance to Haitians to avoid mission creep. Muraski's outbound counterpart openly shared his frustration over his inability to help the impoverished, noting that "his soldiers had a hard time not being able to help the Haitians directly; give them food and actually help them. He said if you want to help them, you give them things you throw in the trash because they eventually get all of it." This seemed obscene to Muraski, but he soon witnessed it on a grand scale. "One of the missions I had was guarding U.S. Army garbage trucks. You would literally have to beat people off the trucks on the way to the dump. Once you got there you had to move people away so they would not get crushed when the trucks dumped their load. But to see little kids picking up food and smiling and saying, Hey, this is great, look what I got today! For my young soldiers, this was tough on them."[76]

Muraski observed that long-established Haitian cultural values of militarism and revenge were still prevalent. Although his men were engineers, his unit provided additional security at the Haitian national prison, a mission normally assigned to military police. Since nation building was not a specified mission, Muraski was ordered to forego making facility repairs "under any circumstances." He found the prison to be a catastrophe.

You went into an open courtyard with a couple of rooms, two or three buildings inside where the prisons were. You had two huge cells with three hundred to four hundred people in each of them. The prison was actually burned, all the mattresses and things, so there was nothing but tangled and burnt metal frames of the beds inside. Human waste was twelve to eighteen inches deep in an open sewer and open kitchen facility; just deplorable. The guards were afraid to go there so we had to assess the situation. The people had disease. A lot of prisoners had gangrene; no way for hygiene. They had one water fountain that was a post and water bubbled out of the top of it. That is where they took showers.

Muraski also noted, "The prison gates were torn off the wall and some [fifteen] prisoners escaped. The guards would then shoot into the escape area, not to warn the prisoners but to warn the local populace who then caught the prisoners and beat the hell out of them. They turned most of them back over to the police. It was interesting that [Haitian] vigilantism was alive and well and they were very effective when they had to be."[77]

As JTF 190/MNF's tenure in Haiti ended, former president Jimmy Carter, Senator Sam Nunn, and General Colin Powell returned on February 23. The Haitians offered a mixed reception to the negotiators who had spared their country bloodshed. Carter was shunned by many of Haiti's elites, who perceived him as a meddler who had forced them into cooperating with thugs instead of crushing the thugs through international military power. Dr. Bryant Freeman remarked,

The most hated man in Haiti today [1997] is Jimmy Carter. There is still anti-Carter graffiti on the walls all over the place and some of it I would not translate. He has been snubbed by the Haitian government, who should have had someone to meet him at the airport and he couldn't understand why [they didn't]. That man did enormous harm. But he was also in communication with President Clinton at the White House. I mean, Carter is a beautiful person, well-meaning but embarrassing. In Haiti, I was embarrassed to be an American because he was so weak. The whole thing was a flop but typical of Carter.[78]

Mid-March witnessed President Aristide preparing for the upcoming elections and the country transitioning to UNMIH. On March 27, USACOM announced that JTF 190/MNF would be redesignated JTF 190 on March 31, signifying that the multinational aspect of operations would fall under UNMIH. Major General Fisher handed over command to Brig. Gen. James T. "Tom" Hill, U. S. Army, a logistician who would oversee the return of U.S. equipment to its home station.

On March 31 UN secretary-general Boutros Boutros-Ghali, the founder of contemporary military interventions, as well as President Clinton and various dignitaries, observed the UNMIH takeover of Haitian operations under the command of Maj. Gen. Joseph W. Kinzer, U.S. Army. Kinzer assumed command not only of UN forces but also of a sizeable U.S. military support contingent that remained. In truth, of the six thousand UN personnel who would assist the government of Haiti as it prepared for its elections, 40 percent came from the U.S. military.

For many of those who served during Operation Uphold Democracy, leaving Haiti came with mixed feelings. While some military personnel thought Haiti was better off in 1995 than previously, others believed that whatever progress had been made would soon fade away. As some Americans donned UN blue berets or blue baseball caps under a new military rubric, Maj. Robert Shaw, SF, summed up the situation this way: "A soldier is a soldier and our primary mission as the army is to conduct the operations and protect the nation in support of the policies that the president sets." UNMIH would reflect his observation.[79]

5

Intervention under the Blue Beret

"I think we gave it the best chance to succeed. But the biggest shortcoming was a very reluctant attitude to try and let the Haitians do things at their own pace."

—COL. DAVID PATTON, commander, U.S. Support Group Haiti

On March 31, 1995, the redesignated JTF 190 conducted a mission handover ceremony with UNMIH. The event signified that the U.S.-led military intervention had stabilized Haiti's situation sufficiently enough to permit a UN peacekeeping force. UNMIH, formed in September 1993 as part of the July 1993 Governors Island Accord, was to have prepared for deposed Haitian president Jean-Bertrand Aristide's return. But the USS *Harlan County* incident of October 1993 delayed matters and ultimately triggered Operation Uphold Democracy. When U.S.-led forces removed Raoul Cédras and his henchmen in October 1994 and the Haitian president returned to office, UNMIH once again prepared to execute its one-year mandate: to assist the democratic government of Haiti in sustaining a stable environment, to professionalize the armed forces while creating a separate police force, and to establish an environment conducive to free and fair elections. The mission, however, required effective military leadership and fastidious staff management to ensure the intervention's success.

Exit Strategy

In early September 1994 Operation Uphold Democracy was nearing execution. Members of the UN's Department of Peacekeeping Operations (DPKO) were simultaneously conducting a mission analysis with the understanding that the U.S.-led invasion would

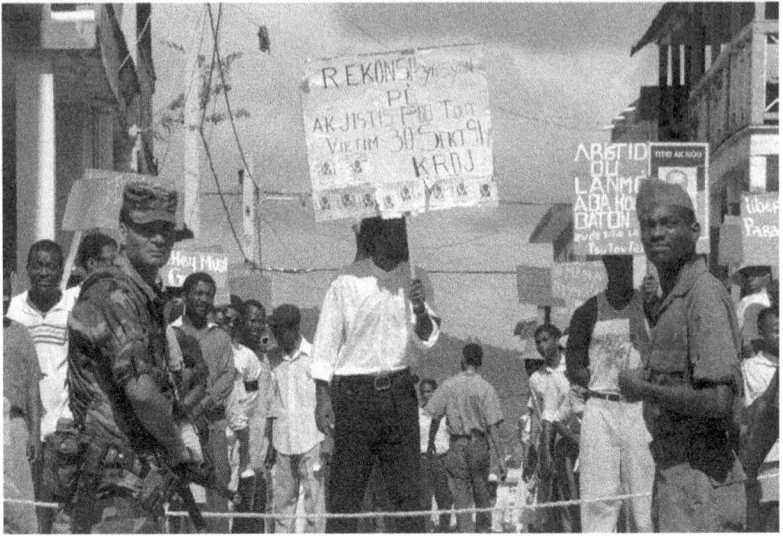

19. Multinational soldiers adopted a relaxed uniform posture during the latter part of Operation Uphold Democracy. Source: Department of Defense.

be limited in duration out of political necessity. UNMIH, the UN's military force assembled for the follow-on peacekeeping mission in continued support of peacebuilding, was to assume mission responsibility once the UN had deemed Haiti's situation to be stable.

Given that the UN would accept mission handover once stability was verified, the force commander on the ground was under considerable pressure to convincingly make that determination. Col. John Lewis, U.S. Army, deployed to Haiti from Fort Leavenworth, Kansas, one day after the intervention began and quickly found himself "in the middle of the goop." A JTF 190/MNF individual augmentee, Lewis was ordered to Haiti from the army's School of Advanced Military Studies to transition the U.S.-led coalition mission to UNMIH. But he soon found himself embroiled within a political and military quandary over how to declare the Western Hemisphere's poorest country to be stable so U.S. troops could leave. Once inside the LIC headquarters complex, Lewis was taken aside by a U.S. general officer "who was not the mission commander." Lewis remembered the closed-door meeting where the general urgently stated, "'The most important thing that you gotta do is to get us outta here. Figure out how to bring this thing to closure so we can get outta here!' And he was a Somalia veteran. So my focus within twenty-four hours of the intervention occurring was developing an exit strategy."[1]

Lewis scrutinized UNSCR 940, the document that set the conditions for determining multinational force success in Haiti. He recalled, "UNSCR 940 set the conditions of what had to be met to get success [as] defined within the operation. They were straightforward and agreed upon. But what I thought initially were four conditions turned into thirty-seven things that had to be met before the UN was ever going to set foot on the ground. How do you show that it [UNSCR 940] has been accomplished? How do you prove it to the [U.S.] National Command Authorities? And how do you get the UN to accept the U.S.'s view when it isn't necessarily what the UN's view is?"[2]

Lewis needed compelling evidence to prove that Haiti was stable. To him, verification meant statistical data. He phoned U.S. police departments in

> Detroit, Los Angeles, etc. and said to give us your crime statistics on rape, murder, break-ins, looting, and riots, whatever. We then laid out the five big cities in Haiti against what had occurred in the last twenty-four hours every day in our backyard. So what you saw was Detroit had more murders that day, Los Angeles had more fights in the street that day, and we started to build a case showing on a graph every day the secure environment of Haiti. And we were sending that to the Joint Chiefs of Staff, the National Command Authorities, the State Department, and the UN.[3]

Lewis also used the media to his advantage:

> What is said is that you cannot manipulate the media, you cannot feed the media untruths. But that does not mean you cannot come up with a strategy for winning the information war. And this was briefed [to U.S. leaders] within the American embassy on D+5. We were going to target the international community and the Amer-

ican public. We targeted the Haitian leadership, the de facto and legitimate governments, and the Haitian population. We wanted to get the media focused upon political things. We would look out about seventy-two hours at [future] operations and then asked, Do we want the media to see it? We voted thumbs up or down. If yes, then we would make sure a media representative was there: going on a block search, watching ships unloading food, watching kids being fed.[4]

To be sure, Lewis was proactively establishing a rapport with media reporters as he legally leveraged them to the U.S. government's advantage.

Nine days into the U.S.-led intervention, Lewis was in a two-vehicle convoy driving through Port-au-Prince. He soon found news cameras at work covering Haitians waiting for food outside a warehouse.

We came around a corner and there is a crowd of four thousand to five thousand Haitians in the street. There must be thirty news cameras from CNN positioned all over the place. It looked like a movie set. And the crowd was noncomplaisant. About the time our vehicles were in the crowd it was as if someone yelled, "Action!" All of a sudden people started beating each other with clubs and tearing doors open and breaking into the warehouse and throwing food out into the street. And it just turned into pandemonium and we're in the middle of this riot. Our [machine] guns are down and we are saying, "Are you kidding me?" The cameras are swinging all over capturing this. People's faces were bloody and caved in. We forced our way through. Five minutes later, we were safe in the U.S. embassy and running upstairs to a secure briefing room. We always had CNN on. And what did we see? You see videotape of my two vehicles moving through the crowd and then getting out around a corner. It had been ten minutes ago and it had already been shown [via live television] to the NCA and the JCS. And the JTF commander [Maj. Gen. David C. Meade] did not even know it had occurred. That is the power of the media.

In the age of instantaneous communications, the U.S. media had broadcast a food riot worldwide and to U.S. government officials long before the intervention commander in Haiti knew what had happened.[5]

Gradually, JTF 190/MNF personnel made progress in convincing UN Security Council members that Haiti was more secure than many American cities. But selling the UN also meant that the Tenth Mountain Division (Light)'s leadership must provide visual evidence by softening its force-protection posture and aggressive approach to operations. Lewis worked hard on this because "it is kind of a hard sell to the UN if we are walking around in a flak vest armed to the teeth everywhere we go. So we did a risk assessment of what we considered to be low-risk areas to where we started conveying guys [there] in soft caps, basic equipment, no fixed bayonets or armored vests." Sending lightly armed troops into secure areas of Haitian cities was captured by the media, who concluded and reported that progress was being made. Lewis explained his calculating logic as, "How you get in is one thing but how you get out is even more important."[6]

Preparing UNMIH

On September 19, 1994, the day U.S. forces entered Haiti; the UN published an eighty-four-page document detailing UNMIH's organizational and operational parameters. The DPKO document outlined a 181-man command-and-control headquarters element (taken from the authorized six-thousand-member force), predeployment training requirements, and other necessities. Yet, because the UN is a non-warfighting entity, DPKO officers could not evaluate participating nations' military doctrine and training procedures or certify that UNMIH members were qualified for their positions. They simply relied on trust.

In truth, UN policy meant assuming that countries involved in UN military operations would provide properly experienced personnel when a mission headquarters formed. This concept was practical but unrealistic given the lack of standardized practices and capabilities among world military forces. Following established procedures, the UN staff identified mission requirements and then solicited support from member nations who volunteered assets.

Once accepted for a UN mission position, each participating individual brought whatever military experience he or she possessed. Some contributing nations sent capable personnel while others were qualified only by their political or familial ties. While most soldiers were fluent in English, the customary communication language for UN operations, others had but rudimentary skills. A UN field headquarters was a true potpourri of military practices.[7]

U.S. military liaison officers at UN headquarters in New York found the DPKO booklet to be impressive but naïve. They, as with many American officials, held strong misgivings about the UN's ability to find sufficiently skilled military officers capable of managing a robust peacekeeping operation. Indeed, the previous year had been disastrous for the United Nations Operation in Somalia II. Several incidents between UN forces and Somali factions were mishandled, with tragic results. On October 3, two weeks before the USS *Harlan County* affair in Haiti, a seventeen-hour firefight in Mogadishu saw eighteen U.S. Army personnel killed and eighty-four wounded while attempting to eliminate the Somali warlord Mohamed Farrah Aidid. Given such recent events in Somalia, U.S. government officials and military leaders doubted the UN's ability to direct effective military operations.[8]

The Clinton administration responded to Somalia critics by publishing Presidential Decision Directive (PDD) 25, "Reforming Multilateral Peace Operations." The directive required U.S. government agencies to assist in "reforming and improving the UN's capability to manage peace operations," including eleven steps "to strengthen UN management of peace operations and [direct] U.S. support for strengthening the UN's planning, logistics, information and command and control capabilities." The PDD was a direct attempt by the U.S. government to shape the course of future UN operations.[9]

Within the DOD, Gen. Gordon R. Sullivan, chief of staff, U.S. Army, viewed PDD 25 as an opportunity to influence the training of UNMIH headquarters personnel. On September 21, 1994, Sullivan directed the U.S. Army's Battle Command Training Program (BCTP), a TRADOC organization that tutored corps and division commanders and staffs, to assist UNMIH with staff training. The mission fell to BCTP's Operations Group Delta, whose members were joint force and multinational operations experts.

One week later, at Fort Leavenworth, Kansas, BCTP leaders assembled a group of experienced army trainers. Lt. Col. Thomas K. "Doc" Adams from the U.S. Army's Command and General Staff College had recently returned from supporting operations in Rwanda, where he had found that "UN headquarters policy was one thing and reality was another." At the Leavenworth meeting, Adams recalled, "What we did was ask, What is it that we are trying to accomplish here? And the answer is, we are trying to take a disparate group of people, military and civilian of various nationalities and ranks, experience, and backgrounds, and try to create a functional UN headquarters, which had never been done before." The discussion continued over "are we doing functional training here and creating an American staff? I took the position that what we were really doing was not trying to create an American-style staff but team building. After some back and forth we agreed that that was probably the essential thing."[10]

While UNMIH training deliberations were underway, twelve members of the UNMIH advance team arrived in Haiti on September 23, 1994. Team members coordinated measures necessary for UNMIH's full deployment, monitored ongoing JTF 190/MNF operations, prepared the headquarters building, and rendered reports to the UN Security Council regarding the implementation of Resolution 940. Later, on September 29, 1994, the Security Council requested the deployment of the remaining sixty-person advance team under Resolution 944, as well as the return of the MICIVIH. The council also agreed to lift UN sanctions one day after President Aristide was reinstated in office.[11]

Deploying and leading UNMIH was a complicated affair requiring a stalwart commander. Temporarily filling the position was a Canadian, Col. William Fulton, the UNMIH chief of staff. Fulton "was warned on a Thursday afternoon [September 8] that I had to be in New York the following Monday to work with the New York planning team, as the head of the advance team. I spent approximately two weeks in New York working with Lt. Col. Willy Vanstraelen from Belgium. Together we worked the structure of the force, the structure of the headquarters, and the initial concept of operations. I was joined by a number of officers from different countries."[12]

Although the UN Security Council desired an immediate UNMIH presence in Haiti, Fulton was blocked from entry by "the UN resident representative in Haiti, [New Zealander] Mr. Ross Mountain, the senior security officer for the UN. I had to deal with him from New York. He was very reluctant to allow us to come into the country bearing in mind that the embargo was still on and there were difficult times. There were major demonstrations in the street to get President Aristide back into the country. The MNF was establishing itself. Mountain basically did not want us to deploy at that time." Bureaucratic hesitancy did not stop Fulton, however. "We made the decision in New York that we would deploy anyway. The American-led MNF had control of the international airport and was tied up with bringing their flights to sustain and build the operation. So we decided to fly into the Dominican Republic and we flew into Santo Domingo. We were assisted by the UN representative there and managed to get control of some UN vehicles that had been put there after they left Haiti earlier in 1994. We contacted the MNF to meet us at the border and they did."[13]

After a restless evening, the UNMIH members drove to the Dominican Republic–Haiti border. After two hours of administrative red tape, they entered Haiti in UN vehicles to be escorted to the capital by Tenth Mountain Division (Light) troops. "We drove through the countryside and people came out in the streets and cheered and clapped," Fulton recalled. "But the closer we got to Port-au-Prince the less prevalent that was. The population was subdued; no smiles, no reaction whatsoever. [There was] a lot of fear in Port-au-Prince." Still, the team arrived safely. By October 5, UNMIH consisted of sixteen military observers, ten military planners, thirteen civilian policemen, and ten administrative staff personnel.[14]

During October 1994, as UNMIH members entered Haiti, U.S. Army leaders concluded that Sullivan's proposed staff-training idea could not appear to be U.S. fixated if the UN was to approve it. Astute U.S. training officers developed a multinational and diverse training concept that made UN participation obligatory and prestigious. During training, UN officials would explain why UNMIH was necessary strategically, to be followed by lectures on organizational procedures given by UN peacekeeping veterans. The UNMIH staff would attend this training and then be formed into small, functional area "syndicates" based on their specialized expertise: operations, logistics, communications, and other areas. The syndicate members would receive focused individual and group training to build the confidence required to work together despite cultural and language differences. After the sessions ended, the syndicates would again become one staff and participate in numerous vignettes replicating real-world situations requiring decision making, management, communications, and reporting. The training period would conclude with an "after action review," a participant-driven discussion of what happened during the vignettes and why, followed by a graduation ceremony.[15]

American officials spent much of November hawking the training plan to the UN Security Council. The UN body was interested, but financial considerations and finding an agreeable training location ruffled a few feathers. It would cost about $500,000 to train the staff in Puerto Rico or $486,000 in Haiti. Some cringed at paying for it. Suitable computer simulations and a satellite communications facility were also needed, such as at Fort Leavenworth, Kansas. UN and U.S. Army representatives eventually settled on an initial training session at Fort Leavenworth to "train the trainers," followed by a second period in Haiti where the trainers would instruct the UNMIH staff. On December 14, 1994, the UN Security Council approved the proposal and requested that it be completed by March 1995.[16]

Finding instructors, however, became a political issue. Adams recalled asking by name for Dr. Bryant Freeman from the University of Kansas Institute of Haitian Studies. To Adams,

> Freeman has thirty years' experience in Haiti, holds advanced degrees, speaks French, Créole, and Spanish [actually Italian], he is an American citizen and so forth. I said that they had to talk with this guy. Well, we can't do that. Why not? Well, he has an agenda. Okay, everybody has an agenda. Well, we do not want to expose our people. Well, why? Well, we got secret agents this guy will know about. Interestingly, there was a Canadian major who was the military intelligence advisor to the UN, although they do not call it intelligence but "information." He also said you can't talk to him. Eventually we got Freeman on board but the intelligence people really did not like it.

Freeman nonetheless proved to be a valued instructor and an asset in establishing contacts in country. He also helped in vetting Haitians seeking employment with the UN. As Adams put it, "People don't present themselves to the UN mission as, Excuse me, but I have participated in at least four certifiable massacres in the past ninety days. They often omit those parts of their résumé. You need somebody who understands the applicants."[17]

Part of the training curriculum covered UN and military terminology, as well as doctrine. Although seemingly pedestrian, such matters were not to be taken lightly. In Somalia, the UN had assumed that military vocabulary was universally applicable to all forces at the basic level, but that proved to be erroneous. Adams explained,

> The UN doesn't have a lot of what we would call the doctrinal things we have adopted in the U.S. But that wasn't hard to do here. The big difference was some of the terminology. What the UN calls peacekeeping is much more inclusive than what the U.S. Army calls peacekeeping. The UN has an excellent term called "complex emergencies" for these situations like Haiti that aren't really peacekeeping and they really aren't humanitarian assistance and they really aren't disaster relief. But they are some uncomfort-

able combination of those things with other elements thrown in and that is useful even though it doesn't depend upon doctrine.[18]

On February 27, 1995, the UN staff trainers arrived at Fort Leavenworth, Kansas, for certification. The group included Brig. Gen. Abdul Ghani from the UN DPKO, military officers with UN experience representing Austria, Canada, and the United States, and civilians from a number of UN agencies and academic institutions. The three-day seminar went over the UNMIH staff training curriculum, which now lasted for six days instead of ten days due to funding constraints. A seminar was held to familiarize everyone with U.S. Army command and staff decision-making procedures, as well as discussions over what was to be accomplished and how that would be achieved.

On March 4, less than one week later, the team arrived in Port-au-Prince, Haiti. Training began at the LIC the next morning. The conference began with welcoming remarks from a number of notable figures, including Maj. Gen. Maurice Baril, a Canadian from the UN; U.S. chairman of the JCS, Gen. John Shalikashvili, U.S. Army; commanding general of JTF 190/MNF Maj. Gen. George Fisher, U.S. Army; and the newly appointed UNMIH commander, Maj. Gen. Joseph W. Kinzer, U.S. Army. Each speaker stressed the training's significance as the first-ever attempt to build cohesion within a UN military staff before mission assumption.

The day's events consisted of information briefings explaining the UN structure, the command relationship between the UN and UNMIH, and how different agencies operated and supported the staff. Some lectures were highly detailed, such as Adams's lecture on the nature of UN peacekeeping operations. A few talks from local UN representatives were less than stellar. The UN signal officer in Haiti was unable to coherently explain how the communications system functioned. Ruth Archibald of Canada, who represented the UN's Commission on Population and Development, Economic and Social Council, was to have covered population issues. Adams noted, "I can recite her presentation fully from memory. She said, 'I've always believed that these presentations should be like a woman's skirt, wide enough to cover everything but short enough to be interesting. Well, I am very busy and have to leave now but I want to thank you for inviting me here today.' Then she stood up and walked out."[19]

The second day began with Dr. Bryant Freeman presenting his understanding of Haitian culture, religion, personal relationships, gestures, and customs. Freeman's role was "to make the observers aware of the history of Haiti, political problems, economic problems, and to supervise courses in Haitian Créole. The attendees underwent intensive [language] classes for two hours a day because 15 percent of Haitians speak some French and 85 percent speak no French whatsoever but Haitian Créole. They are related but different, as Spanish is to Portuguese or Dutch to German." Before he began, however, two U.S. and Canadian Military Intelligence officers again protested his presence and vehemently proclaimed that he was an academic with an agenda and should leave. After much ado, the dust settled and Freeman made his presentation, which was well received.[20]

The remaining days consisted of syndicate training involving decision making and crisis management with a computer-driven exercise to assess the workshop attendees' ability to practice their skills. Adams and others were shocked by what transpired. "We had expected that everyone would have shown up for the first day. Then attendance would drop each day. But that did not happen. The workshops were well attended and seemed to go longer than scheduled. In one workshop on the civil military operations center we basically had to blow them out of there with dynamite. They were really interested in that." In truth, the training had focused on precisely what the officers would be doing, which piqued their interest. Moreover, the staff members had no difficulty conducting twenty-four-hour operations during the computer exercise. In less than two days, the UNMIH staff responded efficiently and effectively to numerous simulated situations, such as pilferage, riots, gunfire incidents, and distinguished visitor arrivals and briefings. When training ended on March 10, everyone in attendance believed that the UNMIH staff was cohesive and competent, which would ring true upon mission execution.[21]

Finding a Commander

As the U.S. Army was preparing to train UNMIH's headquarters staff, the UN searched for a mission commander. Given that 40 percent of UNMIH's total troop strength would contain U.S. personnel, an American general officer was to be nominated for command. That officer turned out to be Maj. Gen. Joseph W. Kinzer, U.S. Army, who at the time was the deputy commanding general of the Fifth U.S. Army at Fort Sam Houston, Texas.

Kinzer related that he "was notified on 9 December 1994 that the chief of staff of the army, Gen. Gordon R. Sullivan, was going to nominate me to be the force commander of UNMIH. I was told to contact [the] deputy chief of staff for operations, Lt. Gen. Paul Blackwell, who said I should prepare to come to Washington DC for some days of orientation. I went on 12 December, the following Monday." Kinzer visited with members of the army staff and JCS "experts who gave me an orientation on where the U.S. Army was with Haiti." General Sullivan "asked me what I needed and I told him some engineering units and I needed some people that I wanted to handpick and he supported me." From there,

> I went to the State Department where I met with Ambassador Frances D. Cook, who was then working with all the contributing countries. Then I met with several other echelons of the State Department to get their perspective and then with Department of Commerce. From there to [Virginia and] USACOM to meet with Gen. [John J.] Sheehan, who had just taken over from Adm. [Paul D.] Miller. Then to the UN in New York, where I was introduced to the political-military peacekeeping organization. I had the opportunity to talk with Madeline Albright, who was then the U.S. ambassador to the UN, and I found out how the UN resolution was crafted with the specific thought of a going-in strategy, an execution strategy, and an end state or an exit strategy. This

was the first time it occurred to me and I thought, somebody has put some real thought into this idea of setting parameters for this operation so that we wouldn't get in there and get stuck.[22]

Experience in international incursions as both an enlisted man and an officer was central to why Kinzer was selected to lead UNMIH. But his collective experience mattered.

It was everything I had done prior to getting this mission, from what I learned as a squad leader as an infantryman to what I learned at the War College and everything in between. The two tours in Vietnam, having been in the Dominican Republic in 1965 as a young lieutenant in the Eighty-Second Airborne Division and seeing how that situation had unfolded and remembering our priorities and how we dealt with OOTW, and then of course Panama and Operation Just Cause. I learned many lessons there of how to get a municipality back on its feet after it had gone through the trauma of a combat operation. Also Field Manual 100-23 [*Peace Operations*] had just hit the street. I read it three times on the way to Washington. It is kind of like reading the Bible, each time you read it you get a little different perspective. It was very helpful for me as I shaped the task organization and crafted the mission statement and set about determining what my intent ought to be, purpose, method, and all those pieces of the operation. I kept going back to the UN resolution as a document that gave me the moral and legal high ground to do what I had to do, from crafting rules of engagement to setting up the task organization of the force and developing a concept of operation.[23]

After getting his personal affairs in order in San Antonio, Kinzer returned to New York and the UN in January 1995. There "I met for the first time the chief of staff of the mission, Col. [William] Bill Fulton from Canada. I met the special representative of the secretary-general, Ambassador Lakhdar Brahimi from Algeria. I saw for the first time that the task organization numbers were six thousand [troops] from twenty-one nations, about nine different languages, and six different religions. Brahimi and I talked about the political and military aspects of the mission along with Fulton. Two days later we went to Haiti as a group."[24]

Once in Haiti, Kinzer met with "the American multinational force, Gen. [George] Fisher, U.S. ambassador [William L.] Swing, and the Haitian government. We had a meeting in the Cabinet Room at the National Palace. I met Mr. Aristide, his special assistant Leslie Voltaire, the prime minister [Smarck Michel], and so on. I really got a feel for what the situation was in Haiti and how the multinational force had shaped the situation and what kind of liaison and conduits that they had established with the Haitian government as a result of the actions of September 1994."[25]

Kinzer returned home briefly and then ventured to Haiti once again for four days in February 1995. On this visit, Kinzer's purpose was

to meet with my own staff [UNMIH], and then talk with [JTF 190/MNF commanding general George] Fisher about the residual force that the U.S. was going to leave there, about twenty-four hundred troops. Fisher left the Second Brigade under Col. [Charles] Chuck Swanick, a cavalry squadron from the Second Armored Cavalry Regiment (Light) from Fort Polk [Louisiana], and so on, and also a logistics piece and a communications piece to support the American contingent. Of course, I was dual-hatted as the U.S. and UN commander. Interesting! In peacekeeping, I don't think any U.S. flag officer had done that before on this order of magnitude, so it was unique. I again met with Haitians and we began to refine our transition training plan.[26]

Kinzer developed a concept for observation and coordination with JTF 190/MNF

for about a week to ten days where our people would watch how their staff operated in this environment. We stood up our own command post two weeks before we took over the mission and basically made the transition with communications and SOPs [standard operating procedures] and things like that and they watched us. When I talked with General Sullivan back in December he mentioned doing a BCTP [session] with my staff. I had already thought about that but I didn't have any money and the UN doesn't pay for training. The UN's approach is that contributing nations train their units but they don't make any provisions for the staff. But we convinced Kofi Annan at the UN to pay for it and we had an exercise in March. We used the Haitian elections as a model. I had about 85 percent of the force attend. It cost the UN $167,000 and lasted six days. We came away with draft SOPs, modified training plans, and we were ready to do it. I hope it becomes a model for the UN. Eventually we had the whole force on the ground and we were ready to go on 31 March 1995.[27]

Transition

On March 31, 1995, mission handover began with a parade to announce that there was a new force, UNMIH, securing Haiti. The UN troops looked professional, but there were internal problems that required immediate attention. During the ceremony, Pakistani troops walked past those from India and would not look at them. Nor would the two forces stand next to each other. Kinzer "had to move the two-hundred-man contingent from India to the other end of the formation, away from the Pakistanis." Regardless, UNMIH was now in charge of supporting the government of Haiti.[28]

Kinzer's major challenge initially was organizing his force on the ground in concert with mission requirements and cultural views. Given that Kinzer was the senior officer for both multinational and U.S. troops, he decided to follow the model established by JTF 190/MNF and place an American officer in charge of the U.S. troops while he remained in overall command of the entire force. He selected Col. David Patton for the position of commander, U.S. Support Group, a headquarters that Patton described as "a bilateral mission performed under the auspices of USACOM and JTF Bravo-type organization, if you are familiar with JTF Bravo and Honduras. It is a command-and-control headquarters to support a series of deployments for training engineer, medical, and civil

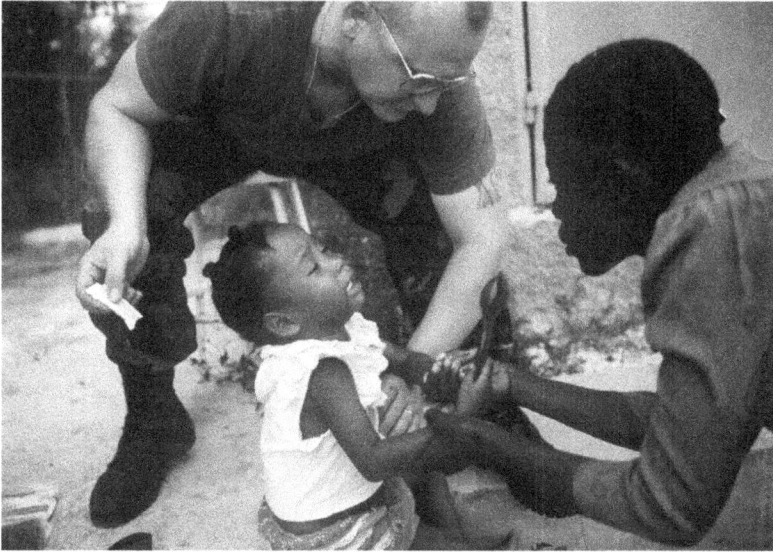

20. A U.S. Army medic provides medical attention to a Haitian family. During UNMIH, U.S. troops established clinics such as this one throughout Haiti. Source: Department of Defense.

affairs units who can come [in this case] to Haiti, train, and as a byproduct of that the government of Haiti and its people receive some development of infrastructure." While the support group headquarters was U.S., it was also multiservice, for "I have an army sergeant major but my executive officer is a navy Seabee full commander. My secretary is a marine and I have two administrative personnel, a navy yeoman and an air force administrative clerk." The U.S. Support Group headquarters under Patton's command allowed Kinzer to focus upon the UN mission without becoming involved in the mundane affairs of U.S. forces.[29]

Kinzer also recalled being influenced by "how we organized for combat in Vietnam and having spent two years over there in the idea of tactical zones: I, II, III, and IV Corps tactical zones." He said, "I did a similar thing in Haiti. I looked at what the mission said, maintain security and stability and create an environment conducive to free and fair elections. That mission drove me to draw the boundaries along political lines that made sense so that when we got into elections support we were all familiar with the boundaries." Upon grasping how Haiti was controlled politically, Kinzer discovered, "There were nine departments in Haiti. We carved those out so a commander could get his arms around his department or tactical zone, if you will. There were two populated areas, Cap-Haïtien in the north and Port-au-Prince in the center. I made Port-au-Prince Zone V and I put an American in charge." Ultimately, the zones covered both urban and rural areas of Haiti. A Pakistani battalion controlled Zone I (Cap-Haïtien), while a Nepalese battalion was responsible for Zone II (Gonaïves). A Dutch/Surinam company was located within Zone III (near Jacmel), and CARICOM forces were in Zone IV (Les Cayes), although, for reasons to be explained later, CARICOM was replaced by a U.S.-led force. Zone V (Port-au-Prince) was under U.S. control and contained the UNMIH headquarters, and Zone VI (northern Port-au-Prince) was occupied by a battalion of Bangladeshi troops.[30]

Diversity does not always mean cohesion, and Kinzer had his share of cultural differences within UNMIH. Kinzer had put

> a Bangladeshi colonel subordinate to an American colonel in Zone V [initially], as had General Fisher. But Fisher had a [U.S.] brigadier general [in charge there]. The Bangladeshi colonel, Col. Abdul Wadood, came to me and said he had a problem. He said that he understood the command relationship and that was fine with him but not back in Dhaka, Bangladesh. It won't play well there, me working for another colonel. I said that I understand. So looking at Port-au-Prince and its environment, it is a pretty big area. I knew elections would be a challenge. So we carved out Zone VI and put the Bangladeshis in charge. It is how you deal with twenty-one different countries, most English-speaking, 45 percent Christian and 45 percent Muslim and the rest other, and you have to build cohesion.[31]

In this military intervention, at least, challenges that required attention existed within the force, not just in Haiti.

By early April 1995, after Kinzer readjusted matters, UNMIH's Port-au-Prince headquarters controlled six subheadquarters in six operational zones: Port-au-Prince with its two sectors, Cap-Haïtien, Gonaïves, Jacmel, and Les Cayes. Five UN infantry battalions (which included a quick reaction force); administrative, logistical, and medical support units; a military police battalion; an engineering unit; aviation and air logistical elements; a military information support team (MIST); and a civil affairs unit were deployed in ten locations: Port-au-Prince, Cap-Haïtien, Fort-Liberté, Hinche, Gonaïves, Port-de-Paix, St. Marc, Jacmel, Les Cayes, and Jérémie. SF elements, most wearing UN blue baseball caps instead of green or blue berets, remained deployed throughout the country in twenty-five locations, a holdover from Operation Uphold Democracy. SF elements were located in each of the six zones in support of UN troops. By early April 1995, UNMIH's military component totaled 6,017 troops. UNMIH's civilian police component stood at 791 members under Chief Supt. Neil Pouliot, a Canadian. UNMIH also contained 122 international civilian staffers, 175 locals, and 12 UN volunteers.[32]

In addition, Kinzer had the zone commanders host a briefing for their counterparts, with the first being Zone V and the UNMIH headquarters. The second was held in Cap-Haïtien, which was under Pakistani control. Kinzer explained,

> We flew a helicopter around and picked up all the leaders and flew to Cap-Haïtien. The Pakistanis brought us into a big tent and showed a film of Pakistan and when we left we had a good appreciation for what Pakistan had done, where it had been, where it was today, and their contributions to peacekeeping operations. After this conference, the Indian lieutenant colonel was shaking hands with the Pakistani colonel. The Bangladesh[is] hosted one, the Dutch, the Canadians, and that is how we built cohesion. I also included the Americans under Col. [Walter L.] "Skip" Sharpe of the Second ACR. He did his briefing at Club Med with of course a beach, swimming pools, and what have you.

Kinzer also discovered immediately that Haiti was not as stable as some imagined. Killings and violence continued. UNMIH forces found themselves at risk but remained cautious about taking coercive measures. Operating under the UN Charter's Chapter VI, Kinzer found it too restrictive for what was actually occurring in Haiti. Conversely, Chapter VII was too permissive in the use of force. Having arrived under Chapter VI obligations but perhaps needing Chapter VII authority at times, Kinzer's troops were in a tenuous situation. He therefore requested that the UN approve what he called a "Chapter VI and a half" circumstance or, put another way, a Chapter VI+ situation, which allowed for self-defense but also more, if needed. That approval came, after some debate.[33]

Mission Execution

Although JTF 190/MNF's Twenty-Fifth Infantry Division (Light) had left a brigade and other units behind to assist UNMIH initially, plans called for replacing them with others once UNMIH had settled in. The Second ACR (Light), along with two infantry companies from the Eighty-Second Airborne Division and other elements, began rotating squadron-sized elements to Haiti in January 1995 and until March 1996.[34] According to regimental executive officer Lt. Col. Kevin C. M. Benson, "We were focused in Zone V." Ironically, Benson had been previously assigned to the Eighteenth Airborne Corps at Fort Bragg, North Carolina, where he had helped design the peacemaking invasion plan for Haiti, OPLAN 2370. Now wearing a blue beret, Benson and his regimental commander "directed forces on operational missions, those being presence patrolling, quick reaction force, and information gathering. We monitored U.S. personnel supply functions and pay problems. We made sure the chaplain got out seeing all the folks. We had PSYOP teams all over the country, although the UN calls them 'military information support teams' (MIST). We had civil affairs all over the country advising UNMIH forces: Indians, Pakistanis, and Bangladeshis, to name a few. Part of our regimental medical company was in Cap-Haïtien running a small clinic and in Les Cayes running a small clinic, as well."[35]

Near Zone V was Zone IV, which encompassed the southern "claw" of Haiti. The area was originally to have been the responsibility of CARICOM forces. However, they lacked "facilities, logistic support, and so forth" and were unable to assume or sustain the mission. Instead, zone control fell to U.S. leadership by default. In March 1995, Maj. Clyde Meeks, SF, assumed command for one month and then Maj. Walter M. Pjetraj, SF, took over. At the time, Pjetraj explained, he "was serving as the S5 [civil affairs staff officer] for Third Special Forces Group (Airborne) but changed jobs and became the zone commander for Zone IV." A junior field grade officer, Pjetraj took charge of "U.S. PSYOP and civil affairs units, Canadian engineers, some Filipinos, plus civilian police elements," among others. His top priority became the forthcoming Haitian regional elections.[36]

As Benson mentioned, UNMIH had PSYOP teams covering the country but not all of them were Haiti experts. Maj. Dorothea M. Burke, a PSYOP officer from Company B, Sixth PSYOP Battalion (Airborne), Fort Bragg, North Carolina, worked within Zone V, after replacing her counterpart from the departing First PSYOP Battalion (Airborne). "I really had little knowledge [of Haiti]," she explained. "Our regional area of responsibility is Africa. So although it is very similar, this was the first time we actually had experience in Haiti. We started off with a transition just to get to know what was going on. We did not make any conscious, deliberate changes. But some changes were made based on our unique unit requirements or our personal own experiences."[37]

June 1995 Elections

In March 1995, as UNMIH prepared to assume its duties, forty-three Haitians died due to vigilantism, a situation reflecting Haiti's continued propensity for social violence. Three more killings occurred in early April. Whether Haiti was now safer than most U.S. cities was debatable. Regardless, despite having argued successfully for Chapter VI+ authority, Kinzer did not unleash it, for UNMIH's military intervention could not end centuries of violent ways that were imbedded in Haitian society and culture.

Countering increased violence as elections neared became worrisome for all concerned. Kinzer soon found his headquarters in support of MICIVIH, which was now responsible for the June 1995 legislative and municipal elections, for a total of eighteen Senate seats, eighty-three deputy positions, 135 mayoral races, and 565 community council races. Kinzer recollected,

> I met with all the leaders of the political parties, forty-five parties, and I got advice from Nguyễn Hữu Đông [Vietnam], the UN representative for the elections. I told Mr. Brahimi that I was a soldier first and a politician second and he said you won't last long unless you reverse that. Nguyễn Hữu Đông said there are forty-five parties but only eighteen viable ones, with twenty-seven hundred people running for twenty-five hundred positions. Everyone wanted personal protection. I said that I am like a window washer but I don't install windows. I will be where I need to be on election day, trust me, and if anything happens I will be able to respond to it.[38]

Conseil Electoral Provisoire (Provisional Electoral Council, or CEP) estimated that over 3.5 million Haitians were eligible to vote. But those numbers originated from a 1982 census and were not current. It was also estimated that 15 to 20 percent of Haitian voters were literate. Handbills and leaflets were of limited value. UNMIH MIST personnel used television and radio broadcasts to convey election information in support of the CEP.

Violence continued through the months of May and June, and UNMIH patrol activity increased. In support of the patrols, U.S. PSYOP teams deployed in cities and rural areas, using loudspeakers, radio broadcasts, and leaflets to convey themes about "supporting the Haitian government, promoting the justice system, setting the conditions for peaceful elections, disarming the population, which was essentially a weapons buyback program, and dealing with Haitian-to-Haitian violence." Unfortunately, conveying those themes was difficult in Haiti. As Capt. Jeffrey White said (and Major Burke confirmed), "Obviously loudspeakers were the most effective because they were face-to-face. We tried to maximize radio, print posters, and newspapers. But if you can't read, you have to rely on pictures. So we have gone to computer graphics, but when you are in a third-world country computer graphics just don't cut it. You need a good illustrator to be able to produce pictures to draw the people."[39]

But getting the message out was more problematic than merely producing images or broadcasting. For Burke,

The main problem is that you can only reach so far. The terrain and the vehicles we had didn't allow for the mobility that we needed. You had your twenty-two teams throughout the country but there are location pockets that in November 1995 still do not know that anybody has been in this country. There is just no contact with them. And here is a good-size number of the population in that category. There are these little villages built in the countryside where there are trails that go off and you never see where they end. There are villages out there that will never get radio and never see a white person short of a missionary. So you don't reach the entire population.[40]

The night before the election, Kinzer accompanied a patrol in Port-au-Prince to see how effective the messages had been within a built-up area. "I am with a rifle platoon," he recalled.

I got dropped off on a street corner and the platoon maneuvered down a couple of blocks. While I was waiting for them, it was about midnight, a little old lady had this kiosk and she was cooking. This guy walks up to me in shorts, sandals, and a tee shirt. He says in English, "Hey guys, how ya doing? Are you going to start World War 3?" I said that we are here to maintain security and stability for the elections tomorrow. I asked if he was going to vote. He said no but would give me his background. He lived in Brooklyn, New York, for fifteen years, graduated from high school in Brooklyn, but got deported because he never became an American citizen. He got in trouble with drugs and guns so they sent him back to Haiti. He told me he was not going to vote unless someone pays him 150 bucks; then he will vote for whoever pays him.

Kinzer added, "He said he had enough smarts and initiative to take charge of his little piece of the city block. But when you do that in

Haiti it sends the message that you got political ambitions. You and your family want to take over this area for you and your family, not for the good of the community. In Haiti, initiative is frowned upon." Col. David Patton concurred with Kinzer. "General Kinzer likes to talk about the legacy of two hundred years of dictatorship in this country. I think he is probably right on the mark. People that have grown up in this country are fearful of taking responsibility, of making decisions, and it is very difficult to try to bring them into a twentieth- or twenty-first-century democracy when they do not have anything to fall back on in the way of values."[41]

Kinzer admitted that UNMIH "had completely underestimated the scope of the support for the election process. Our mission was not to support it directly, it was to create an environment conducive for free and fair elections, translate that into security and stability." But the more UNMIH worked with MICIVIH, he discovered that CEP, "was inept at what they were doing. They didn't know how to plan. They didn't know how to organize. They didn't know how to coordinate let alone execute. The logistics infrastructure was just appalling." The Haitians were unable to print the voter registration forms. In what might be considered "mission creep," Kinzer "sent people to California to print them. They printed four million copies. We transported them back into country. Then we had to distribute them to eleven thousand potential voting booths throughout the country. I think there were 9 regions, 137 districts, and then the subsets of the districts. They could vote 420 people per location. So we had to register everybody, consolidate all the names, and put it into a database."[42]

On March 20, 1995, two Boeing 727s arrived in Haiti filled to capacity with voter registration forms. UNMIH officers were frustrated, for the Haitians had "no plan to receive or secure them. No plan to account for them." At this point Kinzer intervened and ordered his officers to fix the situation. "In two and half hours," Kinzer noted, "one captain and one lieutenant, two of my guys, put together a whole plan and the facility to receive, store, and sort this stuff to include floodlights, tables, and all kinds of stuff. The Haitians could no more have done that than the man in the moon." UNMIH exasperation mounted, for, as Kinzer stated, "Every time you turned around we were confronted with, for lack of a better word, 'shits.' I mean every time you turn around, Oh, we forgot this, Oh, we don't have a plan for this, Oh, we are going to hire a bunch of guys off the street to stack this stuff up but, Oh, we don't have any money to pay them. So UNMIH has to go to USAID and get some money out of the electoral support fund to pay them."[43]

Having UNMIH troops interfering in Haitian matters was something the UN wanted to avoid. Kinzer agreed in principle: "The challenge was to send the message that this was a Haitian election done with UN support, not a UN election. So I had the dilemma of making sure the facilities were secure enough that the process could occur without being overbearing so it would look like the UN was running the elections." Still, he had to tone down his can-do approach, despite his instincts. To avoid the appearance of election tampering,

> We would sortie into town by the voting booth, kind of check it out, go down the road, park, and then do some foot patrols. My guys developed methods to provide security but not be obtrusive. So we provided escort for the filled-out ballots back to a central collection point. But Haitians were notorious for not paying their workers so they wouldn't come in and count them. So we would have to go to USAID with one of the CEP people and pick up money, come back, and then make the Haitians pay their workers. We did not want to take charge of the ballots; we helped them move them. All of my commanders were very sensitive to that.[44]

Major Pjetraj noted that many ballots were incorrectly printed or actually inspired violence, most likely so that Aristide's Lavalas party would win the elections. In one case

> there were four candidates for an office but only one made it onto the sheet and that was a Lavalas candidate. So the other three were not Lavalas and wanted to know why they are not on the sheet. The CEP did not tell them why. They did not proclaim to

the people why their candidate is not there. So you get apathy. We had ballots being burned because this is their mentality: if I can't have it, you *won't* have it. If my candidate is not on the list, we are going to destroy things and make it null and void because it is not a fair election.

In another instance a candidate was shot "by an individual from a powerful family who had attempted to become a candidate but was not on the list because he was not Lavalas. The other guy [who was shot] was a good guy and on the list and was Lavalas. He was at a conference and a handgun was pushed through a window and shots were fired. You have social groups, power groups, familial groups, and if they are prevented from representing their constituents they react and this is what you get." Indeed, the June 1995 Haitian election reflected a third-world nation being pushed into administering and comprehending democratic processes that were alien in concept to many and difficult to fathom quickly. But as far as Pjetraj was concerned the election results did not matter anyway. "It is my opinion," he said, "that it was more important for the U.S. newspapers and the media to perceive this election as a success than it was for the Haitians to perceive this as a success."[45]

The disorganized CEP made UNMIH support for the elections challenging. Within the Second ACR (Light) Zone, Benson observed,

In Zone V and everywhere within the UN areas we had to secure the ballots and protect the government officials from violence who were distributing the ballots. Then we had to know where the polling places were. But we could not physically locate there due to Haitian law. So we had to disappear but be close enough to get back if there was a disturbance. The first hurdle was there were some workers who refused to move ballots the night before the election because they weren't being treated right by the Haitian government. They didn't have any water, they didn't have any food, blah, blah, blah. And we had to step in and help because the important thing was to get the election set up. Distribution first, then collecting the ballots, and then protection of the ballots returning to the counting area, and then when those were done we had to further protect the ballots as they were collected and put them into a warehouse at the LIC.[46]

Benson reported that dealing with Haitian illiteracy when voting was tricky. "The ballots all had to have pictures either of the candidate or the symbol of the political party. A lot of people were illiterate and would recognize a symbol or face and then make a mark. One of the elections was almost held up because some party complained that the symbol was not right or not the right color. The Haitians had to deal with that but we had to be involved in the distribution of corrected forms, collection, and all of that." One would imagine that the Haitian election process would improve after the June cycle but that was not the case, for the same issues plagued "both the August and September elections." Whether this was by design or happenstance is open to debate.[47]

After the June elections and into the fall of 1995, UNMIH forces continued to patrol cities and rural areas. The Second ACR (Light) "put out an average of two patrols during the day and one or two patrols at night. So we constantly had GIs on the street." In a dramatic contrast with the early days of the U.S.-led intervention in 1994,

> part of the patrol instructions was to stop and talk to people, smile at them, and wave at the kids. Every patrol had a linguist, mostly of Haitian descent and some from the Defense Language Institute [in California]. The SF guys were out there [in the countryside] in small teams. Overall I think they had a positive effect because there were always Americans out there and the Regular Army guys did some wonderful things, as did reservists as we rotated special operations forces through. I think they had more interaction than anybody because they lived out there day to day and so they depended upon their dealings with the populous for security.

Remarkably, the confusing security situation that had plagued JTF 190/MNF early in the 1994 intervention had dissipated enough in one year to permit UNMIH troops to engage the population, a testament to those who came before them.[48]

The great debate for the moment, however,

> was when do we take off Kevlar helmets and the flak jackets and not mount the caliber .50 and the M60 machine guns to demonstrate that there is a safe environment? This went back and forth. We finally resolved that we still going to wear helmets because we are in Humvees and the streets are really bad and we don't want anyone cracking their skull open. We will take off the flak jackets but we will have them nearby. Then we stopped patrolling with the .50 caliber machine guns mounted. We just had M60 machine guns, again not up and visible but ready for action. I told everybody it was like the cavalry in the American West.[49]

The less aggressive uniform posture went into effect in July 1995, after the June elections concluded.

Another Mission Handover

Mission fatigue coupled with the forthcoming Haitian election cycle of June and August 1995 had contributed to the Tenth Mountain's replacement by the Twenty-Fifth Division in January 1995. Similar considerations had brought in the Second ACR (Light). In the summer of 1995 another unit replacement occurred when the First Brigade, 101st Airborne Division (Air Assault) from Fort Campbell, Kentucky, supplanted most of the light cavalry forces. On October 13, 1995, when the Haitian government announced that presidential elections were to be held on December 17, UNMIH and U.S. leaders had already planned for a unit rotation to be completed beforehand.

Col. Jack Donovan, the First "Bastogne" Brigade commander, 101st Airborne Division (Air Assault), was "notified that we had this mission by Eighteenth Airborne Corps the very latter part of July. It is a very short notice. We were told it was a brigade headquarters and two infantry companies. That presented some unusual problems because I was taking units from other camps, on post [Fort

Campbell, Kentucky], and other stations and making a patchwork quilt, if you will, to come down here and execute this mission. As soon as I found out that I had the rose pinned on me a few of us came down here on a recon."[50]

After visiting with his counterpart in Haiti, Donovan returned to Fort Campbell to prepare his unit. While the Second ACR (Light) headquarters provided Donovan with "reams of staff work and mission stuff," he also reviewed PowerPoint "briefing slides. From that we deduced the tasks that are going to be asked of us and we guessed about 95 percent right, actually." Preparation included a leadership-training program involving "several personnel from the NSC and Major General Kinzer. I sent my two infantry companies to Fort Polk, Louisiana, where they meshed with the Second Squadron Second ACR and [focused on] building interaction in how they are going to work together."[51]

As with the divergent mission approaches taken by Tenth Mountain and SF troops during Operation Uphold Democracy, the 101st's infantrymen held a different view of the mission than the ACR's cavalrymen. Donovan recalled,

> We were criticized that once we got down here [Haiti] the infantry guys were too aggressive in their approach. We were highly trained at kicking doors in and taking down rooms and taking down buildings. I understood that all along and I was fully conscious of what I was doing. What I wanted to do was when we came here our guys would know they would not need to be that aggressive because of the local situation and we would throttle back. But if you are called to go into a building and it is a hostile takedown then you know that you have been trained to that standard so you are very comfortable in that.[52]

Donovan was fully aware of what this mission meant for the 101st and its historical record. He needed augmentation troops "to not screw it up." Taking over from a robustly manned cavalry regiment meant that his brigade needed more personnel due to the differences between his unit's assigned strength and what was actually required in Haiti. But his requests for reinforcements went unheeded. Donovan recalled,

> At the time we were at Fort Campbell, our division headquarters was of no assistance whatsoever. It is not a slam against them. They had other things that they were concerned with and so we had to fend for ourselves. The biggest challenge was getting the people to man the joint headquarters down here because a division mission, the Twenty-Fifth Infantry Division, had been scaled down to an ACR. So we are trying to fill positions with what had been once filled by a division. Very difficult when you go to your division commander and say I need fifty extra people and they say, "Bullshit, take your brigade headquarters and that's it."[53]

As a brigade commander, Donovan was not one to avoid confrontation. He soon went to his division commander, and "I told Maj. Gen. [John M.] 'Jack' Keane, the commanding general, at how proud we were of the 'Screaming Eagle' patch. But if you want to become famous, just let us go ahead and screw this thing up. Everybody remembers the patch. So we can't go down there and screw this thing up because that would have bad repercussions for everybody, the least of which would be the great 101st." Still, Donovan knew that the "Screaming Eagle" patch might be on his left shoulder but "this patch on the right shoulder is a UN patch. We are not U.S. guys doing things unilaterally, we are part of a UN force and so we have to keep that always in the front of our minds."[54]

After one week of joint operations between the 101st and the Second ACR (Light), mission handover occurred on October 26. For Donovan, it went well. "Everyone talks about buzz words like 'seamless transition' and all that stuff. I have got to tell you from my perspective it truly was a seamless transition because Second ACR made the investment right from the start and constant dialogue back and forth, fax, telephone, email, whatever." The First Brigade, 101st Airborne Division (Air Assault) was now a UN unit, for the first time in its history.[55]

In October Donovan's brigade

pretty much took over what the cavalry unit was doing with the patrolling and with the quick reaction force. You also have to know the force laydown, where things are and who is responsible for what zone. The tough part was trying to get your arms around the layout of the city of Port-au-Prince. You got maps but some of the streets do not have names. It's very congested. Things go real fast. When you are up to driving downtown, things go very, very fast. Trying to find a street that maybe had gone to a different angle than what you thought and what would look like on a map means it is easy to get disoriented downtown.

To alleviate some of the navigational problems, patrols had local linguists as escorts, but "sometimes they are good guides and sometimes not. But those are some of the learning things that we had to assimilate once we got here."[56]

Donovan had a policy that all members of his unit had to accompany one daylight patrol and one nighttime patrol, each lasting about six hours. On October 31 Donovan joined a patrol in Port-au-Prince.

It was Halloween and it was about 2300 [11:00 p.m.] at night and we were literally walking in the shit downtown, ankle deep in trash. A couple of guys had night vision goggles on and there was nobody around. All of a sudden on the street to the left 250 people showed up. *Rara* bands; out having a good time, drunk, celebrating Halloween. The staff sergeant in charge stopped the patrol. First inclination is that we have a problem. So we hunker down in the shadows and we watched. I am just a free rider [observing]. So the sergeant eyeballs the situation and decides to lay low; we will follow them but at a distance. Let's not incite them or piss them off because then we will have a problem we can't control. They're not starting trouble. A couple of Haitians at the tail end turned around and looked and then they just kept on going.[57]

UNMIH's mission did not become easier as time passed. With the First Brigade on the ground but a few weeks, President Aristide's cousin, Jean Hubert Feuille, was killed on November 9. Pro-Lavalas supporter Gabriele Fortunet was wounded. Aristide lashed out, threatening to remain in office for three more years due to his term being curtailed by the 1991 coup. Although he soon reversed his thinking, the forty-two-year-old president soon undertook a whirlwind of last-minute actions. He fired his police chief, announced plans to marry his legal advisor, the Haitian American Mildred Trouillot, and phased out the miniscule Haitian navy, replacing it with a coast guard. Many of these decisions upset powerful Haitian stakeholders, and tensions ran high within the country.

The violence against Aristide supporters, however, also threatened UNMIH's credibility in maintaining stability. For his part, Donovan was quick to act. He knew of a problem area in the Artibonite Valley, Petite Rivière. The locals had been disruptive and, as Donovan related, "We need to encourage the people of that particular region to maintain law and order, secure a stable environment, which is part of our mission statement, our charter, respect the Haitian National Police [HNP], and build up some trust in the new HNP. So what we did was scheduled a [helicopter insertion] mission for o-dark-thirty in the morning. We did not want to intimidate them, but when they woke up they would look around and there is a cavalry and infantry company team surrounding the village."[58]

After planning the operation in detail and inserting the troops via helicopter,

> We basically came through the village with loudspeaker teams and announced that isn't it great that you have a wonderful constitution that allows you to freely elect your president and by the way it is two weeks from now. The people did not really understand the elections; they liked Aristide and wanted to leave him in there. It doesn't work that way. We also broadcasted that you have the new HNP here. We put an arm around one of them and walked around telling the people that they will help you solve problems.

We then walked a portion of the force into the marketplace, promulgating our themes, and at 8:30 a.m., after four hours, we were out of there. We left the impression that these guys can come in from anywhere in the middle of the day or night, drop in on us if we are screwing up, and they can provide relief or put the hammer on us. I brought Haitian public affairs with us to have them broadcast what we were doing over their media. They told a better story, amplified it, and achieved better results. It seemed to work well with no further problems.[59]

As UNMIH forces attempted to maintain stability, many pundits believed that Aristide was contributing to public unrest by his unwillingness to separate himself from his personal philosophies. Some suspected that Aristide deliberately caused elections to be dysfunctional in an attempt to stay in office. Regardless, his often-radical rhetoric led Zone IV commander Major Pjetraj to flatly state that Aristide "was a communist." Patton put it differently, saying,

Aristide could have done more. He could have made public statements that would have made a lot of difference in this country. I don't think he ever totally embraced the democratic process, for one thing. Economically he never said the right things to try to reengage the Haitian business community or the international community at large. He tap-danced around all of those issues because he knew he couldn't condemn capitalism. He couldn't condemn international investment because the U.S. and the international community that had put him back into power and were supporting him made it clear that those particular ideals [democracy and capitalism] had to become part of the future of this country.[60]

Nevertheless, the International Republican Institute's assessment coincided with the two UNMIH military officers' observations. Institute staff reported, "Haiti is a broken-down nation in need of enlightened leadership and measured support. It is also a fact, however, that this leadership and support exists in limited quantities."[61]

UNMIH election security for the presidential election followed similar patterns as in the previous elections. But unique to this election cycle was that UNMIH's mission would end soon afterward, in February 1996, prompting mission handover to the UNSMIH. As early as May 1995, Kinzer cogitated about the eventual mission handover "and explained this to Aristide. He went ballistic. In November we had another meeting with the Haitian leadership and the outcome was the establishment of functional area working groups with a Haitian in charge. Some did it reluctantly. Some did it with vigor."[62]

Regarding election support, Colonel Donovan had the advantage of lessons learned from the previous election cycles. He placed responsibility for CEP election coordination with Capt. Ed Sullivan: "I sent him here for about three weeks during one of their runoff elections so he could see the election process. He then became my election guru. He ran the elections for this country, from the U.S. standpoint anyway, from a trailer over at the airport. This guy is phenomenal; he ran a goddamn national election."[63]

Lavalas candidate René Préval won the Haitian presidential election with 88 percent of the popular vote. According to observers, CEP procedural measures had improved significantly, but the turnout was apathetic, at 15–28 percent across the districts. The International Republican Institute noted that election-day incidents were few; the "preemptive security blanket provided by the United Nations military forces (UNMIH), in conjunction with the Haitian police, again enabled citizens to vote without significant personal risk." Issues continued, however, with ballot privacy and accountability.[64]

With the elections over and UNMIH's mandate ending in February 1996, Kinzer explained, "the [force] drawdown started in December. We moved the Indian contingent out and we started to draw down U.S. forces. We had an SF plan and the least engaged came out first. We looked to have it all zeroed out by 15 April." Kinzer also had to leave behind some non-U.S. assets to support UNSMIH, which consisted of thirteen hundred Canadian and Pakistani troops under Canadian leadership.[65]

21. A crowd gathers outside Haiti's National Palace to welcome Aristide's return. Source: Department of Defense.

President René Préval was sworn into office on February 7, 1996, marking the first time in Haitian history when two democratically elected presidents exchanged power. Knowing that UNMIH was to depart in a few weeks, Préval requested that they remain in country until June. While Préval's request was approved, Kinzer nonetheless transferred command to Brig. Gen. J. R. P. Daigle, a Canadian, on March 1, 1996. Kinzer left without fuss. "We had a change-over ceremony but it was not elaborate and we didn't do it at the National Palace. We did it at the Bangladesh parade field, brought in elements of all forces, and did the change of command there."[66]

UNMIH's departure on June 30, 1996, ended the U.S. military's role in Operation Uphold Democracy and UNMIH. Kinzer left the country by air on March 2, returning to San Antonio, Texas. In May 1996 a ten-day conference was held at Carlisle Barracks, Pennsylvania, to capture lessons learned and to produce an after-action report. Kinzer "wanted no more than twenty-five pages. I wanted to get at the salient points of the mission, the concept of operation, how we accomplished it, what the task organization looked like, the major challenges we had and how we dealt with those, and what we learned. Anything longer than twenty-five pages, nobody will read it. The people that need to read it, won't. The final document was twenty-two pages long, but there is more data available. It is at the Peacekeeping Institute at Carlisle Barracks."[67]

As UNMIH disbanded, U.S. and international troops returned to home station or civilian careers. For some, their time in Haiti had been an opportunity to complain by "pissing and moaning about six months away from all the Thanksgiving and Christmas and New Year's stuff. That is one way to look at it." But many others who participated in both operations came to understand that "this is an interesting mission. Like, wow, this is real."[68]

6

Aftermath

"When I was in Les Cayes [in October 1994], and I have pictures of it, this Haitian lieutenant had two [human] skulls on his desk, you know, two skulls. The U.S. Army Rangers had found out by talking to someone that one of them was about a year old and the other one was about three months old because you can still see the blood. The blood was still in the skull."

—MAJ. ANTHONY LADOUCEUR, U.S. Army

This study investigated what happens to individuals who plan, execute, and view military interventions. Haitian American Anthony Ladouceur's encounter at a FAD'H headquarters in Les Cayes, a city of seventy-two thousand people, is but one example. Perhaps the Haitian officer had executed his victims and their remains were personal trophies. Conceivably they symbolized an alleged mystical vodun power that the lieutenant leveraged to frighten the superstitious. Regardless of why the skulls were there, the FAD'H officer was quickly run off. Over one year later, Ladouceur remained shaken and remembered the incident as if it had happened yesterday.

Immediate Outcomes

Few people who are accustomed to Western-style living standards understand what transpires in the third world. In the case of military interventions into developing nations, oral histories provide valuable insights that most books simply overlook. Many of the men and women in this study remembered the Haitian intervention because they witnessed unimagined levels of filth, disease, and depravity. Capt. Doni Colon was nearly overpowered by the stench emanating from heaps of human waste and rotting garbage at Port-au-Prince International Airport and in the streets. Col. James M. Dubik ordered truckloads of putrefying animal carcasses to be removed from a butcher's store. Col. Mark D. Boyatt recalled seeing disfigured people who were victims of junta brutality. Maj. Robert Shaw and others felt empathy for Haiti's impoverished citizens who barely managed to exist in hovels or in prisons but were unable to help them directly due to U.S. government concerns over "mission creep." M. Sgt. Edison Andre, a Haitian American, recollected that his former country simply smelled differently than he remembered it.

In March 1996, months after having left Haiti, Ladouceur still harbored guilt after having assisted "this Haitian lady with five kids. The kids did not have shoes. The boy was running around with no pants on. They lived in a shack. So I had fifty dollars American. I gave it to her but hopefully that won't get me in trouble." His testimony and those of others speak to a significant issue uncovered in this study: a command's inability to psychologically prepare their soldiers for the sensory overload of military intervention. Even as the force struggles to impose its will on the civilian population, the soldiers are wrestling with their own demons as they attempt to cope with what they are experiencing. During Operation Uphold Democracy, operational strain played some role in three suicides, while nearly a dozen soldiers were evacuated due to psychological trauma. While much has been said about the effects of combat on the human psyche and about post-traumatic stress, little attention has been given to the effect of peacemaking, peacebuilding, and peacekeeping missions on the people involved. The so-called human dimension of war, the moral factors that permeate military operations, certainly requires attention in military interventions, for the evidence here suggests that mission demands and post-traumatic stress affected participants to some degree.[1]

The oral histories also address the UN's core belief about what military intervention is supposed to accomplish, which is to stabilize a bad situation in order to create peace. The U.S-led Operation Uphold Democracy and the follow-on UNMIH have been acclaimed as success stories in lessening the rampant abuse of Haiti's citizens by the junta, as Ladouceur witnessed in Les Cayes. Between September 19, 1994, and March 31, 1995, military and civilian forces removed the junta, returned Haitian president Jean-Bertrand Aristide to office, provided security to Haitians amid continued social upheaval, confiscated weapons, assisted Haiti's civil administration, mentored the judiciary, trained a new police force, provided hurricane disaster relief, and prepared the Haitian people for elections. The complex mission ended with few casualties. The subsequent mission handover to UNMIH on March 31, 1995, was uneventful due to a U.S. Army–contrived UN staff training program, effective leadership, and coordination between headquarters. After transition, UNMIH troops protected international personnel and key installations, continued to professionalize the FAD'H until Aristide disbanded them, and worked toward attaining a politically separated, civic-minded Haitian police force and border patrol. They also assisted Haiti's government and its electoral body, the CEP, through three election cycles before mission handover to the UNSMIH on June 28, 1996.

While evidence for mission success is plentiful, the oral histories in this book reveal details about preventive diplomacy that question its effectiveness. The missionary couple Willard and Margaret Squires lived in Haiti during the embargo and noted that few people seemed bothered by it, while others did not even know what it meant. Colonel Boyatt revealed that the wealthy, the embargo's supposed target, continued to live in luxury while Haiti's tottering economy was destroyed and the already exploited poor endured additional suffering. Militarily speaking, armed intervention in Haiti was a chaotic venture because a peaceful solution preempted the invasion. While no one desires untold death and destruction from war, the U.S.-led operation had been planned strategically as a peacemaking combat incursion to be followed by postconflict peacebuilding. Even with multiple planning options, the expected conditions on the ground were not in place when the assault terminated at the last minute. The junta and its forces were

22. An Argentinian MNF arriving for training in Puerto Rico. Source: Department of Defense.

not vanquished but remained in control and were dangerous. The invading force that had prepared mentally and tactically for war then changed; the astonished Eighty-Second Airborne Division went home and the Tenth Mountain Division (Light) entered the country. The Tenth Mountain, which at the time was a reserve force for the combat operation, found itself tossed into a risky and uncertain peacekeeping situation that it was not totally prepared to undertake. Uncertainty meant that force protection soon dominated the mission while population engagement was minimized, as evidenced by the behavior of conventionally trained combat troops. Haitian civilians, military interventionists, and the junta and its forces alike were confused over who was responsible for what. The "in your face" combat posture taken by the Tenth Mountain, an approach that its leaders justified as using intimidation to protect the force, did little to change the public's perception that militaries exist to browbeat civilians.

The Tenth Mountain's methodology in stabilizing Haiti has both its advocates and its faultfinders. The oral histories add to this dialogue by underscoring that the division leadership failed to appreciate Haiti's history and its social views of military power and to prepare their troops accordingly. In truth, some military practitioners at the Eighteenth Airborne Corps took time to study Haiti's history, but only regarding the U.S. military occupation of the early twentieth century. Their inquiry was motivated by a desire to resolve contemporary strategic and operational issues. But the *longue durée* of Haiti's military history was largely overlooked by the intervening forces. Established patterns of military and police power on the island of Hispaniola had woven themselves into Haiti's societal fabric over the centuries and created strongly held opinions about people in uniform: soldiers and paramilitary troops are agents of those who pay them to use force or the threat of it to impose their will upon the people. In truth, the Tenth Mountain Division's aggressive behavior and force-protection efforts to secure themselves and prevent casualties unwittingly confirmed this cultural viewpoint. While some Haitians cheered the American troops upon arrival, their standoffishness caused many Haitians to later view them as collaborators instead of saviors.

As the oral histories indicate, the target nation's cultural baggage regarding military authority contributes to, hinders, or may even prevent intervention success. In war, analyzing centuries of interaction between a country's military and its society may be inconsequential; countries are ravaged and populations conquered. In interventions involving armed soldiers who are to create stability, civil cooperation is an operational necessity. Appreciating what military power has meant historically to the targeted population is vital and warrants careful scrutiny before the intervention begins.

The nineteenth-century Prussian military theorist Carl von Clausewitz aptly noted that a strong intellect is necessary to overcome the chance and uncertainty of war. An OOTW demands the same ability. The interviewees in this work indicated that a strong mind was required in Haiti to overcome people who perceived that the U.S. Army was in league with the FAD'H. Riots and upheavals typically occurred in Haiti's urban areas but less so among the rural population, where rebellion in Haiti had typically fermented. Quelling the disturbances fell to conventionally trained soldiers who took an overtly aggressive approach that made earning public cooperation problematic. In contrast, SF soldiers lived among the historically defiant rural people every day in an aware but calm posture that earned public trust. Problems were few. Astute reporters immediately picked up on the operational disparity between the "two American armies." The Department of Defense evidently noticed as well. John Ballard noted that replacing the assertive Tenth Mountain Division (Light) in January 1995 with the more relaxed Twenty-Fifth Infantry Division (Light) reflected operational considerations, including mission fatigue. Still, by the time of the rotation, the JTF 190/MNF commander had announced that Haiti was stabilized, a conclusion reached by comparing the frequency of Haitian instances of violence with violence in daily life in United States cities. While JTF 190/MNF was undoubtedly successful in meeting UN requirements for stability, oral history interviewees reported an immediate easing of social tension once the Hawaii-based division assumed the mission. UNMIH continued the Twenty-Fifth Infantry's operational approach.[2]

As this study elucidates, there is little doubt that the UN sends soldiers and police monitors and trainers into situations "beyond their ken." Approving a military intervention to occur is one thing, but commanding and controlling it is another. The eyewitnesses in this study indicated that UN members deferred the gritty details of planning soldierly operations to professional military officers, as indicated by how OPLANS 2370, 2380, and 2375, as well as the last-minute 2380+, were created. In truth, some military personnel prefer it this way and see civilian authorities as meddlers. In the case of Haiti, the UN had a multinational staff within its Department of Peacekeeping Operations produce strategic guidance for creating and fielding a force. But those officers did not create the operational plans, for they did not have standing forces of their own. The Haiti case also showed that the UN of 1994, as with the previous League of Nations, was not capable of managing complex military interventions. Surrogates were required to plan the intervention, which in this case involved the United States, with its robust military and convoluted security system. In considering Haiti and the UN operations that have followed it, the list of countries with the capacity to plan, execute, and sustain a military intervention is rather short.[3]

The oral histories also divulged what happens when the UN leadership assumes that participating nations will provide properly equipped and experienced personnel when intervening. In Haiti, the U.S. government and its military outfitted certain contributing nations' forces with weapons, ammunition, vehicles, and uniform accoutrements, including insignia, boots, socks, and underwear. U.S. military officers, albeit with U.S. government assistance, spent considerable effort and taxpayer funds finding contributing nations, establishing training camps and transporting forces to them, training soldiers, obtaining air-conditioned hotel rooms for international policemen, and deploying forces to Haiti.

Furthermore, multinational augmentees are trained and educated in their own military culture, but the UN does not prepare them to command and control the multinational operations it approves. The UN simply has no expertise to train an operational headquarters. With UNMIH, UN staff training occurred only because of President William J. Clinton's presidential directive in the aftermath of Somalia in 1993 and U.S. Army chief of staff Gen. Gordon R. Sullivan's willingness to organize the training. The UNMIH commander and his headquarters staff members appreciated the mission-focused training that carried over into mission execution, but the UN has not adopted this procedure as routine. Military culture also affected the force itself; the UNMIH commander expended considerable effort in stroking egos and making mission adjustments during the operation to achieve force harmony.

Long-Term Outcomes

Where promilitary interventionists often point to immediate outcomes to support their views, antimilitary interventionists tend to revisit events once the operational fog has lifted. Haiti's list of postintervention foibles is long. Numerous election cycles have transpired since UNMIH's departure in June 1996, albeit with varying levels of voter participation, periodic violence, and administrative untidiness. But government turmoil continues; constitutionally mandated senatorial elections were finally held in August 2015 after a three-year hiatus. Approximately 18 percent of eligible voters cast ballots. Elections were canceled in twenty-two districts; positions remain occupied by previously elected officials, are vacant, or have been filled by nonelected appointees. Haiti's long-standing militarized society has changed to some degree absent the FAD'H. While potential exists for the Haitian Border Police and the revamped HNP to become true public servants, the endemic mismanagement, corruption, and lack of funding appear overwhelming. The HNP remains weak; finding qualified candidates for the academy is difficult. The prison system is overcrowded due to lack of funds, questionable arrests, and lengthy pretrial waiting periods.[4]

But important evidence for what military intervention means in the long term also comes from oral histories. Many participants commented on their efforts when departing the country in the 1990s. To many, resolving Haiti's woes was far more complicated than what official briefings and bulleted lists of accomplishments suggested. Some soldiers doubted that progress would be possible in Haiti unless centuries-old issues were settled. The Haitian-born Maj. Anthony "Tony" Ladouceur believed that the power and security difficulties raised by Haiti's culture had yet to be fully addressed. "Haiti has a problem," he said, "because everyone wants to be president. Until you change that mentality you are not going to change Haiti itself. Once Haitians get power, they just suck the resources, the money, out of Haiti." UNMIH's Col. David Patton had similar concerns about well-entrenched Haitian government practices regarding policing. Patton commented, "There are concerns about them [the HNP] becoming politicized. I think it is basically because of the cronyism that exists here. So many leadership positions are filled by friends regardless of their skills. Personal loyalty means a lot more than any type of actual skills here." Maj. Jeffrey Morris of JTF 190/MNF observed that civic-mindedness was absent within the populace. He said, "I think if you put most Americans in that kind of environment they would immediately start trying to improve things and find ways to make things better. But in the case of Haitians, I am not sure everyone has that motive." The Haitian-born M. Sgt. Eddison Andre concluded that perhaps the interventions did more harm than good for U.S.-Haitian relations.

Our perception is that we've come here, we've taught democracy, we did good, we're leaving, we planted the seed. But Haitians are saying that we've always had democracy over here, we've just never had the stability for it to grow. So you have not taught us anything. You have not really helped us. You are creating chaos because you wiped out the army [FAD'H] that was a stable force. It [the army] was wrong but it was stable and respected. It should have been molded and changed. But the fact that it was whoosh, gone, and you bring in a bunch of young kids who don't know what they are doing. Now you have opened it up for true chaos and possibly an opportunity to destroy democracy.[5]

Other participants, however, were more optimistic. Col. Mark D. Boyatt believed that Haiti's difficulties could be overcome with proper leadership. "The Haitian people are not lazy," he stated. "They are incredibly hard working, if they have a goal, if anyone can show them an out, if anyone can show them a reason." Maj. Robert Shaw believed that Haitian lives had been improved to some degree because of the intervention. He recalled Cité Soleil, the poorest Port-au-Prince district, the day after the U.S.-led intervention began. "The children had no clothes. It was bad. There was overwhelming stench everywhere. And it was very dangerous, no one trusted anyone." But when he returned in March 1996, things were better. By then, "people trusted some people. They tried to clear the streets. There was one main street that was cleared of garbage. You could drive down there. There was food and medical supplies and things like that." Maj. Jeffrey Miser, who was with JTF 190/MNF, also believed that the intervention had improved lives. "They understood that we were there to protect them. They can sleep at night."[6]

Perhaps what bothered intervention veterans most was that UN and U.S. government policy makers believe that imposing foreign military power on an unschooled, impecunious population actually assists in establishing or furthering democracy. In November 1995 Maj. Dorothea M. Burke explained her view:

> I think we associate democratizing Haiti with peaceful elections and a transition government. People have a majority vote and the people know who they're going to vote for. But they still do not know what democracy is. For them, democracy is water, electricity, roads, food on the table, jobs. If you ask them what democracy is, they don't know. If you ask a typical American to explain democracy, I do not think you will get the same answer from them. Some Americans do not know what it is. So to come into Haiti militarily and say we democratized it I think is pretty ignorant on our part. We can't even explain it ourselves and put it into simple terms that need to go to an illiterate population to educate them to put it into practice. They're moving toward democracy but there is a lot of work to be done.[7]

Haiti, absent an educated populace, a stable economy, and a sense of civic virtue and power sharing, remains a work in progress.

Furthering democracy in Haiti required establishing "security and stability," the raison d'être for UN, OAS, and U.S. leaders and representatives to use military force through JTF 180, JTF 190/MNF, and UNMIH. Yet a 2013 security report from the U.S. Department of State noted that the "stable and secure environment" declared by the JTF 190/MNF commanding general in January 1995 had vaporized or perhaps had merely been an illusion to begin with. The Department of State assessed Haiti as "critical" in the categories of crime and violence, two indicators of a secure and stable environment. Haiti's rating stemmed from the island nation "being unique among Caribbean States" in suffering from a "lack of tourism, scarcity of foreign investment, and inferior infrastructure." Economic difficulties encouraged pickpockets, robbers,

23. A well-armed Tenth Mountain Division (Light) soldier distances himself from Haitians. Population engagement is essential for intervention success, but force protection often takes priority. Source: Department of Defense.

and kidnappers, along with the occasional home invasion to attack tourists and locals alike. While the 1994–96 interventions sought to disarm the population through weapons buyback programs and outright confiscation, firearms remain plentiful and are easy to obtain. Lawbreakers continue to use firearms, knives, and other weapons such as ax handles and sticks to threaten, wound, or kill people, even in broad daylight and in public areas. Moreover, JTF 190/MNF and UNMIH commanders had paid careful attention to outward signs of stability such as public cleanliness and street maintenance in order to demonstrate improvement. By 2015 trash and human waste had once again piled up along the roads. Manholes absent their covers made driving perilous at best.[8]

Social statistics also indicate that Haiti has made little progress since the military intervention. In 2015 the assistance group Haiti Partners cited UN and U.S. government data to reveal that 59 percent of Haitians live on less than two dollars per day. About one-quarter of Haitians—24.7 percent—live in extreme poverty, on just over one dollar per day. Nearly 85 percent of rural Haitians are illiterate. Only half of the country's school-age children attend classes. Of that half, 60 percent leave school by the sixth grade. Only 15 percent of teachers are qualified; 25 percent have never attended secondary school. Although it costs $131 per child to attend classes for one year, Haiti's average annual per capita income is $660. Given such meager earnings, a Haitian family cannot manage to educate several children at once even if financial assistance is available. Building democratic institutions depends upon an educated populace, as well as a means to generate substantial revenue to realize their expectations. In some cases, such as in World War II–era Germany and Japan, it may also require being conquered. Haiti lacks all of these characteristics.[9]

Since the 1990s, Haiti has received continued foreign assistance as various armed forces help it to maintain what had been declared a secure and stable environment in January 1995. In a curious twist on what happened to Haiti in 1915, the six-month-long 1994 U.S.-led multinational intervention has now evolved into a long-term multinational intervention commitment. Since March 31, 1995, seven UN military and police rotations in support of the Haitian government have maintained a near-continuous extraterritorial presence on Haiti's sovereign soil. Personnel rotate, so there is little continuity and lessons often have to be relearned. The first UN mission after the U.S.-led incursion was UNMIH, which departed in June 1996. It was replaced by the thirteen-hundred-man Canadian- and Pakistani-led UNSMIH, which provided security and worked with Haitian law enforcement from June 1996 until June 1997. In June 1997 UNSMIH withdrew and the UN Transition Mission in Haiti (UNTMIH) took over, fifty military and 250 policemen from eleven foreign countries who secured Haiti while assisting the police. In November 1997, as UNTMIH members exited, a Haitian government request for continued foreign assistance resulted in the UN Civil Police Mission in Haiti (MIPONUH), three hundred civilian police from eleven nations who mentored Haitian law enforcement officers until March 15, 2000. The

International Civilian Support Mission in Haiti (MICAH), led by eighty UN technical advisors from eleven nations, then took over, only to depart in February 2001, when its mandate ended. Aristide, who again became president when Préval left office, did not request further UN assistance.

On February 29, 2004, the three-year reprieve from a foreign troop presence ceased when Haiti underwent additional political turmoil, violence, and instability. Strong social upheaval and external pressure caused Aristide to flee Haiti yet again, this time to the Central African Republic and later to South Africa. To steady the country, the U.S. government ordered a battalion of U.S. Marines to execute Operation Secure Tomorrow, yet another security and stabilization mission that later became a UN Multinational Interim Force (UNMIF), including 500 French, 160 Chilean, and 100 Canadian troops. Although less robust than Operation Uphold Democracy, the six-month-long mission was nonetheless the third U.S. military presence and sixth UN force intercession in Haiti's history.

With UNMIF's conclusion in July 2004, UN troops began the seventh force rotation, the United Nations Stabilization Mission in Haiti (MINUSTAH), under UNSCR 1542. MINUSTAH comprises sixty-seven hundred military and thirty-two hundred foreign aid assistants seeking "to restore a secure and stable environment, to promote the political process, to strengthen Haiti's Government institutions and rule-of-law-structures, as well as to promote and to protect human rights." For now, MINUSTAH's mission continues.[10]

The U.S. government supports MINUSTAH militarily through its U.S. Southern Command (USSOUTHCOM), a Florida-based joint operational headquarters that monitors Caribbean crises. On January 13, 2010, USSOUTHCOM responded to a 7.0-magnitude earthquake in Haiti that killed 230,000 people, including 130 Americans, and left two million people homeless. Under Operation Unified Response, a twenty-two-thousand-member multiservice (joint) U.S. military task force provided sixteen aid distribution sites for medical support, as well as food, water, power generators, trash and sewage removal, desalinization equipment, temporary structures, and security teams. U.S. armed forces supported Haitian government and international aid agencies with displaced person assistance while military engineers rebuilt the docks in Port-au-Prince. On March 24, 2010, the mission ended and the U.S. troops departed.

Although UN military stability operations have continued since 2010, Haiti continues to experience domestic security issues. Demonstrations between Haitians and the police periodically flare up and often turn vicious. Foreigners are not immune to local hostility; the American missionary George Knoop was stabbed to death in his Delmas-area home within Port-au-Prince on May 13, 2014. However, the seventy-seven-year-old Chicagoan's brutal murder did not preclude U.S. president Barack H. Obama from signing into law the congressional bill S1104, the Assessing Progress in Haiti Act, on August 8, 2014. The law requires "the Department of State to report to the Congress on the status of recovery and development efforts in Haiti following the 2010 earthquake in that country." The act also mandates annual reports through 2017 and "a three-year strategy to promote economic development and build professional and responsive governmental institutions in Haiti, and provide quarterly briefings to the Congress on the implementation of that strategy." About $712 million annually in U.S. financial assistance supports the strategy. Yet despite the inflow of millions of dollars in U.S. foreign aid, the fifty-five-year-old American missionary Roberta Edwards was murdered in Haiti and a small child was kidnapped from her car on October 10, 2015. Money alone will not end Haiti's propensity for violence or solve its problems.[11]

Given Haiti's domestic perils and what that can mean, USSOUTHCOM is tasked with responding to a future Haiti crisis. In support of the 2014 act, the headquarters has a number of specified missions, including humanitarian assistance, reducing illegal drug flows, interdicting illegal immigration, and preventing mass migrations to the United States. The latter charge came to the fore as the West African Ebola outbreak threatened U.S. citizens in 2014. On October 7, 2014, when visiting the National Defense University in

Washington DC, USSOUTHCOM commander Gen. John F. Kelly, USMC, opined that if the Ebola virus entered Haiti, a panic would ensue "that will make 68,000 unaccompanied [Hispanic] minors [illegally entering the U.S.] look like a small problem." "Haiti," he said, "has no ability to deal with it," and thus the prospect of thousands of Haitians fleeing their island home for the United States would not be unreasonable. Fortunately, the Ebola threat did not materialize in Haiti, and thus what the U.S. military might have done about it remains unknown.[12]

For all that the two military interventions accomplished or did not accomplish from 1994 to 1996, one should consider that foreign ground forces had occupied an independent Haiti but once prior to September 19, 1994. It is therefore helpful to recall the words of Jean-Jacques Dessalines, the rebel leader and Haiti's first emperor. On April 28, 1804, after having ethnically cleansed his country of about five thousand French men, women, and children, he proclaimed, "Never again shall colonist or European set foot on this soil as master or landowner. This shall henceforth be the foundation of our Constitution." While U.S. and UN troops may not be masters or landowners, their overt foreign military presence has clearly influenced Haiti's fate.[13]

In light of Dessalines's 1804 declaration, the oral histories of Operation Uphold Democracy and UNMIH participants increase our understanding not only of military interventions and those who plan, execute, and observe them but also of what a foreign military and police presence in Haiti has meant over 190 years later. The two 1990s missions were not just brief sojourns to realize UN, OAS, and U.S. strategic objectives or, as one U.S. Army officer dryly explained, "an opportunity to go on a real-world mission because it does verify all the training you have done." The security, stability, and assistance objectives aside, Operation Uphold Democracy was the second U.S. military presence upon Haitian soil in the twentieth century, which later led to a third presence in 2004, a substantial U.S. disaster-relief mission involving twenty-two thousand troops in 2010, and millions of U.S. dollars in foreign aid. More significantly, the 1994 U.S.-led operation pried open the door for seven UN military and civil police missions; the seventh one is continuing for now. What will come of them is unclear. The interviewees quoted in this book, at least, would surely agree that any successful military intervention means that once you leave you need not return.[14]

APPENDIX

Oral History Interviewees

Oral histories are primary sources. They are crucial for better understanding past events by filling in gaps in the historical record. They also assist in verifying or disproving the accuracy of historical documents and other material.

Oral history in the American historical tradition is nothing new. U.S. Army historians have incorporated eyewitness testimony into official histories of numerous American wars and interventions. Oral history has enjoyed popularity within America's colleges and universities, given the increase in the number of public history programs and usage of oral history within scholarly work. The U.S. government offers research grants to oral historians seeking to record people's lives for posterity.

The oral histories used in this book resulted from the Haiti Oral History Project (HOHP), conducted by a group of military officers and civilians who worked for the federal government. I helped organize and lead the effort. A few interviewers were trained oral historians but most held but a rudimentary understanding of what oral history work entailed. They did an admirable job nonetheless. Still, while each interviewer was diligent in asking appropriate questions and acknowledging on tape who was being interviewed, where, and when, some failed to identify themselves. Decades later, their unidentified voices cannot be affiliated with the name of a particular interviewer. Compounding the issue is that the flimsy cassette tapes have degraded over time and can be difficult to understand. Rather than guess at the identity of the person or persons conducting a specific oral history session, I attribute all interviews to HOHP, for the project was a team effort.

HOHP members interviewed individuals during and after the military intervention. We were fortunate to have at our disposal U.S. Army Command and General Staff College students and faculty at Fort Leavenworth who had participated in Operation Uphold Democracy or UNMIH, as well as civilians who also played a role. They willingly agreed to be interviewed. HOHP personnel also traveled to military headquarters within the United States and Haiti to meet with key personnel.

Interview preparation entailed studying books and articles on Haitian history, reading contemporary newspaper and magazine accounts of the intervention, and drawing upon years of training and education in the procedures involved in planning and executing military operations. We used personally purchased cassette recorders, although we occasionally had access to a professional camera crew and used them when possible. Most interviews in the United States occurred in offices while seated around a table or in hotel rooms. We structured the interviews with prepared questions for consistency, although deviation naturally occurred because each interviewee had a unique experience. In Haiti the discussions took place within Port-au-Prince's Light Industrial Complex buildings, various Special Forces locations, and a hotel. Some talks were "walking discussions," recorded while accompanying patrols in towns and cities.

The list of interviewees below represents but a small group of the thousands of men and women who planned, executed, or observed the 1994–96 Haiti military intervention under U.S. and UN leadership. I thank them for their interviews and what they underwent while assisting the Haitian people.

Lt. Col. Thomas K. Adams, staff trainer, UN Mission in Haiti, Department of Joint and Multinational Operations, U.S. Army Command and General Staff College, Fort Leavenworth, Kansas. Interview conducted by HOHP at Fort Leavenworth, Kansas, May 11, 1995.

M. Sgt. Eddison Andre, First Psychological Operations Battalion (Airborne), Eighth Psychological Operations Group (Airborne),

U.S. Air Force, Fort Bragg, North Carolina. Interview conducted by HOHP at Port-au-Prince, Haiti, November 10, 1996.

Lt. Col. Phillip J. Baker Jr., commander, Embarkation Forces, UN Mission Support Team, USS *Harlan County*, Combat Studies Institute, Fort Leavenworth, Kansas. Interview conducted by HOHP at Fort Leavenworth, Kansas, July 9, 1997.

Lt. Col. Kevin C. M. Benson, chief of plans, G3, Eighteenth Airborne Corps, Fort Bragg, North Carolina. Interview conducted by HOHP at Port-au-Prince, Haiti, January 20, 1996. Benson also served as the executive officer, Second Armored Cavalry Regiment (Light), under UNMIH, and his interview reflects both experiences.

Maj. James C. Boisselle, military information officer, Military Information Support Team, Ninth Psychological Operations Battalion (Airborne), Fourth Psychological Operations Group (Airborne), Fort Bragg, North Carolina. Interview conducted by HOHP at Fort Leavenworth, Kansas, March 25, 1997.

Col. Mark D. Boyatt, commander, Third Special Forces Group (Airborne), Fort Bragg, North Carolina. Interview conducted by HOHP at Fort Leavenworth, Kansas, April 14, 1998.

Maj. Dorothea M. Burke, commander, Company B, Sixth Psychological Operations Battalion (Airborne), Fourth Psychological Operations Group (Airborne), Fort Bragg, North Carolina. Interview conducted by HOHP at Port-au-Prince, Haiti, November 10, 1995.

Maj. Peter Cafaro, communications officer, U.S. Army Space Command, individual augmentee to Eighteenth Airborne Corps, Fort Bragg, North Carolina. Interview conducted by HOHP at Fort Leavenworth, Kansas, April 16, 1996.

Maj. Clayton Cobb, executive officer, Ninth Psychological Operations Battalion (Airborne), Fourth Psychological Operations Group (Airborne), Fort Bragg, North Carolina. Interview conducted by HOHP at Fort Leavenworth, Kansas, March 24, 1997.

Capt. Doni Colon, cargo operations officer, Tenth Mountain Division (Light), Fort Drum, New York. Interview conducted by HOHP at Port-au-Prince, Haiti, January 15, 1996.

Lt. Col. Edward P. Donnelly, J5 Plans and Policy, U.S. Atlantic Command, Norfolk, Virginia. Interview conducted by HOHP at Norfolk, Virginia, December 5, 1995.

Col. Jack Donovan, commander, First Brigade, 101st Airborne Division (Air Assault), Fort Campbell, Kentucky. Interview conducted by HOHP at Port-au-Prince, Haiti, February 9, 1996.

Maj. Jack Doyle, J5 Plans and Policy, U.S. Atlantic Command, Norfolk, Virginia. Interview conducted by HOHP at Norfolk, Virginia, December 5, 1995.

Col. James M. Dubik, commander, Second Brigade, Tenth Mountain Division (Light), Fort Drum, New York. Interview conducted by HOHP at Fort Leavenworth, Kansas, June 8, 1995.

Professor Bryant Freeman, director, Haitian Studies Institute, University of Kansas, Lawrence. Interview conducted by HOHP at Fort Leavenworth, Kansas, May 5, 1997.

Col. William Fulton, Canadian Army, chief of staff, UN Mission in Haiti, Port-au-Prince. Interview conducted by HOHP at Port-au-Prince, Haiti, January 10, 1996.

Maj. Robert Geddis, brigade intelligence officer S2, Second Brigade, Twenty-Fifth Infantry Division (Light), Schofield Barracks, Hawaii. Interview conducted by HOHP at Fort Leavenworth, Kansas, April 10, 1997.

Maj. Steven C. Gomillion, assistant S3 operations officer, 110th Military Intelligence Battalion, Tenth Mountain Division (Light), Fort Drum, New York. Interview conducted by HOHP at Fort Leavenworth, Kansas, March 4, 1999.

1st Sgt. Louie E. Hough, Headquarters Support Company, First Battalion, Third Special Forces Group (Airborne), Fort Bragg, North

Carolina. Interview conducted by HOHP at Fort Lamantin, Haiti, November 11, 1995.

Maj. Michael Hoyt, plans and operations chaplain, Eighteenth Airborne Corps, Fort Bragg, North Carolina. Interview conducted by HOHP at Fort Leavenworth, Kansas, March 14, 1996.

Maj. Christopher Hughes, Combined Arms Assessment Team, Center for Army Lessons Learned, Fort Leavenworth, Kansas. Interview conducted by HOHP at Fort Leavenworth, Kansas, November 14, 1995.

Lt. Col. Phil Idiart, J5 Plans and Policy, U.S. Atlantic Command, Norfolk, Virginia. Interview conducted by HOHP at Norfolk, Virginia, December 6, 1995.

Lt. Gen. Joseph W. Kinzer, commanding general, UN Forces in Haiti, Port-au-Prince. Interview conducted by HOHP at Fort Sam Houston, San Antonio, Texas, June 2, 1998. Kinzer was promoted to lieutenant general after the UNMIH ended.

Maj. Anthony Ladouceur, special assistant to the commanding general, Joint Task Force 180, Eighteenth Airborne Corps, Fort Bragg, North Carolina. Interview conducted by HOHP, Fort Leavenworth, Kansas, March 10, 1996.

Col. John Lewis, individual augmentee, Transition Planning Team, Tenth Mountain Division (Light), School of Advanced Military Studies, Fort Leavenworth, Kansas. Interview conducted by HOHP at Fort Leavenworth, Kansas, July 28, 1995.

Maj. Gen. David C. Meade, commanding general, Tenth Mountain Division (Light), Fort Drum, New York. Interview conducted by HOHP at Stafford, Virginia, [day and month inaudible], 1998.

Maj. Jeffrey Miser, executive officer, 548th Corps Support Battalion, assigned to Tenth Mountain Division (Light), Fort Drum, New York. Interview conducted by HOHP, Fort Leavenworth, Kansas, April 4, 1997.

Maj. Jeffrey S. Morris, contingency contracting officer, Fort Hood, Texas. Interview conducted by HOHP, Fort Leavenworth, Kansas, February 17, 1999.

Maj. Richard J. Muraski Jr., company commander, Sixty-Fifth Engineer Battalion in support of Second Support Brigade, Twenty-Fifth Infantry Division (Light), Wahiawa, Hawaii. Interview conducted by HOHP at Fort Leavenworth, Kansas, March 11, 1997.

Lt. Col. Berthony Napoleon, political/military advisor to the commanding general, Eighteenth Airborne Corps and UN Multinational Force Haiti, Port-au-Prince, Haiti. Interview conducted by HOHP at Port-au-Prince, Haiti, January 15, 1996.

Maj. Nancy A. Nycamp, Joint Task Force and Multinational Force intelligence collection manager, Twenty-Fifth Infantry Division (Light), Schofield Barracks, Hawaii. Interview conducted by HOHP at Fort Leavenworth, Kansas, April 22, 1997.

Lt. Col. Christopher Olson, J5 Plans and Policy, U.S. Atlantic Command, Norfolk, Virginia. Interview conducted by HOHP, Norfolk, Virginia, December 5, 1995.

Col. David Patton, commander, U.S. Support Group, Haiti, Port-au-Prince. Interview conducted by HOHP at Port-au-Prince, Haiti, December 6, 1995.

Maj. Walter Pjetraj, civil affairs officer, Zone IV commander, UN Mission in Haiti, Third Special Forces Group (Airborne), Fort Bragg, North Carolina. Interview conducted by HOHP at Port-au-Prince, Haiti, January 13, 1996.

Former captain Lawrence P. Rockwood II, counterintelligence officer, G2 Military Intelligence Division Staff Section, Tenth Mountain Division (Light), Fort Drum, New York. Interview conducted by HOHP at Port-au-Prince, Haiti, October 31, 1996.

Maj. Horacio E. Schwalm, commander, Team B, Third Special Forces Group (Airborne), Fort Bragg, North Carolina. Interview conducted by HOHP at Fort Leavenworth, Kansas, March 20, 1997.

Maj. Robert Shaw, liaison officer, Joint Special Operations Command, MacDill Air Force Base, Florida. Interview conducted by HOHP, Fort Leavenworth, Kansas, March 12, 1996.

Reverend Willard S. Squires Jr. and Mrs. Margaret Squires, episcopal missionaries, Diocese of Haiti, Port-au-Prince, Haiti. Interview conducted by HOHP at Fort Leavenworth, Kansas, February 15, 1997.

Col. Jonathan S. Thompson, commander, Twentieth Engineer Brigade (Task Force Castle), Fort Bragg, North Carolina. Interview conducted by HOHP at Port-au-Prince, Haiti, October 17, 1994.

Maj. John Valledor, company commander, Company B, Third Battalion, Fifteenth Infantry, Twenty-Fourth Infantry Division (Mechanized), Fort Stewart, Georgia. Interview conducted by HOHP at Fort Leavenworth, Kansas, March 3, 1999.

Maj. Kristin B. Vlahos-Schafer, brigade intelligence officer S2, 525th Military Intelligence Brigade, Eighteenth Airborne Corps, Fort Bragg, North Carolina. Interview conducted by HOHP at Fort Leavenworth, Kansas, October 16, 1995.

Capt. Jeffrey R. White, executive officer, Military Information Support Task Force (MIST), Company B, Sixth Psychological Operations Battalion (Airborne), Fourth Psychological Operations Group (Airborne), Fort Bragg, North Carolina. Interview conducted by HOHP at Port-au-Prince, Haiti, January 5, 1996.

NOTES

All interviews were conducted by HOHP; full details can be found in the appendix.

Introduction

1. Ladouceur, interview.
2. Colon, interview.
3. Boutros-Ghali, *Agenda for Peace*.
4. Corey, *Just War Tradition*; Talentino, *Military Intervention*, 151–57; Haass, *Intervention*; Antizzo, *U.S. Military Intervention*; Geddis, interview.
5. Everett, *Oral History*, i–77.
6. Government Accounting Office, *National Drug Control Budget*. Costs total about $51 billion per year. Whitfield, "Group of Friends."
7. Kinzer, interview.

1. Haitian Culture and Military Power

1. Gonzalez, "From Cannibals to Mercenaries," 26–27.
2. Morison, "Route of Columbus," 261–63.
3. Cook, "Sickness, Starvation, and Death," 351–53.
4. Gunther, "Hispaniola," 764; Cook, "Sickness, Starvation, and Death," 352.
5. Sluiter, "Dutch Maritime Power"; Covington, "Drake Destroys St. Augustine," 83.
6. Dubois and Garrigus, *Slave Revolution*, 10.
7. Simpson, "Haitian Politics," 487; Dubois and Garrigus, *Slave Revolution*, 10–11.
8. Cap-Français is also referred to as Cap-François, Cap-Henri, and Le Cap. Shen, "History of Haiti."
9. Simpson, "Haitian Politics," 487; Garrigus, *Before Haiti*, 110.
10. Clark, "Role of the Haitian Volunteers," 357–59.
11. Clark, "Role of the Haitian Volunteers," 362–66; Lawrence, *Storm over Savannah*, viii–ix.
12. Girard, "Rêves d'Empire," 392.

13. King, *Blue Coat or Powdered Wig*, 236–38. *Marrons* were also referred to as *maroons*, meaning brownish crimson in color.

14. Chatman, "There Are No Slaves," 146; Shacochis, *Immaculate Invasion*, 22;. Bailey, Maguire, and Pouliot, "Haiti."

15. Knight, "Haitian Revolution," 108–9.

16. Dubois and Garrigus, *Slave Revolution*, 25.

17. Dubois and Garrigus, *Slave Revolution*, 26.

18. Dubois and Garrigus, *Slave Revolution*, 27–29.

19. Chartrand and Back, *Napoleon's Overseas Army*, 12–13.

20. Chartrand and Back, *Napoleon's Overseas Army*, 13–15. The small U.S. Army was responsible for securing the border from Canada to Florida and from the Atlantic to the Mississippi River. Compare that mission with the Haitian army having to occupy a space smaller than modern-day West Virginia.

21. Chartrand and Back, *Napoleon's Overseas Army*, 15–16.

22. Louverture banned vodun as a religious practice and made Roman Catholicism the official religion. The colony, however, still affiliated itself with France, its purpose being to establish equality and to be autonomous but also to receive French citizens' benefits. There were twenty-two versions or revisions of the constitution until the 2012 version, which is in effect as of the writing of this book.

23. Matthewson, "Jefferson and Haiti," 220. Rochambeau was the son of Jean-Baptiste Donatien de Vimeur, Comte de Rochambeau, who fought for the United States during the American Revolution.

24. Dubois and Garrigus, *Slave Revolution*, 36–37.

25. Chartrand and Back, *Napoleon's Overseas Army*, 16–17.

26. Dubois and Garrigus, *Slave Revolution*, 37.

27. Knight, "Haitian Revolution," 113. I will refer to the nation as "Haiti" for consistency.

28. "Haitian Constitution, 1805"; Schmidt, *United States Occupation of Haiti*, 21.

29. "Haitian Constitution, 1805."

30. Bryan, "Independencia Efimera."

31. "Military in Haitian History."

32. Grant, *Papers*, 21:145–47; Levine, "Frederick Douglass, War, Haiti"; Hickey, "America's Response." Navassa Island was claimed on September 19, 1857, by Peter Duncan, an American sea captain, under the Guano Island Acts of August 18, 1856. Haiti disputed the claim. On July 7, 1858, U.S. president James Buchanan issued an executive order upholding annexation and authorizing military action to enforce it. A lighthouse was later added. The U.S. Supreme Court, in *Jones v. United States* in 1890, found that Navassa Island must be considered as "appertaining" to the United States. The island is currently maintained as an unincorporated territory under the management of the U.S. Department of Fish and Wildlife.

33. Tierney, "America's 'Black Vietnam'"; Corbett, "Rule of Faustin Soulouque."

34. Small, "United States and the German 'Threat.'"

35. Mobley, "Haiti," 1:269.

36. U.S. Marine Corps, *Small Wars Manual*.

37. Laguerre, *Military and Society in Haiti*, 107; Dupuy, *Prophet of Power*, 35. The Haitian coast guard formed in the 1930s and varied in size over the years, often having fewer than ten small boats. The Haitian air force had few aircraft.

38. Hooper, "Monkey's Tail Still Strong," 165.

39. Aristide was defrocked in 1988 by Pope John Paul II.

40. Père Lebrun came from a tire commercial where the advertiser, Lebrun, put his head through a tire. Lavalas is from Haitian Créole meaning "flood" or "avalanche." It is the rainwater runoff that flows down Haiti's mountains and washes everything clean. Fishel, *Civil Military Operations*, 210; Girard, *Clinton in Haiti*, 34–35.

2. Preventive Diplomacy and Military Intervention

1. Oswald Johnston, "OAS Sending Team to Warn Junta in Haiti," *Los Angeles Times*, October 3, 1991.

2. United Nations, "United Nations Mission in Haiti Background." The contingency plan was identified as CONPLAN 2367. It had been developed several years earlier, during President Ronald Reagan's administration.

3. United Nations, Resolution 47/20.

4. United Nations, "Haiti-MICIVIH."

5. United Nations, "United Nations Mission in Haiti Background."

6. Freeman, interview.

7. "Haiti Faces Oil Embargo, No Blockade," *Chicago Tribune*, June 17, 1993.

8. Freeman, interview.

9. Morrell, "Governors Island Accord"; "Governors Island Accord."

10. United Nations, "United Nations Mission in Haiti Background."

11. United Nations, "United Nations Mission in Haiti Background."

12. United Nations Security Council, Resolution 867.

13. Baker, interview.

14. Baker, interview. Ernst was TRADOC's deputy chief of staff for training.

15. Pezzullo, *Plunging into Haiti*, 183–84.

16. Baker, interview.

17. Baker, interview.

18. Baker, interview.

19. Baker, interview. Nation building and nation assistance have many definitions. For my purposes, nation building involves enhancing state institutions. It may involve creating or overhauling a government as well as creating or modifying inherent cultural values to foment a sense of commonality among

people. Nation assistance is civil or military aid, such as training, security, foreign internal defense, or other missions defined by international or U.S. law.

20. Baker, interview.

21. Baker, interview.

22. Pezzullo, *Plunging into Haiti*, 186–87; Baker, interview.

23. Pezzullo, *Plunging into Haiti*, 183–87; Riehm, "uss *Harlan County* Affair," 32; Nairn, "Our Payroll."

24. Baker, interview.

25. Baker, interview; Riehm, "uss *Harlan County* Affair," 33.

26. Freeman, interview; Baker, interview; Riehm, "uss *Harlan County* Affair," 33.

27. Riehm, "uss *Harlan County* Affair," 33.

28. Baker, interview.

29. Riehm, "uss *Harlan County* Affair," 34–35.

30. Baker, interview; Riehm, "uss *Harlan County* Affair," 35.

31. Freeman, interview.

32. Freeman, interview; United Nations, "Haiti Background Summary."

3. Planning a Military Intervention

1. United Nations Security Council, Resolution 875; Ballard, *Upholding Democracy*, 65; Donnelly, interview. The UN security clearance system is different than that of the United States, and UN officers from countries other than the United States were not cleared to know what was being discussed.

2. Donnelly, interview.

3. Donnelly, interview.

4. Shaw, interview; Donnelly, interview; White House, "Multilateral Peacekeeping Operations." Compartmented information is typically reserved for Top Secret clearances with additional "sensitive compartmented information." In this case, the compartment designation was used to restrict information access to a limited number of personnel.

5. Shaw, interview; Ballard, *Upholding Democracy*, 65.

6. Ballard, *Upholding Democracy*, 65–66.

7. Boutros-Ghali, *Agenda for Peace*.

8. Benson, interview. At the time of this interview, Benson had been promoted and was serving with the United Nations Mission in Haiti. JTF 180 was the result of the 1980 creation of a rapid deployment joint task force concept to deploy U.S. forces quickly by air and also sea to global contingencies. JTF 180 not only included the Eighteenth Airborne Corps and the Eighty-Second Airborne Division but also the Tenth Mountain Division (Light), the 101st Airborne Division (Air Assault), and the Twenty-Fourth Infantry Division (Mechanized). Forces from these units would deploy to Haiti between 1994 and 1996.

9. Benson, interview.

10. Benson, interview. Benson credits his ability to perform this detailed task to the education he received at the School of Advanced Military Studies, a second-year course that follows training at the Command and General Staff College at Fort Leavenworth, Kansas. At the time, School of Advanced Military Studies faculty and army staff selected but fifty-two volunteer officers a year into their Advanced Military Studies Program, a highly competitive program that focused on operational planning and mission execution. Graduates received special staff positions throughout the army and the moniker of "Jedi Knight," a title taken from the individuals of *Star Wars* movie fame who studied under Yoda.

11. Benson, interview. Aspin resigned on December 15, 1993, and left office on February 3, 1994. William J. Perry replaced him.

12. Benson, interview.

13. Benson, interview.

14. Benson, interview.

15. United Nations, "United Nations Mission in Haiti Background."

16. Benson, interview.

17. Benson, interview; Avril, *From Glory to Disgrace*, 68–69.

18. Kretchik, Baumann, and Fishel, *Invasion, Intervention, "Intervasion,"* 47–56.

19. Donnelly, interview; Idiart, interview.

20. Donnelly, interview; Kretchik, Baumann, and Fishel, *Invasion, Intervention, "Intervasion,"* 44; U.S. Department of State, Office of the Historian, *History of the National Security Council*. The NSC was created by Public Law 80-253, approved July 26, 1947. Upon taking office, President Clinton revised the NSC system to include the PDD and the PRD. The NSC organization in the Clinton administration included an NSC Principals Committee. Here, Cabinet members discussed and finalized issues without Clinton's personal participation. An NSC Deputies Committee acted as the senior sub-Cabinet interagency forum. This included levels of IWGs, which convened regularly to review and coordinate the implementation of PDD and PRD in their respective areas, such as Haiti. The system was in place but not fully tested at the time of Operation Uphold Democracy.

21. Kretchik, *U.S. Army Doctrine*, 232–34; Ballard, *Upholding Democracy*, 71.

22. Kretchik, Baumann, and Fishel, *Invasion, Intervention, "Intervasion,"* 66–69.

23. Ballard, *Upholding Democracy*, 76–77.

24. Ballard, *Upholding Democracy*, 78.

25. Ballard, *Upholding Democracy*, 74.

26. Meade, interview.

27. Ballard, *Upholding Democracy*, 87–88.

28. Vlahos-Schafer, interview.

29. Dubik, interview.

30. Dubik, interview.

31. Meade, interview.

32. U.S. General Accounting Office, *Cuba*.

33. Olson, interview. Contributing nations included Jamaica, Trinidad and Tobago, Belize, Guyana, Bahamas, Barbados, and Antigua and Barbuda.

34. Olson, interview.

35. Donnelly, interview; Doyle, interview.

36. Donnelly, interview; Olson, interview; Idiart, interview.

37. Idiart, interview.

38. Idiart, interview. ICITAP was created in 1986 to help prosecute key human rights violation cases in El Salvador while enhancing the criminal investigative capacity of Latin American security forces.

39. Idiart, interview.

40. Idiart, interview.

41. Clinton, "Address to the Nation on Haiti."

42. Meade, interview.

43. Ladouceur, interview.

44. Larry Rohter, "Showdown with Haiti: Diplomacy; Carter, in Haiti, Pursues Peaceful Shift," *New York Times*, September 18, 1994, http://www.nytimes.com/1994/09/18/world/showdown-with-haiti-diplomacy-carter-in-haiti-pursues-peaceful-shift.html.

4. Conducting a Military Intervention

1. Kretchik, Baumann, and Fishel, *Invasion, Intervention, "Intervasion,"* 120; Shacochis, *Immaculate Invasion*, 81. Task Force Mountain consisted of the division's field artillery element and additional divisional troops. The unit would locate in Port-au-Prince, along with the division headquarters and the First Brigade Combat Team. Part of its mission was to administer Tenth Mountain Division forces and thus free the JTF 190/MNF commander from routine aspects of the intervention. Schwalm, interview.

2. Meade, interview; Shaw, interview; Department of the Army, *Operations*, 2–11, 13–14.

3. Hoyt, interview. "Command climate" is how military personnel describe the leadership "tone" of an organization. A unit commander sets the tone. In this case, Hoyt believed that the commanding general had set a strict tone that many people found oppressive.

4. Meade, interview. In 1994 Brown and Root Corporation, officially Kellogg Brown and Root, Inc., was a Houston, Texas–based firm under Halliburton Energy Services. During the Haiti intervention the company provided construction, cooking, fuel distribution, and other services under a government contract. The company hired military veterans and retirees, many of whom were experts in their fields and valued for their experience and skill. Many of these

employees, however, were not physically fit and suffered heart attacks and other ailments such as skin cancer. Brown and Root employees who required medical attention in Haiti used U.S. government (military) health care facilities as part of the contract.

5. Department of Defense, DOD Dictionary.

6. Boyatt, interview.

7. Bill Glauber, "Marine Landings Meet Surreal Haitian Welcome: U.S. Intervention in Haiti." *Baltimore Sun*, September 21, 1994, http://articles.balti moresun.com/1994-09-21/news/1994264042_1_haiti-marines-landing-craft; Boyatt, interview.

8. Squires and Squires, interview; Boyatt, interview; Colon, interview.

9. Andre, interview.

10. Ladouceur, interview.

11. Meade, interview; Boyatt, interview.

12. Kretchik, Baumann, and Fishel, *Invasion, Intervention, "Intervasion,"* 95-97; Ballard, *Upholding Democracy*, 108-10.

13. Vlahos-Schafer, interview; Miser, interview; Cafaro, interview; Colon, interview.

14. Thompson, interview.

15. Thompson, interview.

16. Shacochis, *Immaculate Invasion*, 79.

17. Idiart, interview.

18. Idiart, interview; Rosser, "USMC Class 38th OCC/BC 3-66 Alumni Profiles."

19. Idiart, interview.

20. Idiart, interview.

21. Meade, interview.

22. Cafaro, interview; Miser, interview; Headquarters, Tenth Mountain Division, *10th Mountain Division Handbook*.

23. Vlahos-Schafer, interview.

24. Freeman, interview; Squires and Squires, interview.

25. Vlahos-Schafer, interview.

26. Meade, interview; Boyatt, interview; Cobb, interview.

27. Freeman, interview.

28. Meade, interview.

29. Meade, interview; Ballard, *Upholding Democracy*, 111-12.

30. Valledor, interview. Task Force Victory had fourteen Bradley armored fighting vehicles, each with antitank missiles and a 25mm gun. Each vehicle had a three-man crew and carried six additional personnel. The vehicles are equipped with night vision sights. Malone, "Armor in Military Operations Other Than War," 112-15.

31. Valledor, interview.

32. Miser, interview.

33. Shacochis, *Immaculate Invasion*, 78.

34. Shaw, interview; Meade, interview.

35. Olson, interview.

36. Dubik, interview; Ballard, *Upholding Democracy*, 114-15; Ladouceur, interview; "Marines Kill 9 Haitians in Confrontation—1 Soldier Wounded in Firefight with Gunmen at Police Station," *Seattle Times*, September 25, 1994, http://community.seattletimes.nwsource.com/archive/?date=19940925&slug=1932484.

37. Dubik, interview.

38. Dubik, interview.

39. Dubik, interview.

40. Gomillion, interview.

41. Vlahos-Schafer, interview.

42. Rockwood, interview.

43. Meade, interview.

44. Rockwood, interview. Rockwood's interview was taped by a Haitian television film crew at a Haitian Studies Association meeting in Port-au-Prince. The crew never provided a copy of the tape, despite several requests. Rockwood's comments are taken from interview notes.

45. U.S. Court of Appeals for the Armed Forces, "Findings of the Appellate Court Proceedings."

46. Vlahos-Schafer, interview. Amnesty International arranged for Ramsey Clark to defend Rockwood.

47. Dubik, interview.

48. Meade, interview.

49. Meade, interview.

50. Meade, interview.

51. Dubik, interview.

52. Dubik, interview.

53. Hughes, interview.

54. Hughes, interview.

55. Napoleon, interview; Geddis, interview; Hughes, interview; Ladouceur, interview.

56. Gomillion, interview.

57. Valledor, interview.

58. Valledor, interview.

59. Hough, interview.

60. Boyatt, interview.

61. Boyatt, interview. A chemlight is a short, plastic, transparent stick with a glass vial inside. The chemicals in the plastic tube are a mixture of dye and Cyalume. The chemical inside the glass vial is concentrated hydrogen peroxide. When the plastic is bent, the glass vial breaks. Shaking mixes the chemicals together, which produces low light for a period of time. Chemlights produce different colored light depending on the dye, in this case green.

62. Schwalm, interview.

63. Schwalm, interview.

64. Schwalm, interview.

65. Ballard, *Upholding Democracy*, 137.

66. U.S. Department of Defense, "Hawaii Unit Replaces 10th Mountain Division."

67. Ballard, *Upholding Democracy*, 136.

68. Meade, interview.

69. Andre, interview; Marcus Mabry, "Haitian Stress Syndrome?," *Newsweek*, October 30, 1994, http://www.newsweek.com/haitian-stress-syndrome-189310.

70. "U.S. Soldier Killed in Shootout with Ex-Haitian Army Officer," *New York Times*, January 13, 1995, http://www.nytimes.com/1995/01/13/world/us-soldier-killed-in-shootout-with-ex-haitian-army-officer.html.

71. Valledor, interview.

72. Valledor, interview.

73. Nycamp, interview. During the operation Nycamp worked within a joint intelligence cell made up of representatives from various civilian and military sources.

74. Nycamp, interview.

75. Muraski, interview.

76. Muraski, interview.

77. Muraski, interview.

78. Freeman, interview.

79. Shaw, interview.

5. Intervention under the Blue Beret

1. Lewis, interview.

2. Lewis, interview. The NCA was a term used by the Department of Defense to designate the president of the United States and the secretary of defense, particularly in regard to the use of nuclear weapons.

3. Lewis, interview.

4. Lewis, interview.

5. Lewis, interview.

6. Lewis, interview.

7. Kretchik, "Multinational Staff Effectiveness," 394–95.

8. Baumann and Yates, *"My Clan Against the World,"* 165–72.

9. White House, "Clinton Administration Policy."

10. Adams, interview. Adams was often called "Doc" due to his having earned a PhD in political science from Syracuse University.

11. United Nations, "United Nations Mission in Haiti Background."

12. Fulton, interview.

13. Fulton, interview.

14. Fulton, interview.

15. Kretchik, "Multinational Staff Effectiveness," 398–99.

16. Kretchik, "Multinational Staff Effectiveness," 399–401.

17. Adams, interview.

18. Adams, interview.

19. Adams, interview.

20. Freeman, interview.

21. Kretchik, "Multinational Staff Effectiveness," 403–6.

22. Kinzer, interview. Ambassador Cook at the time was deputy assistant secretary of state for regional security affairs, Bureau of Political-Military Affairs, a position he held from 1993 to 1995.

23. Kinzer, interview.

24. Kinzer, interview.

25. Kinzer, interview.

26. Kinzer, interview. At the time, the Second Armored Cavalry Regiment was designated "Light." After returning from the Persian Gulf War in 1991, the regiment returned to Germany but was then reassigned to Fort Lewis, Washington. Once there the regiment's ground squadrons were converted from Abrams tanks and Bradley Fighting Vehicles into a light cavalry unit consisting of Humvees mounted with antitank missile launchers (TOWs), Mark 19 grenade launchers, caliber .50 machine guns, M60 machine guns, and the SAW. The redesignated Second ACR (Light) was then stationed at Fort Polk, Louisiana, in 1992.

27. Kinzer, interview. Despite the success in training the UNMIH staff and glowing reports from those who attended the sessions, the UN has not trained any operational headquarters staff since.

28. Kinzer, interview.

29. Patton, interview.

30. Kinzer, interview.

31. Kinzer, interview.

32. "United Nations Mission in Haiti Background."

33. Kinzer, interview. Kinzer's request for a "Chapter VI and a half" situation will be referred to as "Chapter VI+" within this book.

34. Benson, interview; Benson, "Report from Haiti," 15. Benson had previously served as the G3 plans officer, Eighteenth Airborne Corps, Fort Bragg, North Carolina.

35. Benson, interview.

36. Pjetraj, interview.

37. Burke, interview.

38. International Republican Institute Staff, *Haiti*, 17.

39. White, interview; Burke, interview.

40. Burke, interview.

41. Kinzer, interview; Patton, interview.

42. Kinzer, interview.

43. Kinzer, interview.

44. Kinzer, interview.

45. Pjetraj, interview.

46. Benson, interview.

47. Benson, interview. There were parliamentary elections in August and September 1995. Lavalas won both elections, with a voter turnout of 31.09 percent.

48. Benson, interview; Boisselle, interview.

49. Benson, interview.

50. Donovan, interview.

51. Donovan, interview.

52. Donovan, interview.

53. Donovan, interview.

54. Donovan, interview.

55. Donovan, interview.

56. Donovan, interview.

57. Donovan, interview.

58. Donovan, interview.

59. Donovan, interview.

60. Pjetraj, interview; Patton, interview.

61. International Republican Institute Staff, *Haiti*, 8.

62. Kinzer, interview.

63. Donovan, interview.

64. International Republican Institute Staff, *Haiti*, 5, 12.

65. Kinzer, interview.

66. Kinzer, interview.

67. Kinzer, interview.

68. Donovan, interview.

6. Aftermath

1. Ladouceur, interview.

2. Durch, *UN*, 2; Clausewitz, *On War*, 101.

3. The list includes the United States, Britain, and France.

4. Human Rights Watch, "World Report 2015."

5. Ladouceur, interview; Patton, interview; Morris, interview; Andre, interview.

6. Shaw, interview; Boyatt, interview; Miser, interview.

7. Burke, interview.

8. U.S. Department of State, Department of Diplomatic Security, *Haiti 2013 Crime and Safety Report*.

9. Haiti Partners, "Haiti Statistics."

10. United Nations, "MINUSTAH."

11. Congressional Budget Office, *Assessing Progress in Haiti Act of 2014*; Abby Phillip, "American Missionary Ambushed and Killed in Haiti; 4-Year-Old Child Abducted," *Washington Post*, October 15, 2015, https://www.washingtonpost

.com/news/acts-of-faith/wp/2015/10/13/american-missionary-ambushed-and
-killed-in-haiti-4-year-old-child-abducted/. The child was later found unharmed.

12. Sam LaGrone, "SOUTHCOM Commander: Ebola Outbreak in Central America Could Cause Mass Migration to U.S.," October 7, 2014, USNI News, http://news.usni.org/2014/10/07/southcom-commander-ebola-outbreak-central-america-haiti-nightmare-scenario; Muraski, interview.

13. Dessalines quoted in Danner, *Stripping Bare the Body*, 53.

14. Muraski, interview. UN military forces in Haiti as of the publication of this book include Argentina, Bolivia, Brazil, Canada, Chile, Ecuador, El Salvador, France, Guatemala, Honduras, Indonesia, Jordan, Nepal, Paraguay, Peru, Philippines, Republic of Korea, Sri Lanka, United States, and Uruguay. Civilian police include Argentina, Bangladesh, Benin, Brazil, Burkina Faso, Burundi, Cameroon, Canada, Chad, Chile, Colombia, Côte d'Ivoire, Croatia, Egypt, France, Grenada, Guinea, India, Jamaica, Jordan, Kyrgyzstan, Lithuania, Madagascar, Mali, Nepal, Niger, Nigeria, Norway, Pakistan, Paraguay, Philippines, Portugal, Romania, Russian Federation, Rwanda, Senegal, Serbia, Spain, Sri Lanka, Thailand, Tunisia, Turkey, United Kingdom, United States, Uruguay, Vanuatu, and Yemen. "Facts and Figures," in United Nations, "MINUSTAH."

SELECTED BIBLIOGRAPHY

Reports and Government Documents

Boutros-Ghali, Boutros. *An Agenda for Peace: Preventive Diplomacy, Peacemaking, and Peacekeeping*. New York: United Nations, 1992. http://www.un.org/en/sc/repertoire/89-92/Chapter%208/GENERAL%20ISSUES/Item%2029_Agenda%20for%20peace_.pdf.

Clinton, William J. "Address to the Nation on Haiti." September 15, 1994. American Presidency Project, http://www.presidency.ucsb.edu/ws/?pid=49093.

Congressional Budget Office. *Assessing Progress in Haiti Act of 2014*. Washington DC: Congressional Budget Office, 2014. http://www.cbo.gov/publication/45499.

Government Accounting Office. *The National Drug Control Budget FY 2013 Funding Highlights*. Washington DC: Government Accounting Office, 2013.

"Governor's Island Accord." GlobalSecurity.org. http://www.globalsecurity.org/military/library/report/1998/kretchik-appendixd.htm.

Haiti Partners. "Haiti Statistics: Haiti by the Numbers." 2015. https://haitipartners.org/about-us/haiti-statistics/.

"Haitian Constitution, 1805." http://www2.webster.edu/~corbetre/haiti/history/earlyhaiti/1805-const.htm.

Headquarters, Tenth Mountain Division. *10th Mountain Division Handbook, Operations in Haiti: Planning/Preparation/Execution*. Fort Drum NY: Headquarters Tenth Mountain Division, 1995.

Human Rights Watch. "World Report 2015: Haiti, Events of 2014." https://www.hrw.org/world-report/2015/country-chapters/haiti.

International Republican Institute Staff. *Haiti: Election Observation Report, 17 December 1995*. Washington DC: IRI, 1996.

———. *Haiti: IRI Assessment of the June 25, August 13, and September 17, 1995, Elections in Haiti*. Washington DC: IRI, October 11, 1995.

"The Military in Haitian History." GlobalSecurity.org. http://www.globalsecurity.org/military/world/haiti/military-history.htm.

Morrell, James. "The Governors Island Accord on Haiti: International Policy Report, September 1993." http://www.haitipolicy.org/archives/Publications&Commentary/governors.htm.

Rosser, Richard C. "USMC Class 38th OCC/BC 3-66 Alumni Profiles." http: //www.usmc-thebasicschool-1966.com/pdf/profile/Rosser.pdf.

Shen, Kona. "History of Haiti, 1492–1805." History of Haiti Project, Brown University, Department of Africana Studies. 2015. http://library.brown.edu /haitihistory/1sr.html.

Special Collections. Combined Arms Research Library. Fort Leavenworth, Kansas.

United Nations. "Haiti Background Summary." http://www.un.org/en/peace keeping/missions/past/unmihbackgr1.html.

———. "United Nations Mission in Haiti Background." http://www.un.org/en /peacekeeping/missions/past/unmihbackgr2.html.

———. "Haiti-MICIVIH." http://www.un.org/en/peacekeeping/missions/past /micivih.htm.

———. "MINUSTAH." http://www.un.org/en/peacekeeping/missions/minustah /index.shtml.

United Nations Security Council. Resolution 867. "Haiti." September 23, 1993. http://unscr.com/en/resolutions/867.

———. Resolution 47/20. November 24, 1992. http://www.un.org/documents /ga/res/47/a47r020.htm.

———. Resolution 875. October 16, 1993. http://repository.un.org/bitstream /handle/11176/52186/S_RES_875%281993%29-EN.pdf?sequence=3&is Allowed=y.

U.S. Court of Appeals for the Armed Forces. Findings of the Appellate Court Proceedings. *U.S. v. Rockwood.* September 30, 1999. http://www.armfor .uscourts.gov/newcaaf/opinions/1999term/98-0488.htm.

U.S. Department of Defense, "Hawaii Unit Replaces 10th Mountain Division in Haiti." News release, number 673-94, December 6, 1994. http://archive .defense.gov/Releases/Release.aspx?Releaseid=297.

U.S. Department of State, Office of the Historian. *History of the National Security Council, 1947–1997.* Washington DC: U.S. Department of State, 1997 . http://fas.org/irp/offdocs/nschistory.htm.

U.S. Department of State, Department of Diplomatic Security. *Haiti 2013 Crime and Safety Report.* Alexandria VA: Overseas Security Advisory Council, Raytheon Corporation, 2013. https://www.osac.gov/pages/ContentReport Details.aspx?cid=14000.

U.S. General Accounting Office. *Cuba: U.S. Response to the 1994 Cuban Migration Crisis.* Washington DC: Government Printing Office, 1995. http: //www.gao.gov/archive/1995/ns95211.pdf.

White House. "Clinton Administration Policy on Reforming Multilateral Peace Operations (PDD 25)." Bureau of International Organizational Affairs, U.S. Department of State. February 22, 1996. http://fas.org/irp/offdocs /pdd25.htm.

———. "Multilateral Peacekeeping Operations." Presidential Review Directive NSC/13. February 15, 1993. http://fas.org/irp/offdocs/prd/prd-13.pdf.

Published Works

Adams, Thomas K. *U.S. Special Operations Forces in Action: The Challenges of Unconventional Warfare.* London: Frank Cass, 1998.

Amnesty International. *On the Horns of a Dilemma: Military Repression or Foreign Invasion?* New York: Amnesty International USA, 1994.

Antizzo, Glenn J. *U.S. Military Intervention in the Post–Cold War Era: How to Win America's Wars in the Twenty-First Century.* Baton Rouge: Louisiana State University Press, 2010.

Arthur, Charles. *After the Dance: Haiti: One Year after the Invasion.* London: Haiti Support Group, 1995.

Avril, Prosper. *From Glory to Disgrace: The Haitian Army 1804–1994.* Boca Raton FL: Universal Publishers, 1999. E-book, http://www.universal-publishers.com/book.php?method=isbn&book=1581128363.

Bailey, Michael, Robert Maguire, and J. O'Neil G. Pouliot. "Haiti: Military-Police Partnership and Public Security." In *Policing the New World Disorder: Peace Operations and Public Security*, edited by Robert B. Oakley, Michael J. Dziedzic, and Eliot M. Goldberg, 215-52. Washington DC: National Defense University Press, 1998.

Ballard, John R. *Upholding Democracy: The United States Military Campaign in Haiti, 1994–1997.* New York: Praeger, 1998.

Baumann, Robert F., and Lawrence A. Yates. *"My Clan Against the World": U.S. and Coalition Forces in Somalia, 1992–1994.* Fort Leavenworth KS: Combat Studies Institute Press, 2004.

Benson, Kevin C. M. "A Report From Haiti: Cavalry in Peacekeeping Operations." *Armor* 104, no. 6 (November–December 1995): 15-17.

Boot, Max. *The Savage Wars of Peace: Small Wars and the Rise of American Power.* New York: Basic Books, 2002.

Bryan, Patrick. "The Independencia Efimera of 1821 and the Haitian Invasion of Santo Domingo 1822: A Case of Pre-emptive Independence." *Caribbean Quarterly* 41, no. 3/4 (September–December 1995): 15-29.

Casper, Lawrence E. *Falcon Brigade: Combat and Command in Somalia and Haiti.* Boulder CO: Lynne Rienner, 2001.

Chartrand, René, and Francis Back. *Napoleon's Overseas Army.* London: Osprey, 1989.

Chatman, Samuel I.. "'There Are No Slaves in France': A Re-examination of Slave Laws in Eighteenth Century France." *Journal of Negro History* 85, no. 3 (Summer 2000): 144-53.

Clark, George P. "The Role of the Haitian Volunteers at Savannah in 1779: An Attempt at an Objective View." *Phylon* 41, no. 4 (Fourth Quarter 1980): 356-66.

Clausewitz, Carl von. *On War.* Edited and Translated by Michael Howard and Peter Paret. Indexed ed. Princeton NJ: Princeton University Press, 1984.

Cole, Ronald H. *Mission to Haiti: Direction and Support of Peacekeeping and Humanitarian Operations, 1994-2000.* Washington DC: Office of the Chairman of the Joint Chiefs of Staff, 2008.

Cook, Noble David. "Sickness, Starvation, and Death in Early Hispaniola." *Journal of Interdisciplinary History* 32, no. 3 (Winter 2002):349-86.

Corbett, Bob. "The Rule of Faustin Soulouque (Emperor Faustin I), March 1, 1847-January 15, 1859." 1995. http://www2.webster.edu/~corbetre/haiti/history/1844-1915/soulouque.htm.

Corey, David D. *The Just War Tradition: An Introduction.* Wilmington DE: Intercollegiate Studies Institute, 2012.

Covington, James W. "Drake Destroys St. Augustine: 1586." *Florida Historical Quarterly* 44, no. 1/2 (July-October 1965): 81-93.

Danner, Mark. *Stripping Bare the Body: Politics, Violence, War.* New York: Nation Books, 2009.

Department of Defense. DOD *Dictionary of Military and Associated Terms.* Joint Publication 1-02. Washington DC: Department of Defense, 2015. http://www.dtic.mil/doctrine/new_pubs/jp1_02.pdf.

Department of the Army. *Operations.* Field Manual 100-5. Washington DC: Department of the Army, 1993.

Dubois, Laurent, and John D. Garrigus. *Slave Revolution in the Caribbean, 1789-1804: A Brief History with Documents.* Boston: Bedford/St. Martin's, 2006.

Dupuy, Alex. *The Prophet of Power: Jean-Bertrand Aristide, the International Community, and Haiti.* New York: Rowman and Littlefield, 2006.

Durch, William J., ed. UN: *Peacekeeping, American Policy, and the Uncivil Wars of the 1990s.* New York: St. Martin's Press, 1996.

Everett, Stephen E. *Oral History: Techniques and Procedures.* Washington DC: Center of Military History, 1992.

Fishel, John T. *Civil Military Operations in the New World.* Westport CT: Praeger, 1997.

Fishel, John T., and Andrés Sáenz, eds. *Capacity Building for Peacekeeping: The Case of Haiti.* Washington DC: National Defense University, 2007.

Garrigus, John D. *Before Haiti: Race and Citizenship in French Saint-Domingue.* New York: Palgrave Macmillan, 2006.

Girard, Philippe. *Clinton in Haiti: The 1994 US Invasion of Haiti.* New York: Palgrave, 2004.

———. "Rêves d' Empire: French Revolutionary Doctrine and Military Interventions in the Southern United States and the Caribbean, 1789-1809." *Louisiana History* 48, no. 4 (Fall 2007): 389-412.

Goff, Stan. *Hideous Dream: A Soldier's Memoir of the U.S. Invasion of Haiti.* New York: Soft Skull Press, 2000.

Gonzalez, Nancie L. "From Cannibals to Mercenaries: Carib Militarism 1600–1840." *Journal of Anthropological Research* 46, no. 1 (Spring 1990): 25–39.

Grant, Ulysses S. *Papers of Ulysses S. Grant.* Edited by John Y. Simon. 30 vols. Carbondale: Southern Illinois University Press, 1967.

Gunther, John. "Hispaniola." *Foreign Affairs* 19, no. 4 (July 1941): 764–77.

Haass, Richard N. *Intervention: The Use of American Military Force in the Post-Cold War World.* Rev. ed. Washington DC: Brookings Institution Press, 1999.

Hickey, Donald R. "America's Response to the Slave Revolt in Haiti, 1791–1806." *Journal of the Early Republic* 2, no. 4 (Winter 1982):361–79.

Hooper, Michael S. "The Monkey's Tail Still Strong: The Post-Duvalier Wave of Terror." In *Haiti: Dangerous Crossroads,* ed. NACLA, 161–73. Boston: South End Press, 1995.

King, Stewart R. *Blue Coat or Powdered Wig: Free People of Color in Pre-revolutionary Saint-Domingue.* Athens: University of Georgia Press, 2007.

Knight, Franklin W. "The Haitian Revolution." *American Historical Review* 105, no. 1 (February 2000): 103–15.

Kretchik, Walter E. "Multinational Staff Effectiveness in UN Peace Operations: The Case of the U.S. Army and UNMIH, 1994–1995." *Armed Forces and Society* 29, no.3 (Spring 2003): 393–413.

———. *U.S. Army Doctrine: From the American Revolution to the War on Terror.* Lawrence: University Press of Kansas, 2011.

Kretchik, Walter E., Robert F. Baumann, and John T. Fishel. *Invasion, Intervention, "Intervasion": A Concise History of the U.S. Army in Operation Uphold Democracy.* Fort Leavenworth KS: Command and General Staff College Press, 1997.

Laguerre, Michel S. *The Military and Society in Haiti.* Knoxville: University of Tennessee Press, 1993.

Lawrence, Alexander A. *Storm over Savannah: The Story of Count D'Estaing and the Siege of the Town in 1779.* Athens: University of Georgia Press, 1951.

Levine, Robert S. "Frederick Douglass, War, Haiti." Special Topic: War, *PMLA* 124, no. 5 (October 2009): 1864–68.

Malone, John T. "Armor in Military Operations Other Than War." Master's thesis, U.S. Army Command and General Staff College, 1996.

Matthewson, Tim. "Jefferson and Haiti." *Journal of Southern History* 61, no. 2 (May 1995): 209–48.

McFadyen, Deidre, and Pierre LaRamée with Mark Fried and Fred Rosen, eds. *Haiti: Dangerous Crossroads.* Boston: South End Press, 1995.

Mobley, Christina. "Haiti." In *The Encyclopedia of U.S. Military Interventions in Latin America,* ed. Alan McPherson. 2 vols. Santa Barbara CA: ABC-CLIO, 2013.

Morison, Samuel Eliot. "The Route of Columbus along the North Coast of Haiti, and the Site of Navidad." *Transactions of the American Philosophical Society,* n.s., 31, no. 4 (December 1940): i–iv, 239–85.

Nairn, Allan. "Our Payroll, Haitian Hit." *Nation*, October 9, 1995. http://www
.thirdworldtraveler.com/Global_Secrets_Lies/HaitiOct95_Nairn.html.

Palmer, Vernon Valentine. "The Origins and Authors of the Code Noir." *Louisiana Law Review* 56, no. 2 (Winter 1996): 363–407.

Pezzullo, Ralph. *Plunging into Haiti: Clinton, Aristide, and the Defeat of Diplomacy.* Jackson: University Press of Mississippi, 2006.

Pouligny, Béatrice. *Peace Operations Seen from Below: UN Missions and Local People.* Bloomfield CT: Kumarian Press, 2006.

Riehm, Peter J. "The USS *Harlan County* Affair." *Military Review* 77, no. 4 (July-August 1997): 31–36.

Schmidt, Hans. *The United States Occupation of Haiti, 1915–1934.* New Brunswick NJ: Rutgers University Press, 1995.

Shacochis, Bob. *The Immaculate Invasion.* New York: Viking, 1999.

Siegel, Adam B. *The Intervasion of Haiti.* Alexandria VA: Center for Naval Analyses, 1996.

Simpson, George Eaton. "Haitian Politics." *Social Forces* 20, no. 4 (May 1942): 487–91.

Sluiter, Engel. "Dutch Maritime Power and the Colonial Status Quo, 1585–1641." *Pacific Historical Review* 11, no. 1 (March 1942): 29–41.

Small, Melvin. "The United States and the German 'Threat' to the Hemisphere, 1905–1914." *The Americas* 28, no. 3 (January 1972): 252–70.

Talentino, Andrea Kathryn. *Military Intervention after the Cold War: The Evolution of Theory and Practice.* Athens: Ohio University Press, 2005.

Tierney, John J., Jr. "America's 'Black Vietnam': Haiti's Cacos vs. the Marine Corps, 1915–1922." *Lincoln Review* 2, no. 3 (Fall 1981). http://www.iwp.edu/news
_publications/detail/americas-black-vietnam-haitis-cacos-vs-the-marine
-corps-1915-22.

U.S. Marine Corps. *Small Wars Manual, United States Marine Corps, 1940.* Washington DC: Government Printing Office, 1940.

von Hippel, Karen. *Democracy by Force: U.S. Military Intervention in the Post-Cold War World.* Cambridge: Cambridge University Press, 2000.

Whitfield, Teresa. "Group of Friends." In *The UN Security Council: From the Cold War to the 21st Century,* edited by David M. Malone, 316–17. Boulder CO: Lynne Rienner, 2004.

Wilkins, Aaron L. *The Civil Military Operations Center in Operation Uphold Democracy.* BiblioScholar, 2012.

INDEX

Page numbers in italic indicate illustrations

Field Manual 100-23, 140

First Brigade, 101st Airborne Division (Air Assault), 65, 67, 72, 78, *99*

First Brigade, 10th Mountain Division (Light), 154, 156, 158

Fisher, George, 120, 121–22, 126, 137, 141, 144

force protection: 78–79, 85–86, 113; Special Operations Forces, 79, 94; Tenth Mountain, 79, 92–93, 166, *173*; Twenty-Fifth Infantry Division (Light), 121–22; UNMIH, *97*, 131

Forces Armées d'Haïti. *See* Armed Forces of Haiti (FAD'H)

Fort Leavenworth KS, 117–18, 133, 136–39

France, xviii, 3–8, 10–13, 17–18, 22

François, Joseph-Michel, 22, 52, 72, 106

FRAPH. *See* Front for the Advancement and Progress of Haiti (FRAPH)

Freeman, Bryant, 27–29, 41–42, 91–92, 94–95, 125–26, 136, 138

French Revolution, impact on Haiti, 6–7

Friends of Haiti (UN group), xviii

Front for the Advancement and Progress of Haiti (FRAPH), 37, 41, 52–53, 81

Front pour 'l Avancement et Progres Haitien. *See* Front for the Advancement and Progress of Haiti (FRAPH)

Fulton, William (Canadian), 133–35, 140–41

Galbaud du Fort, Thomas Francois, 8

Garde Coloniale (army reserve), 9

Garde d'Haïti (Gendarmerie d'Haïti), 19–20

Garde Presidentialle, 20

Garrett, William B., III, 48–9

Gendarmerie d'Haïti. *See* Garde d'Haïti (Gendarmerie D'Haïti)

Germany, 17–18, 174

Ghani, Abdul (UN DPKO), 137

Gifford, Robert B., 69

Gomillion, Stephen C., 103, 112

Gordon (tropical storm), *114*, 116–17

Gorelick, Jamie S., 69

Governors Island Accord (1993), 29–31, 37, 44, 127

Granderson, Colin, 42, 53

Grant, Ulysses S., 16–17

Great Britain, presence in Haiti, 7–9, 12–13, 17

Great Inagua Island, Bahamas, 54, 61

Guantánamo Bay, Cuba, 21, 26, 41, 54, 57, 65, 67

Gurkhas, 113

Haiti: civil war of (1806–20), 15; communications in, 51; constitution of (1805), 13–15; and 2010 earthquake, 175–76; and 1995 elections, 147–54; embargo on (1993–94), 28–29, 42–44, 57, 59, 83–84, 134, 165; foreign debt of, 18; government, 15, 19–22, 147–49, 161, 165; illegal drugs and, xviii, 58, 176; independence of, 12–13; literacy in, xviii, 174; and Marine Corps Intervention (1915–30), 18–19; and public's attitude toward military, 1, 6, 12–16, 20–21, 125, 167; and public's attitude toward violence, 4, 12–13, 31, 147, 151–2, 173; refugees in, 57–59

Haitian National Police (HNP), 48, 53, 55, 69–70, 122, 158–59

Haitian national prison, 103, 105, 124–25

Harrison, Benjamin, 17

Hill, James T. "Tom," 126

Hispaniola, xvii–xviii, 2–4, 8, 13, 16

HNP. *See* Haitian National Police (HNP)

Hough, Louie E., 114

Hoyt, Michael, 79

Huddleston, Nikki, 39

Hughes, Chris, 110–11

ICITAP. *See* International Criminal Investigation and Training Program (ICITAP)

Idiart, Phil, 69–71, 89–90

International Civilian Mission in Haiti (MICIVIH), 27–28, 30–31, 42, 44, 53, 133, 147–48, 150

International Civilian Support Mission in Haiti (MICAH), 175

International Criminal Investigation and Training Program (ICITAP), 60, 69, 70, 122

International Police Monitors (IPM), 68-70, 88-90, 122
International Republican Institute, 159, 160
IPM. *See* International Police Monitors (IPM)

Jackson, Andrew, 16
Jade Green (planning cell), 45-48
JCS. *See* Joint Chiefs of Staff (JCS)
Jefferson, Thomas, 12, 16
Joint Chiefs of Staff (JCS), 26, 31, 39, 45-49, 130, 139
Joint Special Operations Command, 52
Joint Task Force Haiti Assistance Group (JTF HAG), 34, 41
Joint Task Force (JTF) 120, 44, 67
Joint Task Force (JTF) 160, 65
Joint Task Force (JTF) 180, 48-55, 56, 67, 71-73, 84, 86, 94, 103, 172
Joint Task Force (JTF) 185, 67
Joint Task Force (JTF) 190, 61-62, 67, 126-27, 168, 172-3
Joint Task Force 190/Multinational Force (JTF 190/MNF): activities of, 85, 92, 95-96, 106, 124, 131; CARICOM and, 97, 100; formation of, 87; and Tenth Mountain to Twenty-Fifth Infantry transition, 117, 121-2; and transition to UNMIH, 125-26, 133, 137, 141-42, 146, 153, 168
Jonassaint, Emile, 73
Jones, Michael, 99
JTF 120. *See* Joint Task Force (JTF) 120
JTF 160. *See* Joint Task Force (JTF) 160
JTF 180. *See* Joint Task Force (JTF) 180
JTF 185. *See* Joint Task Force (JTF) 185
JTF 190. *See* Joint Task Force (JTF) 190
JTF 190/MNF. *See* Joint Task Force 190/Multinational Force (JTF 190/MNF)
JTF HAG. *See* Joint Task Force Haiti Assistance Group (JTF HAG)

Keane, John M. "Jack," 156
Kelly, John F., 177
Kelly, Raymond W. "Ray," 70, 88-90, 122
King Henry I (of Haiti). *See* Christophe, Henry
Kinzer, Joseph W., xx, 126, 137, 139-47, 148, 149-51, 155, 160-62

Knoop, George, 176

Ladoucer, Anthony "Tony," xiii, 73, 85, 101, 111, 163, 164, 170
Langdon, John, 45
Las Isla Espanola. *See* Hispaniola
Lavalas (political party), 22, , 102, 151-52, 160, 189n40
Le Cap. *See* Cap-Haïtien, Haiti
Leclerc, Charles Victor Emmanuel (French), 10-11
Lemay, Jean-Jacques, 32
Léopards (counterinsurgency unit), 21, 25, 30
Lewis, John, 128-31
LIC. *See* Light Industrial Complex (LIC)
Light Industrial Complex (LIC), 85, 87
Lincoln, Abraham, 16
Louverture, Toussaint, 7-11
Luciano, Geraldo D., 120
Lüders Affair, 17-18

Magloire, Paul E. (Haitian), 19
Mallory, Guy, 41
Malval, Robert, 30, 32
maréchaussée (rural police force), 5-6
Meade, David C.: activities of, 85, 95, 106-9, 121, 124, 130; command climate of, 79; force protection and, 86, 90, 92-93, 103, 113; on *Mount Whitney*, 72; and opinion on departure, 119-20; and opinion on invasion, 62-63, 77; and opinion on special forces, 79-81, 99-100; Rockwood case and, 103-5
media, influence and use of, 37, 59, 66, 101, 129-31, 152, 158-59
MICAH. *See* International Civilian Support Mission in Haiti (MICAH)
MICIVIH *See* International Civilian Mission in Haiti (MICIVIH)
Milice Civile. *See* Tontons Macoutes (Milice Civile)
military information support teams (MIST), 145, 148
Miller, Paul D., 40, 45, 49, 51, 60-61, 67, 72-74, 123, 139
MINUSTAH. *See* UN Stabilization Mission in Haiti (MINUSTAH)

www.ingramcontent.com/pod-product-compliance
Lightning Source LLC
Chambersburg PA
CBHW030410100426
42812CB00028B/2909/J